# Wealth, Whiteness, and the Matrix of Privilege

# Wealth, Whiteness, and the Matrix of Privilege

## The View from the Country Club

WILLOW INTERNATIONAL LIBRARY

Jessica Holden Sherwood

LEXINGTON BOOKS
A division of

ROWMAN & LITTLEFIELD PUBLISHERS, INC.
*Lanham • Boulder • New York • Toronto • Plymouth, UK*

Published by Lexington Books
A division of Rowman & Littlefield Publishers, Inc.
A wholly owned subsidiary of The Rowman & Littlefield Publishing Group, Inc.
4501 Forbes Boulevard, Suite 200, Lanham, Maryland 20706
www.lexingtonbooks.com

Estover Road, Plymouth PL6 7PY, United Kingdom

British Library Cataloguing in Publication Information Available

**Library of Congress Cataloging-in-Publication Data**

Sherwood, Jessica Holden, 1972–
  Wealth, whiteness, and the matrix of privilege : the view from the country club
/ Jessica Holden Sherwood.
       p. cm.
  Includes bibliographical references and index.
  ISBN 978-0-7391-3412-2 (cloth : alk. paper) — ISBN 978-0-7391-3414-6
(electronic)
  1. Clubs—Membership. 2. Clubs—Social aspects. 3. Women. 4. Race. 5.
Equality. I. Title.
  HS2519.S54 2010
  367—dc22                                                    2010025182

∞ ™ The paper used in this publication meets the minimum requirements of
American National Standard for Information Sciences—Permanence of Paper for
Printed Library Materials, ANSI/NISO Z39.48-1992. Printed in the United States
of America

For Jesse, still and always.

# Contents

# List of Tables

# Acknowledgments

This project would not have been possible without the participation of the interviewees. I thank them all for inviting me into their homes and offices, giving willingly of their time and thoughts. I appreciate those who opened their address books to refer me to other club members, and especially the important early contacts whose endorsement of my research smoothed the way to securing more interviews. I'm grateful.

An interviewee who reads this book might be surprised by how critical it is. I'll borrow here from Julie Bettie, who also wrote a critical book about people she liked. As Bettie writes in her Acknowledgments, "my analysis is not meant to be critical of individual people, but of the social systems, processes, and ideologies present in our culture that recruit individual actors and inform their actions."[1]

It has been a long road from those interviews to the publication of this book, but at least it hasn't been lonely. I am grateful to all of these people for giving me some company along the way: Maitrayee Bhattacharyya, Woody Doane, Corey Dolgon, G. William Domhoff, Heather Johnson, Helen Mederer, and Barb Silver. I also acknowledge fondly all the 2006–2010 leaders in Sociologists for Women in Society. I have learned so much working in SWS. I also feel fortunate to have worked in the executive office with Candace Hindle, Kristen Baxter, Theta Pavis, Rachel Weisz-Smith, and Donna Russo Morin.

Many thanks to Michael Sisskin at Lexington Books for accepting this project and working with me to bring it to completion.

Molly Lang and I have been friends throughout graduate school and beyond. It is still wonderful to talk with her as we both work to combine motherhood with sociology careers.

In addition to Molly's friendship, I was buoyed through graduate school by my mentor Barbara Risman. I have learned much from Barbara's example of living one's principles, including putting social capital processes to feminist use. I thank her for wisely chairing my dissertation committee, and also thank committee members Richard Della Fave, Amy Halberstadt, Michael Schwalbe, Don Tomaskovic-Devey, and Susan Ostrander. I'm grateful for Susan's generosity in adopting me and my dissertation, despite the distance between our departments.

I'm pleased to thank my mother for both scholarly and personal reasons. A longtime resident of "the Heights"—going unnamed here—she was an invaluable informant. Our regular conversations helped me a lot in conducting interviews. When I had a baby during dissertation writing, her loving care of the infant Abigail allowed me to keep going. Our family is very indebted to Grandma.

By now, Abigail is eight and her sister Ellie is six. I am grateful that they understand the importance of my work and are proud of me. Of course I am so proud of them.

My partner in parenting and so much more is my husband, Jesse. I know that this road has seemed interminable, and Jesse has my apologies and appreciation. I am grateful to the point of awe for his patience and caretaking. Jesse has been my best company on life's road, and I am pleased to dedicate this book to him with all my love.

## NOTE

1. Bettie, Women Without Class: Girls, Race, and Identity. Berkeley: University of California Press, 2003, page x.

# Introduction

Growing up, my heritage felt lopsided. I seemed always to know that my mother was the grandchild of Jewish immigrants from Russia. My father's side of the family, by contrast, seemed generic and colorless. I now recognize that mistaking oneself for a generic, blank, default group is a sure sign of belonging to a privileged "unmarked" group.

When, as a child, I asked my father to identify his ethnic heritage, he said something indistinct about being a mixture of English, French, and other, and taught me the acronym "WASP." White Anglo Saxon Protestant. So then I embraced being half Jewish, half WASP. When I consider what led me to this particular research study, part of the answer rests in that identity I grew up with and its feelings of partial belonging. I confess to Gatsbyesque mixed feelings toward WASP life, being both repelled and attracted like a confused magnet.

I grew up with class privilege as well as white privilege. Being unmarked/superordinate on both statuses kept them both invisible to me. I've gotten benefits from my social location, like the people in this book; but as we'll see, this dual privilege is a detriment when it comes to recognizing and understanding inequalities.

As a graduate student in sociology, I concentrated in the area of class, race, and gender inequalities. With my classmates I learned about the perspectives and challenges of poor people, people of color, and women. But I was compelled by the occasional reminder to "study up," and remember the unmarked sides of those hierarchies too. I was a preppy

WASP, at least in part, so I thought it made sense to tackle the study of other privileged people.

I got underway gathering data: I interviewed members of the most exclusive country clubs in one area of the northeastern United States. These interviews were surprisingly pleasant—I was braced for the possibility of hostility—and I visited some wonderful homes and offices in the process.

As I analyzed my completed interviews, a controversy erupted in the news. The *New York Times* anticipated it by asking in 2001, "Why don't men and women play golf together?"

In 2002, there was protest that golf's top tournament, the Masters, was to be played at a golf club that admitted no women. This protest about a golf tournament drew attention to all-male clubs just as a similar protest in 1990 drew attention to all-white clubs. The *New York Times* announced that "Some Golf Clubs Are Still a Man's World"; the article considered whether golfers—especially the nonwhite Tiger Woods—had an obligation to protest the tournament's location, and it noted the debate over "Which Private Clubs Are Acceptable. And Private."[1]

I greeted news coverage of my research topic with, once again, mixed feelings. I find exclusion by gender just as deplorable as exclusion by race, and it was frustrating that this wasn't equally obvious to everyone else. But the good news was that my work is relevant: it enters an ongoing conversation in America. This book can address the implicit question: Who cares? What difference does it make if a private club is exclusive? Several answers to that question are to come in the chapters that follow.

In chapter 1, I introduce the country clubs and their members. We'll follow the process of joining the club or of being rejected from it for incompatible personal style. We'll learn why people join and value these organizations. The clubs will be placed in context, showing why they are significant to social scientists, or anyone else curious about the reproduction of class, race, and gender inequalities.

The following three chapters report on club members' talk in terms of *accounts* they give. "Accounts," in this sense, are things people say to justify or excuse something that might appear questionable. Chapter 2 covers members' accounts for their clubs' exclusiveness by class and culture. In several ways, members either justify the exclusion, or deny that any real exclusion is happening at all. For example, one member made this awkward attempt at denying exclusiveness: he pointed out that after initiation fees, club membership—at about $5,000 per year—is just as affordable as renting a beach house for a couple of weeks.

Chapter 3 expands on this talk about exclusiveness and composition by covering the clubs' racial-ethnic makeup. Aware of a reputation for segregation, club members point proudly to the fact that they have diversified in recent years. Impossibly, each club lays claim to being more diverse than the others. However, the truth is that token diversity exists within considerable cultural unity. American racial discourse is often characterized as "colorblind," but members' emphasis on diversity is an interesting exception to that. We'll see how the clubs' diversification, which was color conscious rather than colorblind, allows exclusion by culture and class to continue.

Chapter 4 moves to members' accounts for women's status within the clubs. Whereas the tradition for nonwhites was exclusion, the tradition for women has been inclusion with second-class status. Some clubs retain the second-class status for women today; some do not. Members have interesting explanations for the differences, and for the second-class status that persists in some clubs. Some clubs bar women from the golf course at certain times, which members justify by noting that club members are mainly hardworking husbands paired with stay-at-home wives. We also see, in the talk about gender, some interesting similarities and differences with the talk about racial groups. A big difference is that members call it natural for women and men to be different and sometimes separate; they would never say that about racial-ethnic groups.

In the Conclusion, I review the accounts club members give, why they do so, and the cultural tools they use. Club members' talk, overall, uses and promotes an ideology that says that inequalities are natural and unproblematic. Ironically, their actions illustrate that inequality is something that people produce, not something that occurs naturally.

The answer to the question, "What difference does it make if a private club is exclusive?" is that it does contribute to reproducing class, race, and gender inequalities. Country clubs are not a special engine in this process, but rather one cog in a very complex machinery. I'll demonstrate throughout the book, and argue in the conclusion, that the machinery is better understood when one takes an inclusive approach, studying—regardless of the particular focus—how the cogs interact and relate to the larger whole.

The Methodological Appendix covers the usual issues of gaining access, analyzing data, and my own feelings toward the population I study. However, two less common topics will also be covered here. First is my use of personal connections—social capital and cultural capital—to get entrée to an elusive population. The irony is that while I used these tools for access, I criticize their organizational use as unjust. The other topic is a discussion of the politics of studying the unmarked. This sort of research can expose the researcher and her institution to risks—real or imagined—that are unique to this population. These risks are not common concerns for social scientists, but it is important to consider which groups do and do not get studied, and why. This too is a part of understanding how inequalities get reproduced.

## NOTE

1. Anderson, "Woods is Not Obliged to Boycott." *New York Times*, 8 December 2002, 8–1; Kuczynski, "It's Still A Man's, Man's, Man's World." *New York Times*, 21 July 2002, 9–1; McGrath, "Why don't men and women play golf together?" *New York Times Magazine*, 29 July 2001, p. 16; Scott, "Debating Which Private Clubs are Acceptable. And Private." *New York Times*, 8 December 2002, W-5. This controversy had a little revival in 2010 with the comeback to golf of Tiger Woods (after a sex scandal) at the Masters at Augusta, the defiantly all-male club.

# 1

✛

# Business and Pleasure

## *The Social Context of Exclusive Clubs*

"We truly believe we are a, y'know, a social institution; however I can tell you I've done business with at least fifteen members of that club—and large, very large transactions."

—Clayton, past president of Oldfamily

Have you ever been confronted with an unusual social occasion that you weren't sure how to dress for? Like many people, you may have sought out advice beforehand. Have you ever experienced negative consequences for an appearance that was somehow "wrong"? That's a tricky question, because you don't always know the effects of your appearance. You could get rejected in some way, and be left wondering if your personal appearance had something to do with it. This is one of the ambiguities you might confront if you tried to join an exclusive country club in the northeastern United States.

This book will let you, the reader, in to these clubs to some extent. You will get to hear what members say about who they admit and who they reject, and why. You'll hear their explanations of: their exclusivity, their racial-ethnic mix, and the status of their women members. Throughout, elements of popular American discourse are used, and the club members' privileges are subtly reproduced and legitimated (reinforced as right and proper).

First, let me introduce the study's country clubs and their members. We will follow the process of joining the club, or of being rejected from it for incompatible personal style. We'll learn whether people join and value

1

these organizations for business, for pleasure, or both. This background provides the context for subsequent chapters, which will focus on the accounts (talk that justifies or excuses) surrounding country clubs. The business question is important because the dominant account is that the exclusion is purely sociable, and therefore harmless. But members do acknowledge that involvement in the club yields concrete career gains— for others, themselves, and their children.

The clubs will be placed in context, showing why they are significant to social scientists, or anyone else curious about the reproduction of inequalities. I'll briefly discuss those inequalities of class, race, and gender: how they intertwine, and how "class" requires a broad definition that's cultural as well as material.

## THE COUNTRY CLUBS

For this research, I focused on four country clubs' members or former members (and three club managers). In chapter 4 about gender, we'll also consider one more club, Northern. Northern isn't as exclusive or prestigious as the rest, and is included just in chapter 4 because of its battles over women's status.

I conducted interviews in 2000 and 2001 in the northeastern United States, primarily in a single urban area: all names of places and people are pseudonyms. For background information on the research process, please see the Methodological Appendix.

The northeastern setting is to some extent culturally distinctive. As the location of the first colonial settlers of (what became) the United States, it is home to the oldest "old money" families in the country. Nelson Aldrich's book by that name describes the "aristocratic," "patrician" consciousness of the region.[1] The WASPs at least are mindful of their historical and social primacy, envisioning themselves at the top of a status hierarchy that is both ethnically specified and patriarchal.[2]

I began my research in an affluent neighborhood I call the Heights, the most elite neighborhood of its metropolitan area. For married couples— this research population—the mean household income in 1999 was about $130,000 (according to Census data for the Zip code of the Heights). This is roughly twice the citywide average. The Heights holds only twenty percent of all of the city's married-couple households, but it is home to a full two-thirds of the ones whose annual income is $100,000 or more.

The Heights is a residential area too small and dense to hold even one golf course. But as its affluence would suggest, it is home to many club members. At least six by-invitation-only country clubs are located within twenty minutes' drive, including the first three clubs introduced next.

**Table 1.1. The Country Clubs**

| Club Pseudonym | Social Reputation | Racial/Ethnic Composition* | Gender Regime** | Interviewees |
|---|---|---|---|---|
| Oldfamily | blue blooded | WASPy with diversity | egalitarian | focal club, most interviewees |
| Rosary | Irish Catholic | Catholic with some diversity | men dominate | pseudonyms start with R |
| Suburban | new money | WASPy with some diversity | men dominate | pseudonyms start with S |
| Waterside | exclusive retreat | WASPy with some diversity | egalitarian | pseudonyms start with W |
| Northern | gender battleground | WASPy with diversity | contested, hostile | only covered in chapter 4; pseudonyms start with N |
| Fiorenza, Tuscan, Venetian | Italian clubs | Italian with some diversity | men dominate, interviewees cite as sexist | none; cited by interviewees |

\*:  No census of the clubs is available; these are estimates based on interviews.
\*\*: See Table 4.1 for details on the gender regime at each club.

## Oldfamily

I begin with a club that I call Oldfamily since it was described to me as an old, family club. The historically important families of the Heights—ones whose names match area streets, buildings, charitable foundations—are likely to belong to this club.[3] Oldfamily is tucked into a busy area a few miles away from the Heights. Its clubhouse is visible from the road, but—as its manager pointedly told me—no sign announces its presence.

The clubhouse is larger but otherwise looks similar to many other old wood frame houses in the northeast. Overall, the property is not so elegant and gorgeous as other nearby clubs; many members take some Yankee pride in its relative simplicity.

On interviewing the manager, I guessed (wrongly) at which door to walk in. There is no entrance where a visitor is greeted by a person behind a desk: the place is arranged not to welcome visitors but, perhaps, to give members the feeling that they are on an extension of their own property.

Interviewees describe the character of Oldfamily as "the Heights white-shoe WASPy club," and that its reputation was of a "typical old Yankee blue blood, sort of . . . stodgy, nose-in-the-air kind of place." With its hundred-year history, Oldfamily traditionally topped the area's prestige hierarchy. People disagree on whether that hierarchy is obsolete or persists today. If nothing else, there are senior Oldfamily members known informally as the "old guard," who embody the conservative traditions of an earlier time.

Some "old guard" members and their predecessors are referenced in plaques and framed photos on the walls of the clubhouse. It is a quiet place with worn oriental rugs and dark wood walls, and picture windows overlooking the well-groomed property. The photos and plaques tell of decades of sporting fun and accomplishment, always outdoors and often multigenerational.

While WASPs have been the mainstay of Oldfamily membership, other people now belong. Oldfamily members include, in small numbers, Catholics, Jews, African Americans, and some other nonwhite members. As far as I can tell, the first African American joined Oldfamily around 1992. One former board president asserts, "I firmly believe that Oldfamily is one of the most liberal, integrated, diverse clubs in this state." However, chapter 3 will critically analyze such statements about club composition.

When it comes to women's status, Oldfamily's history is unusual. The club was originally founded by both men and women, and *de jure* (officially) gender equality has always been the rule. However, positions of power have only recently become open to women and there was a *de facto* (unwritten) expectation in recent history that some prime times for golfing be reserved for men. But in the last decade, equality has been explicitly reasserted. Although power at Oldfamily still belongs mostly to men, the club's history of *de jure* gender equality helps women succeed in their efforts toward *de facto* equality.

## Rosary

Rosary is another highly selective club in the area. It's located, like Oldfamily, a few miles from the Heights neighborhood. It has the feel of an urban park: rows of houses at the borders overlook stately old trees on manicured grounds inside. The layout of Rosary is oriented toward golf, as is the interest of its members. Rosary does have a swimming pool and tennis courts, as does Oldfamily. But while Oldfamily members talk about their well-rounded recreational facilities, Rosary members speak overwhelmingly of the quality of their golf course. The windows of the dining room, and the veranda just outside those windows, overlook the first tee.

Though Rosary began, a hundred years ago, as another WASP club, it developed into the club for Irish Catholics. One member speculates that in the post-war era, Rosary's leadership decided that admitting the Irish was better for the health of the club than continuing a losing competition with Oldfamily for prospective WASP members. Most locals know it only as the traditionally Irish club. Like Oldfamily, it has broadened its membership in recent years to include members of other ethnic groups.

Today, Rosary attracts those interested in top-notch golf; the members are affluent, but usually not from "old money." It is primarily known as a place for the enjoyment of businessmen, with family use secondary. The majority of members have stay-at-home wives. Rosary reserves prime golf times for men only. Recently the restrictions were changed from being gender specific to, technically, "Principal members" having more privileges than "Restricted members." But *de facto*, women's status remains low at Rosary.

## Suburban

As its pseudonym suggests, Suburban is located in Littletown, a bit further away from the Heights and its nearest clubs. But its reputation is comparable to Oldfamily and Rosary in terms of exclusiveness. Most of the members of Suburban live in Littletown. But the fact that some are drawn from the Heights testifies to the club's standing.

Suburban has the luxury of more acreage than the first two clubs. It boasts gorgeous vistas and a practice golf range separate from its eighteen holes. It is oriented more toward families than businessmen, with junior sports programs and other activities. Littletown itself seems to draw affluent families; it is known as a more transient community than the well-established Heights. In contrast to Oldfamily, Suburban's reputation among club members is one of "new money" and an attendant lack of refinement. Still, its history is of WASP exclusiveness. But like Oldfamily and Rosary, this exclusiveness has softened in recent years to include members of other ethnic groups.

The country club seems to play a bigger role in the lives of Suburban members than it does for Oldfamily members. The club is right in Littletown where most members live. One member wryly noted that the short drive allows people to have an extra drink at the club. And, Suburban consists of many families with children and stay-at-home mothers. While this leads to greater usage of the club, it also seems to justify women's second-class status. As at Rosary, there are times every week when women are barred from the golf course.

## Waterside

Waterside is different from the three preceding clubs in important ways. Its nearby location and strictly exclusive membership practices lead me to include it in this study. But, it lacks the hundred year history of the three preceding clubs, having opened only recently. Instead of being operated by its members, Waterside is a for-profit venture by a corporation. So rather than select potential members on social bases (as delineated below), Waterside's management screens applicants by charging exorbitant fees. The initiation fee is over $100,000.

The club is so new that its social reputation is nearly nonexistent. All of my interviewees are familiar with Oldfamily, Rosary, and Suburban. When Waterside is mentioned, people either haven't heard of it or refer solely to how expensive it is rather than to the character of its membership.

For their payments, Waterside members get to enjoy the feel of an exclusive private retreat. The club's scenic setting is removed from the urban area; in contrast to Suburban, it does not have a core of members who make heavy regular use of the club. In fact, Waterside often represents the second or third country club where one belongs. It seems to draw members who want a place to go for a "treat" in their social or business lives.

Probably because of its newness, Waterside seems to lack distinctions of gender and race/ethnicity, beyond the high financial hurdle. It is not a family-oriented place. Its manager says: "If you're going to project a certain type of image and a certain style, you just can't have children. I mean I say children—if you're a twelve-, fourteen-year-old kid, sensible, can look smart in a jacket and tie and behave yourself at the dinner table without throwing peas, then fine." But Waterside is designed primarily as a retreat for adults.

## THE INTERVIEWEES

I conducted forty-five interviews in all. My emphasis was Oldfamily members, of whom I interviewed twenty-one. The sample also includes interviews with five Rosary members, six Suburban members, and three Waterside members. I interviewed the general managers at Oldfamily, Rosary, and Waterside. I also interviewed seven members of Northern, but those will be included only in the chapter about gender. The thirty-five interviews with members of the four clubs described above are the core of the sample.

Pseudonyms for members of Rosary, Suburban, and Waterside begin with the letters R, S, and W, respectively (and N for Northern in chapter 4). Names beginning with other letters are for Oldfamily members. In the interest of preserving anonymity, I will not provide profiles of individuals. Instead, here are the characteristics of the sample as a whole.

Of the thirty-five core interviewees, twenty-one are men and fourteen are women. Eight of the men have served on their club's board of governors, five at Oldfamily. Board members are overrepresented here because people wanted to give me referrals who were knowledgeable and influential, leading board members to be named more often than they would have at random.

Two of the women are single, never married; all of the other thirty-three have children, and all are married (some remarried) except for a pair who are currently divorced. The interviewees range in age from about forty to about seventy, with the median in the fifties.

Three of them, all Oldfamily members, are men of color; two more Oldfamily men are Jewish. Overall, six interviewees are Catholic, and the remainder are Protestant, in heritage if not in practice.

Eighteen of the members live in the Heights, including two thirds (or fourteen) of the Oldfamily members. Twelve of thirty-five belonged to their club during childhood; eleven more belonged to a different country club, generally because they grew up elsewhere. The remaining minority did not grow up as country club members. Oldfamily members in this sample are evenly split in thirds between having grown up there, or at another club, or none at all. Overall, most interviewees have been members of their country club for well more than a decade.

These people are affluent, but not uniformly in the elite in the sense of belonging to the upper-class group that controls social institutions.[4] Descendants of the city's most prominent families of the nineteenth century are included, but they are outnumbered today. Certainly some members, as CEOs or inheritors, are very wealthy. But with the stark exception of Waterside, club costs are not prohibitive to the upper-middle class: initiation fees range from $10,000 to $20,000, and annual dues are around $5,000. Nobody I talked with suggested having difficulty paying the costs, although occasionally cost was mentioned as a reason not to add another membership at an additional country club. The interviewees work in law, finance, insurance, real estate, institutional administration, and a few other sectors.

## BECOMING A MEMBER

For the twelve interviewees who had attended their club since childhood, becoming a member was never much of an issue. It is virtually automatic for junior members to become full members if they choose to. Young adults becoming full members receive a break on initiation fees, and are often allowed to skip the waitlist that holds candidates when the club is at full capacity. And of course, growing up in a country club provides assurance that, if full membership is desired, one will have both acceptable personal style and friends to support the application.

Others, of course, had to go through a more rigorous process of joining. I'm told that the process is as follows. I focus on the Oldfamily club, but it is quite similar at Rosary and Suburban.

The most conservative stance is that one must wait until invited by a member to join, because to bring up the matter oneself is too forward.

Marian, who joined in the early 1980s, recalls, "I remember when we were interested in joining, because it had a pool and a place to take the kids, I called one person who was a member and she was horrified that I would call and ask because you were supposed to be approached." However, that view is no longer dominant today. Generally, a candidate's interest in membership will become known through casual social interaction with current members. Most people now consider it acceptable for a candidate to express interest in joining, but presumably not to a member whom they have just met for the first time.

One might know club members socially, through business, as neighbors, via golf, or by doing volunteer work together. Not a single person I spoke with expressed any difficulty at identifying Oldfamily members, which is certainly a selection effect. There is an "everybody knows everybody" feel to the area; this population is characterized by multiple ties (e.g., neighbors who are also involved together in their children's private school). But to know an Oldfamily member, it would be sufficient to have just one of the usual routes (not that everyone has even one)—residential proximity, nonprofit/volunteer involvement, business tie, or playing golf. While the development of connections is an important *product* of club membership, some social capital is also a *prerequisite* for admission.

A club member serves as sponsor or proposer for the candidate. If the sponsor is savvy, their first task will be to mention the candidate's name to influential members, usually those on the board of governors. (There is a facilitating membership committee, but admissions decisions are made by the board.) This way, others' reactions to this candidacy can be gauged early on. This step is technically optional, but is considered wise because it's best to hear negative feedback as early in the process as possible.

The candidate, or sometimes the sponsor, also identifies another club member to second the application.

The first *official* step the sponsor takes is to arrange or request a cocktail party or something similar, for the candidate and the aforementioned influential members to meet and mingle. Sometimes one cocktail party will serve this function for a handful of candidates.

The event is sometimes at the sponsor's home, or often at the Oldfamily club itself. The event is a chance to, quote, "get looked over by the board of governors," who can again provide negative feedback to the proposer if they so choose.

If first impressions are favorable, the candidacy is announced to all members. At Oldfamily, names of candidates are included in members' monthly mailings; other clubs post the names on an internal bulletin board. This gives all members the opportunity to object to the candidate if they so choose. A member can write a letter to the board stating their objection; or less formally—and perhaps anonymously—simply register their objection in conversation with a member of the board or the membership committee.

If a candidate receives any negative feedback, then the board must weigh the negative against the positive, namely, at least two members who are promoting the candidacy. If the negative feedback comes from multiple sources, that will usually kill the candidacy. If only one member objects, they will not always prevail. It depends in part on the importance of the person objecting. Harold muses about proposing a candidate: "If along the way I had gotten any negative feedback *from someone who's important* and said 'oh, I don't like that guy,' I would have just squashed the membership there" [emphasis added]. In past years, one board member's objection would suffice to kill a candidacy, as the proverbial "black ball" suggests. But in an effort to make things more fair, Oldfamily has done away with that rule and board members now must discuss the matter until they reach an agreement, and a lone dissenter will probably not prevail.

So, the board can decide against a candidacy after the optional first step, or the cocktail party, or the circulation of the name. If they reach a negative decision, they notify the proposer. Often this notification is vague and euphemized. John recalls proposing someone to another similar club: "I couldn't get past that level. So I finally got in touch with the chairman of the membership committee and he said, he said that 'this name is not getting any support.'" Though the proposer can ask for an explanation, none is required. Many people agree that the proposer, or at least the candidate, usually knows or should know the reason for their denial. An Oldfamily board president says, "Nine times out of ten, the people being proposed know *exactly* why it is they're being—not being considered." (Typical reasons why are listed below and in the next chapter.)

The proposer notifies the candidate of the bad news, again often with euphemism. Ken recalls the rejection of an acquaintance: "Actually it was someone else on the board who had a lot more clout than I did, who got back to him and told him. He gave him the sort of soft shoe: 'there's a long waiting list now, and, blah blah blah,' just kind of discouraged him." Candidate and proposer alike must accept the decision and have no recourse against it. This way, the application is dropped before it is ever officially submitted, and therefore an embarrassing official rejection need not take place.

However, if the candidacy has survived thus far, *then* the membership committee issues an application to the candidate. The official application consists of letters of support from the proposer and seconder, and the candidate's completed application form and monetary deposit. But as you have guessed by now, this application is little more than a formality, the true screening having already happened. Once accepted, the candidate joins the club or the waiting list if, like many area clubs today, the membership is at its maximum number.

The steps in the process are designed not just to allow for subjective judgments about applicants' desirability, but to *encourage* them. Those judgments can hasten or prohibit one's acceptance into the club. The process also seems designed to be opaque and mystified, probably as an added measure of "protecting privacy." (It may also be a safeguard against burning a bridge by overtly insulting someone who could, in the future, hold greater status and power.) At the same time, though, the process wears the cloak of formal bureaucracy. Referring to rules can soften a rejection, as in the aforementioned use of the "long waiting list" to reject a candidate. Sociologist Diana Kendall also studied exclusive organizations, and notes similarly that "the bureaucratic structure . . . provides the [members] with the means whereby they can retain the exclusivity of the organization's membership and 'hand-pick' new members."[5]

The next question is the criteria on which candidates are screened. Of course, one must first know a club member for sponsorship, and second be able to afford to join. Though club initiation fees in this study range from $10,000 to over $100,000, it is not enough to clear this hurdle. One must be able to signal appropriate class membership. When I ask people about the criteria for membership, their answers usually resonate with this signaling, and the general concept of cultural capital.[6] Personality/behavior, interests, and appearances are all mentioned by different members:

Theresa: If somebody needed to show up already drunk at the party, doesn't mean that there isn't plenty of excessive drinking that goes on there, but if somebody needed to be really obnoxious when they showed up, or if somebody needed to be insulting or somebody really needed to be obnoxious in any possible way, I think they probably wouldn't get in. I think it's that leftover WASP style: perhaps be nice, be proper, that people still want to see. They want to see an effort toward it.

Harold: One of the last things that you go through at the club when you're being considered for membership is you're brought to this cocktail party and you're introduced to all these people, you know, and as long as you don't get too drunk or molest some guy's wife, you know that you're gonna get in.

Larry: It had to do with things like: it's an interesting person, it's somebody that's doing something that's out there and involved, it's somebody who's influential because they are doing things, somebody who could afford to belong. . . . But the common ground was finding people that are *interesting* to be with. And because it's also a sports club, finding people that are interested in the sports aspects of it.

Clayton [*a former board president, explaining why the party now comes early in the process rather than at the end*]: Yet, we've had occasions where people have gotten to that last point, and it's been thumbs down, because they . . . I'll never forget, somebody arrived in a black shirt with a white tie and suit on, and it just wasn't Oldfamily, you know? It just wasn't—and bing, out they went.

Harold: I heard of one other guy who got to the party and didn't get in. He showed up with a black shirt on and a white tie. Didn't make it. So you know, what can I say. Oh, and I heard of a woman who didn't get in too. She showed up with red shoes on. [*Laughs*] That's why she thinks the reason is, but who knows what the reason is.

Interviewees also cite bad business dealings as cause for objection: this might just mean that some past transaction or partnership ended on bad terms, or there could be charges of unethical conduct. Sometimes, a member will object to the candidacy of a business competitor, but that complaint is usually insufficient on its own.

Parker [*board member*]: There may be certain people who look at a club as a way, as a business development opportunity and they would rather not have their competitors being on their turf.
Q: Is that sometimes enough to keep a candidate out?
Parker: I can think of a couple of those situations. It was quite obvious to most people on the board. We have to tell them: not, we understand what your hidden motivation is. "We understand your objections, but we think on balance that there are more people, there are a lot of people who are in favor of this person." We don't confront them on their hidden agenda.

Members would also consider a candidate undesirable who has a public record of philandering, notable drunkenness, or criminal activity. (Perhaps because of their normality, discreetly private affairs and drunkenness can be overlooked in otherwise ideal candidates.) Talk about the "fit" of new members will be expanded on in the next chapter; for now, the following quote from Donna sums up the discernment. "I once had someone say this to me at another club, that you should put up someone who you want to sit next to at a dinner party. And if you don't want to sit next to them, don't put them up and don't write a letter."

## DOES BUSINESS HAVE A PLACE?

The reputation of country clubs is that, once admitted, participation can be helpful for one's career. I was interested to discover that members, usually men, often acknowledge the place of their careers in their club memberships. One in every five interviewees told me they joined at least in part for business reasons. Examples:

Richard: After graduating college, my wife and I moved to [another city] and golf wasn't all that big a part of our lives. It was to me to the extent that a lot of my business colleagues were playing golf and that kind of thing, so I played occasionally, and then we moved back here, it became evident to me that I needed a place where I could entertain prospective clients.

John: When I moved [here] in 1981, my boss in fact said, "you should join Oldfamily." There was a certain sort of social pressure there. He said, "it would be good for business and good for you to do that."

Q: So you've never gotten interested in taking up golf?
   Frank: No. For me, the country club, a lot of it is more business. I do a lot of business dinners. . . . We have outings for our customers and things like that. That's what I use the Oldfamily for.

Ken: I joined simply because I wanted to play golf, and I also joined because as president of [this company], I was aware that there were six or seven board members who were members there. And I felt that at my level professionally, I probably should . . . have a membership, to . . . have a high level of visibility, not only with people associated with [this company], but other key people in the community.

Walter: I think the people who are looking to belong [at Waterside], again not only the economic aspect, but perhaps they had a reason to have a second or third club or need for one away from their normal club, and I think in my case, I think it's not unique in that at your regular club, there's a lot of friendships and back-slapping, but you may not necessarily want that if you're bringing in clients and having, you know, you want to create a very private kind of an atmosphere and an exclusive atmosphere and that's really what that's all about over there. So if you have that kind of need to entertain people and you don't want to do it at your primary club because there's too much sort of informalness to it, you have a place like that where it's, it is a lot more exclusive.

It is generally known that a company might facilitate club membership for an employee whose job entails schmoozing. Ralph says: "It's prestigious to be able to get there [Rosary] to play, and people love the opportunity to play there, so if you have an employee that's a good golfer and he says 'yeah, I can join but I can't afford it,' well, 'we'll find a way that you can afford it.' That happens a lot of places."
   Even those who don't say business was a reason to join say that membership can be useful. This happens primarily in two ways: first, as Frank notes above, business contacts can be invited to golf outings. This strengthens relationships and increases the contacts' goodwill toward the member. Second, ties formed or strengthened at the club can bring in new business. In both these business-friendly processes, golf is central. It is either the treat used to please business contacts, or the vehicle for bonding and creating new business relationships.
   But despite this usefulness (or perhaps because of it), interviewees speak ambivalently about the place of business at clubs. A few interviewees

contend that business has no place at their club; others, more realistically, acknowledge that it does—unofficially.

This same ambivalence appears in elite clubs in Texas. Sociologist Diana Kendall notes that "clubs officially frown on members conducting business," but also that many members "believe that social and economic networking are one and the same thing," when done with appropriate discretion.[7]

The officially/unofficially tension over business appears in my interviews:

> Q: It seems like there's also a rather blurry line between social life and business life—?
>
> Clayton: Very, ah good point. Because some people do join clubs strictly for business. They want to go out and develop business associations etc. We discourage that at Oldfamily, because we truly believe we are a, y'know, a social institution; however I can tell you I've done business with at least fifteen members of that club—and large, very large transactions. I consider that an outcome, or a result of friendship, as opposed to a "I went out looking for business."

Clayton's emphasis on the primacy of friendship can be read as a deflection of the criticism that those who are excluded from Oldfamily are harmed economically. Also:

> Q: So I'm wondering how someone who's new in town could first get in, so you think work is a typical way?
>
> John: Yeah. These people don't like to say that, but it is true.

> Richard: The club exists for social purposes. They don't frown upon necessarily you prospecting for business, but it is not something you do overtly.

This last quote is telling: there is a set of norms, not so much about what one can do, as about *how* one does it. Norms are unwritten rules, of course, but if they were codified they would look something like this:

- The official position is that the country club is for recreation with friends and family, and there is no place for business.
- One exception to the above is that a member may bring business contacts to enjoy the club.
- Actual business transactions and overt salesmanship are unacceptable at the club.
- If a member happens to need a stockbroker/accountant/realtor/etc., he may find he knows one in a fellow member. In-depth conversations should happen elsewhere, but brief overtures at the club are acceptable.

- Friends (or those who want to earn "points" socially) help each other with their careers when possible.[8]

Here is an example of an acceptable process:

Donna [*describing how she gained a client*]: I took someone out last week, who was a referral from a friend of her father's, who played golf with a friend of my father's. . . . There's an example of, I guess, you know, talking about the good old boy network.

And here is an example of an unacceptable one:

Ralph: [*describing a member who supervised a member-guest tournament*] This guy . . . sold the tournament a bunch of his own—he was in the jewelry business—jewelry, and in each gift, he had his business card. The guy was so out of order, such poor taste, that he was brought before the board and told that this was wrong, we never expect it to happen again, and so forth and so on. . . . The board voted to throw him out, but we had to check whether we could legally or not. And before we found the answer out, he resigned.

So, the official rule banishing business can be bent, with finesse. Scholars of the elite have long known that clubs are incubators for business connections.[9] It's a valuable component of cultural capital to know the unwritten rules. A study of elite prep schools notes that part of what students learn there is an understanding of acceptable rule-bending.[10] Someone lacking this knowledge can lose out, either by bending the rule crassly (as above) and risking ostracism, or by adhering to the rule and failing to help their careers. However, club members try to avoid granting a membership in the first place to someone who lacks the requisite cultural knowledge to behave discreetly.

## SOCIOLOGICAL SIGNIFICANCE
## OF EXCLUSIVE COUNTRY CLUBS

Beyond the anecdotes, what is the point of studying exclusive clubs? As I did the study, I had to address the implicit "so what?" question. Like many students, I've become educated and concerned about inequalities. Often, studying inequalities opens a window on the lives of those oppressed by hierarchies of class, race, and gender. But there are insurmountable limits to a scholarship of inequality that only examines the oppressed. To fully understand inequalities, and have hope of reducing them, we must also "study up."

Sociologist G. William Domhoff argued years ago that Marxists' enthusiasm for class revolution has led them to focus excessively on the working class. Domhoff issues a reminder to look up, emphasizing "the ruling capitalist class, for it is the major initiator of action. It usually sets the terms of the interaction with the working class."[11]

Michelle Fine noted the tendency, especially with qualitative research, to always study "the Other," or the marked side of every categorical distinction. When social scientists do that, they are participating in the othering done by dominant groups; they are "re-marking" the groups, as Breckhus puts it. Also, the collective neglect to study the dominant contributes to the sanitization of their lives, keeping their dysfunctions hidden. Similarly, Susan Ostrander encourages people to study up because "a lack of knowledge about elites contributes to obscuring and therefore maintaining their position in society."[12]

The study of privileged and unmarked groups is too rarely undertaken, but it has an important place in the social sciences. First, these groups should receive scrutiny just as other groups do, so that we can understand the ways in which they are similar to and different from their counterparts who receive more scholarly attention. Second of all, each dimension of inequality can only be understood if both sides of the equation are considered. As Domhoff did for class, scholars of race and gender point out that even the best understanding of minorities and women, respectively, will always be incomplete unless the talk and action of whites and men are also understood.[13]

I am grateful for all I have learned from the above authors, but I've become uncomfortable with the term "studying up." Since the "up" concept reinscribes superordinate status, it makes a tiny contribution to legitimating the status quo. I now speak instead of studying the privileged and the unmarked.

I conducted this study to focus on the people who have disproportionate power in shaping the public discourse and the material conditions that produce and reproduce the inequalities. In other words, people with class, race, and gender privilege must be investigated; and I found them through their club memberships. This study opens a window on two aspects of privilege: the ways people build and selectively share it, and also the ways that wealth privilege, white privilege, and male privilege generally reinforce each other. This is the first study I know of that brings an intersectional approach to the study of elites and near-elites. The "matrix of privilege" has not, until now, received the same attention as the matrix of domination.[14]

The social life, leisure, and recreation of the upper classes typically involve things that "not just anybody" can participate in. This is no accident; many upper-class people work to ensure that they mingle only (or primarily) with those who are like themselves economically, culturally, and often on the basis of race or ethnicity. Homophily—mixing with people like yourself—is the norm and an important theme.[15] It's important for the following five reasons.

First: the social interaction is instructive. People have arranged to ensure that the young members of the class are properly socialized into upper-class lifestyle and culture. These initiates—including select adult newcomers—learn the unwritten rules of social life, and they learn the importance of conforming to them. Clubs, along with the right address, schools, and connections, are all recognized as important parts of grooming the next generation to assume their "proper place."[16]

The second reason exclusive homophily is important is that it demarcates, again and again, a division between "us" and "them." Homophily emphasizes a group's distinctiveness, and exclusivity emphasizes its superiority. This boundary work is important regarding race as well as class. Prominent theorist Patricia Hill Collins notes: "Issues of purity and separation, whether of geographical space or . . . forms of symbolic space, appear central to maintaining unjust power relations of race, class, nation, and ethnicity in the United States."[17]

Upper-class boundaries are emphatically *not* drawn by finances alone; one cannot simply buy one's way into acceptance. Signaling (and reading) class is an extensive, detailed project, one that may, for those who didn't grow up belonging, take years to master.[18] Sketching a sense of "us" can begin at elite prep schools, where homogeneity and isolation breed solidarity. Elites do talk of the educational benefits of prep school, but also say: "You don't go to private school just for your education. You go there to be separated from ordinary people." In Susan Ostrander's classic study, the elites she asked about class spoke not of finances, but of being well born, having a prominent social standing, and being superior in a historical, social, or moral sense.[19] Her interviewees acknowledge the exclusivity of their social clubs, and voice appreciation that they are selective on more than just financial criteria. Membership is open only to those whom the existing members consider "congenial."

A third reason homophily is important is that it enables and encourages homogeneous marriages. Any group would dissipate if its members married outsiders; but class distinctiveness and strength is preserved as long as upper-class members marry each other. This is too crucial a matter to be left to chance; many forces combine to reduce the occurrence of "mixed marriage." "Considerable class, school, club, residential, and racial segregation characterize upper class ways of life," which minimizes exposure to unworthy romantic partners.[20] Further, a suitable pool for dating and mating is served up to the youth: their parents and other women organize debutante balls and other invitation-only dances, partly to create a marriage marketplace for the next generation.[21] Country clubs are one important site of such organizing. This is an important function wealthy women serve in the division of class labor. There may be an unspoken awareness within the upper class of the importance of in-marriage for class preservation.

The fourth and fifth aspects of homophily are interrelated, and concern the building of a network of connections and of class consciousness. It is well known that career and financial success depend not just on one's human capital, but on social capital or network ties. The connections fostered at schools, social clubs, and other rarefied sites are recognized as important in every macro-oriented study of elites.[22] Again, though it's unspoken, I believe there's an awareness that part of the purpose of social exclusivity is to hoard the valuable connections that are forged during the mostly homophilous interactions.

The final important quality of exclusive homophily is that it breeds a classwide consciousness and loyalty. Having usually come from similar backgrounds, members of the power elite feel a psychological and social unity. Their intermingling at prep schools and country clubs helps create a sense of class membership.[23] Despite American mythos, upper-class lives are less about individuality than about membership. Indeed, the crucible of prep school is about "melting down the refractory metal of individualism into the solid metal of elite collectivism."[24] The national elite network, with its multiple board memberships and social connections, fosters loyalties beyond one's own family and/or firm. Such a "classwide" mentality is crucial for rising to the very top, since it will ensure that class interests (and not just company interests) are advocated.[25] Exclusive homophily helps build a sense of oneself as a member of the upper class. It can also allow for the development of "elite think," characterized by acceptance of racial-ethnic and gender inequalities and an obliviousness to those not in the upper class.[26] The power elite is a bit more diverse today, but is still unified by a sense of class privilege that transcends its demographic profile. In fact, class consciousness in America is at its greatest in the upper class.[27]

Now that I have outlined the characteristics of upper-class social exclusiveness—socialization, emphasizing distinctiveness, encouraging in-marriage, building connections and class consciousness—it's time to consider exactly what "class" means here, and how it interacts with hierarchies of race and gender.

## CLASS, BROADLY

In classical social theory, class was defined narrowly in terms of one's work and pay. Matters of style and interaction were considered to be often related to class, but logically separate from it.

Contemporary scholars are broadening the definition of class beyond work and money. They—we—are including consideration of not just what you produce, but what you consume, and how and with whom. We recognize that people create the meanings of class distinctions not just at work, but also in family relationships, leisure activities, and through cultural and moral boundaries.[28]

Remembering the intersections of class, race, and gender inequalities reminds us to broaden the analysis of stratification beyond the workplace. In the United States and globally, the class structure is intertwined with structures of race and gender. A growing body of scholars argue that anyone who studies class must take these other hierarchies into account.[29] While not always focused on inequalities, intersectional scholars make a compelling case for studying class and race and gender together.

One goal of this project is to meet the challenge of analyzing class, race, and gender inequalities as interlocking rather than separate. Another goal is, even though the analysis is mainly about ideas, to consider the influence of material social structure. Material social structure influences people with privilege, just as it influences everyone else; remember that structure doesn't just constrain, it also enables.[30] As shown in the above discussion of homophily, country clubs are one important context where people help reproduce a social structure marked by inequalities. The coming chapters will focus more on cultural than structural reproduction. But we'll keep social structure in mind, as we consider the importance of financial and other resources for accomplishing exclusion.

## INTERSECTING INEQUALITIES

A more recent intellectual call than the one to "study up" is the call to conceive of race, class, and gender as interlocking axes of oppression.[31] The challenge is to think of race, class, and gender not as independent hierarchies, but as mutually constitutive: the class hierarchy is raced and gendered, the gender hierarchy is classed and raced, and the race hierarchy is classed and gendered.[32]

Since the concept of hierarchy is fundamentally relational, it also means that these three axes are always in play, for everyone. I disagree with the notion that black women serve, or should continue to serve, as "quintessential intersectional subjects."[33] Gender is about men as well as women, class is about the wealthy, and race about whites.

By definition, the categorical membership of these "unmarked" groups is less salient; the intersecting hierarchies can be forgotten. As Peggy McIntosh shows about being white, part of its insidiousness is that the unmarked category often seems invisible, is considered "neutral."[34] I will attempt to keep all three major dimensions *out* of hiding. Here is a preview of an intersectional perspective on the people of this study.

## Class as Gender and Race Specific

The class hierarchy in America is created by the system of capitalism. This has traditionally been a system wherein the people with some ownership over the means of production are able to profit from the value of work done by those who own nothing but their laboring abilities. Things are more complicated today under late industrial capitalism, with its stock ownership and layers of business managers; but capitalism, and a supportive government, are the reasons why America has such a pronounced hierarchy of class.

And yet, people in this study are not merely "classed actors," neutral and unified. There is internal variation just as there is among all persons; people's gender and race influences some of this variation.

The upper classes are gendered in the following ways. Perhaps most important, it has traditionally been overwhelmingly men whose income and assets qualify them for the top economic stratum. Women generally qualify as wives or inheriting daughters; even wealthy heiresses turn their own fortunes over to their husbands' control.[35] This is a sign that wealth is not a direct road to power. It's also a reminder that compulsory heterosexuality is an important influence on how men and women relate.[36] Gender relations in the upper classes remain male-dominant. The norms of masculinity and femininity influence the identities, behaviors, and relationships of upper-class people, as they do in every class.

Overwhelmingly, the upper classes are "raced white." The above discussion of exclusive homophily, with its dual emphasis on admitting only similar others and on intergenerational continuity, hints at racial segregation traditionally hidden behind class segregation. Whiteness has been until recently a definite requirement for belonging in exclusive clubs and other elite contexts. Today, nonwhites are granted admission; but the contexts remain culturally white. Those nonwhites—indeed, any non-WASPs—who belong to the clubs in this study are assimilated enough so that they do not disturb the arguably racist "comfort zone" that dominates members' conception of who does and does not belong. Also, the persistent overlap between the categories of white and affluent subtly strengthens class and race inequalities, because each dimension of inequality is lent legitimacy by its alignment with the other.

## Gender as Class and Race Specific

As noted, heterosexual partnerships are part of the cultural prescription for men and women. In the upper class, this yields couples where each has a role to play in reproducing the class structure. Traditionally, men have organized the workings of government and business to maintain the status quo that provides them with wealth; their wives, meanwhile, have

performed much of the work described above of orchestrating homophilous social lives (as well as philanthropic work). Today the roles have
blurred together somewhat; but compulsory heterosexuality still influences
the lives of men and women in the upper classes in unique ways. Capitalism's extreme economic inequality helps men/husbands buy the compliance of women/wives who are subordinated within the upper classes.

Another distinct aspect of upper-class gender relations is its appearance
of liberalism. I was surprised to learn that, contrary to my expectations,
the most elite club is not the most conservative about women's status;
quite the opposite. In the upper classes, a man's power is assured and
unshakable: through high public status and control of family wealth, his
dominance is never in question. Gender relations in the upper classes remain male-dominated, but in a subtle rather than a dramatic fashion.

Given the race-class overlap, these gender relations have a distinctly
white cast to them. Men such as the ones in this study are proud of, and
receive praise for, their gender liberalism. The "kinder, gentler" displays
of masculinity are contrasted with men who are not WASPs, who are
denigrated in racial-ethnic terms as less progressive and more chauvinis-
tic.[37] Thus, gender here is race-specific as well as class-specific, as I will
show in chapter 4.

## Race as Class and Gender Specific

American race relations are a unique outcome of the country's history,
immigration patterns, and economic system. Some even argue that economic inequality is the source of racial inequality: that in the absence of
the struggle for resources created under capitalism, racism would wither
away.[38] Given my interest in the *reproduction* of inequalities, I tend not to
participate in the search for original root causes. But certainly, the American racial hierarchy should be considered in the context of the system of
capitalism that fosters group (as well as individual) competition over
scarce resources.

In this population, the most obvious way race is specified is that it has
been nearly impossible for nonwhites to climb to the top of the socioeconomic heap. The upper class was traditionally all white, and even today
it is raced white, though a few nonwhites belong. As Zweigenhaft and
Domhoff show, those nonwhites who have gained entry into the power
elite have done so by assimilating into white culture.[39] The few nonwhites in this study, with their golf games and newscaster's comportment, bear this out.

This study also shows that ethnic distinctions, even within the group
considered white, sometimes seem just as important as racial ones. In
the northeastern setting of the research, racial-ethnic hierarchy has

traditionally been overlaid on economic hierarchy. People have traditionally drawn racial-ethnic group boundaries, with social and economic consequences. When members consider the question of who does and does not belong in their club, they build on, and sometimes reproduce, these racist discourses.

Race is gendered here, too, because of the truism that the upper classes are more open to men than women arrivistes. Though blacks are closer than whites to gender parity in earnings, this disappears at the top of the economic scale: for nonwhites as well as whites, the very top earners are more likely to be men than women.[40] The nonwhite club members in this study are all men, which may also reflect that the dominance required to arrive at the door of the club appears more fitting, to existing members, as part of a man's rather than a woman's identity. Chapter 3 will cover the racial-ethnic composition of the clubs, and how members explain it.

I hope that the foregoing discussion helps illuminate the ways in which class, race, and gender all matter, for the unmarked as well as the marked. I find it very difficult to address all three axes at exactly the same time, and the chapters to follow do indulge in some conceptual segregation between class, race, and gender, reflecting the way that interviewees think and talk. But the book as a whole paints an intersectional picture that, I hope, does justice to the scholarly call to consider the matrix of oppression—or in this case, the matrix of privilege.

## NOTES

1. Aldrich, *Old Money: The Mythology of America's Upper Class*. New York: A. A. Knopf, 1988.

2. WASP stands for White Anglo-Saxon Protestant, a term commonly used by my interviewees, including when they characterize their country clubs. It reflects the fact that white Catholics receive some of the same "othering" treatment that nonwhites do.

3. cf. "Old Name Families" in Kendall, *The Power of Good Deeds: Privileged Women and the Social Reproduction of the Upper Class*. Lanham, MD: Rowman & Littlefield, 2002.

4. My interviewees are not all elites in the sense used by Mills (*The Power Elite*. New York: Oxford University Press, 1956) and van Dijk (*Elite Discourse and Racism*. Newbury Park, CA: Sage, 1993).

5. Kendall (2002:162).

6. Bourdieu, "Cultural Reproduction and Social Reproduction." In *Power and Ideology in Education*, edited by Jerome Karabel and A. H. Halsey. New York: Oxford University Press, 1977.

7. Kendall, *Members Only: Elite Clubs and the Process of Exclusion*. Lanham, MD: Rowman & Littlefield, 2008, page 100. She also reports (on page 97) similar bonding via golf.

8. Kendall (2008:90) points out that when members are conscious of their organization's exclusivity and prestige, it makes them more likely to help one another, thus maintaining a benefit of belonging.

9. Domhoff, *Who Rules America?* Englewood Cliffs, NJ: Prentice-Hall, 1967; Domhoff, *The Powers That Be: Processes of Ruling Class Domination in America*. New York: Random House, 1979; Domhoff, *Who Rules America Now?: A View for the '80s*. New York: Simon & Schuster, 1986; Dye, *Who's Running America?: Institutional Leadership in the United States*. Englewood Cliffs, NJ: Prentice-Hall, 1976; Useem, *The Inner Circle: Large Corporations and the Rise of Business Political Activity in the U.S. and U.K.* New York: Oxford University Press, 1984.

10. Cookson and Persell, *Preparing For Power: America's Elite Boarding Schools*. New York: Basic Books, 1985.

11. Domhoff (1979:xiv). The "studying up" term was coined by Nader in "Up the Anthropologist: Perspectives Gained from Studying Up." In *Reinventing Anthropology*, edited by Dell Hymes. New York: Vintage, 1969.

12. Fine, "Working the Hyphens: Reinventing Self and Other in Qualitative Research." In *The Handbook of Qualitative Research*, edited by Norman K. Denzin and Yvonna S. Lincoln. Thousand Oaks, CA: Sage, 1994; Breckhus, "A Sociology of the Unmarked: Redirecting Our Focus." *Sociological Theory* 16, no. 1 (1998): 34–51; Ostrander, "'Surely You're Not in This Just to Be Helpful': Access, Rapport, and Interviews in Three Studies of Elites." *Journal of Contemporary Ethnography* 22 (1993), page 7.

13. For an example on race, see Morrison (*Playing in the Dark: Whiteness and the Literary Imagination*. New York: Vintage, 1992); for gender, see Connell (*Gender and Power*. Palo Alto, CA: Stanford University Press, 1987).

14. Matrix of domination is from Collins (*Black Feminist Thought: Knowledge, Consciousness, and the Politics of Empowerment*. New York: Routledge, 1990); "matrix of privilege" from Disch ("General Introduction." In *Reconstructing Gender: A Multicultural Anthology*, 4th ed., edited by Estelle Disch. Boston: McGraw-Hill, 1997, page 6). Disch coined that phrase and is unaware of its use anywhere else (personal communication 2010).

15. For a review of the homophily concept, see McPherson, Smith-Lovin, and Cook, "Birds of a Feather: Homophily in Social Networks." *Annual Review of Sociology* 27 (2001): 415.

16. Ostrander, *Women Of The Upper Class*. Philadelphia: Temple University Press, 1984; Daniels, *Invisible Careers: Women Civic Leaders From the Volunteer World*. Chicago: University of Chicago Press, 1988; Keller, "The American Upper Class Family: Precarious Claims on the Future." *Journal of Comparative Family Studies* 22 (1991), page 170.

17. Collins, *Fighting Words: Black Women and the Search for Justice*. Minneapolis: University of Minnesota Press, 1998, page 214.

18. Keller (1991:173).

19. Prep school is the focus of Cookson and Persell (1985); the "separated" quote is from Ostrander (1984:85).

20. Keller (1991:165).

21. Daniels (1988), Kendall (2002), and Ostrander (1984).

22. Mills (1956) notes that the "Power Elite" are tied together in a web that makes use of schools, social and political clubs, firms, vacation resorts, and so on.

Useem (1984) writes of social clubs as important nodes for the "Inner Circle." Attending a prestigious club or school confers not just status for its own sake, but also an entry into a valuable web of connections. Zweigenhaft and Domhoff (*Diversity in the Power Elite: How It Happened, Why It Matters*. Lanham, MD: Rowman & Littlefield, 2006, page 231) note that those women and minorities who enter the power elite are disproportionately likely to have attended a top school.

23. Mills (1956:282).

24. Cookson and Persell (1985:124).

25. Useem (1984).

26. Kendall (2008, chapter 7).

27. cf. Ostrander, "Class Consciousness as Conduct and Meaning." *The Insurgent Sociologist* 9 (1980): 38. On the demographics, see Zweigenhaft and Domhoff (2006).

28. An early example is Warner and Lunt, *The Social Life of a Modern Community*. New Haven, CT: Yale University Press, 1941. Others since are Bourdieu (1977), Bettie (*Women Without Class: Girls, Race, and Identity*. Berkeley: University of California Press, 2003), Lamont (*Money, Morals, and Manners: The Culture of the French and American Upper-Middle Class*. Chicago: University of Chicago Press, 1992), Yodanis ("Producing Social Class Representations: Women's Work in a Rural Town." *Gender & Society* 16 (2002): 323), and Reay, who calls class "a complicated mixture of the material, the discursive, psychological predispositions and sociological dispositions" ("Rethinking Social Class: Qualitative Perspectives on Class and Gender." *Sociology* 32 (1998), page 259).

29. On class and race, see e.g. Bonacich ("A Theory of Ethnic Antagonism: The Split Labor Market." *American Sociological Review* 37 (1972): 547); Collins (1998), and Glenn ("The Social Construction and Institutionalization of Gender and Race: An Integrative Framework." In *Revisioning Gender*, edited by Myra Marx Ferree, Judith Lorber, and Beth B. Hess. Thousand Oaks, CA: Sage, 1999); on class and gender, see e.g. Acker ("Hierarchies, Jobs, Bodies: A Theory of Gendered Organizations." *Gender & Society* 4 (1990): 139); Kessler, Ashenden, Connell, and Dowsett ("Gender Relations in Secondary Schooling." *Sociology of Education* 58 (1985): 34); and Mies (*Patriarchy and Accumulation on a World Scale: Women in the International Division of Labour*. London: Zed Books, 1986).

30. Giddens, *The Constitution of Society*. Berkeley: University of California Press, 1984.

31. Germinal work in this young tradition comes from Collins (1990), Crenshaw ("Mapping the Margins: Intersectionality, Identity Politics, and Violence Against Women of Color." *Stanford Law Review* 43 (1991): 1241), hooks (*Feminist Theory: From Margin to Center*. Boston: South End Press, 1984), and Hull, Scott, and Smith (*But Some of Us Are Brave*. Old Westbury, NY: Feminist Press, 1982). All these authors are women of color, and no coincidence. Their own lived experience led them to see the insufficiency of the scholarship of the time, as suggested in the saying "all the women are white, all the blacks are men, but some of us are brave" (Hull, Scott, and Smith 1982). As people "marked" on two axes of domination, black women rejected a single-axis analysis of the world.

More recent treatments of intersectionality include Choo and Ferree ("Practicing Intersectionality in Sociological Research: A Critical Analysis of Inclusions,

Interactions and Institutions in the Study of Inequalities." *Social Forces* 28 [2010], 129), Davis ("Intersectionality as a Buzzword: A Sociology of Science Perspective on What Makes a Feminist Theory Successful." *Feminist Theory* 9 (2008): 67), Denis ("Review Essay: Intersectional Analysis: A Contribution of Feminism to Sociology." *International Sociology* 23 (2008): 677), McCall ("The Complexity of Intersectionality." *Signs* 30, no. 3 (2005): 1771), and Weber (*Understanding Race, Class, Gender and Sexuality: A Conceptual Framework*, 2d ed. New York: Oxford University Press, 2009).

32. cf. "The various gestures of class performance never exist outside of race and gender meanings" Bettie (2003:191).

33. Nash, "Re-Thinking Intersectionality." *Feminist Review* 89 (2008), page 1.

34. McIntosh, "White Privilege and Male Privilege: A Personal Account of Coming to See Correspondences Through Work in Women's Studies." In *Race, Class and Gender: An Anthology*, edited by Margaret Anderson and Patricia Hill Collins. Belmont, CA: Wadsworth, 1992.

35. Ostrander (1984).

36. Rich, "Compulsory Heterosexuality and Lesbian Existence." In *Powers of Desire: The Politics of Sexuality*, edited by Ann Snitow, Christine Stansell, and Sharon Thompson. New York: Monthly Review Press, 1983; Rubin, "The Traffic in Women: Notes on the 'Political Economy' of Sex." In *Toward an Anthropology of Women*, edited by Reyna Reiter. New York: Monthly Review Press, 1975.

37. Messner ("Men as Superordinates: Challenges for Gender Scholarship." In *Privilege: A Reader*, edited by Michael S. Kimmel and Abby S. Ferber. Boulder, CO: Westview Press, 2003) writes of "kinder, gentler" masculinity.

38. See e.g. Carr, *"Color-Blind" Racism*. Thousand Oaks, CA: Sage, 1997.

39. Zweigenhaft and Domhoff (2006).

40. Morris and Western, "Inequality in Earnings at the Close of the Twentieth Century." *Annual Review of Sociology* 25 (1999): 623.

# 2

# Denials and Justifications

## *Club Members Account for Exclusivity*

"People who are interested in food, and people that are interested in wine, tend to have gotten there ostensibly because they can afford to be there. It's hard to do those things when you're poor. And so it's almost: who enjoys the kinds of things we enjoy who are also part of what this core is."

—Larry, Oldfamily member

Can you think of a time when you had to explain yourself—your actions, your inactions? The student reader may have had to explain her/himself recently to a parent or a teacher. Though you weren't thinking of it at the time, consider now these typical circumstances: [1]

- An explanation or account is called for when a person's conduct is in some way questionable. This depends on the cultural context: what's perfectly normal and unnoticed in one society may be questionable in another.
- The person doing the explaining uses available cultural tools to provide a socially acceptable account.
- So, culture is complex: some cultural ideals or tools may call your behavior into question, yet at the same time you'll use other cultural ideals or tools to explain yourself.

Members of country clubs where admission is deliberately exclusive have some explaining to do. This chapter discusses the accounts the members offer: why they need to give accounts, the cultural tools they use in doing so, and the significance of well accounted for exclusion.

The American ideal of equal opportunity calls club members to account for their exclusion, as illustrated recently by two public controversies about country clubs. In 1990, the golf world was embarrassed by the revelation that Shoal Creek, a club hosting a PGA (Professional Golfers' Association) tournament, was defiantly all-white. Public pressure forced changes at Shoal Creek and in the policies of the PGA and other golf organizations.[2]

More recently, the National Council of Women's Organizations protested against the Augusta National Golf Club for its exclusive membership policies. This protest garnered significant attention in the media, where the subject of Augusta's gender exclusion led to the subject of racial-ethnic exclusion as well.[3] Reactions in the form of opinion columns and letters to the editor were divided: some supported Augusta. Others attacked exclusiveness as discrimination harmful to women and minorities.

In the northeastern United States, where this study is located, criticism of private clubs has appeared occasionally in local newspapers. At Northern, women members filed a discrimination complaint and eventually sued. This prompted considerable coverage, including a newspaper article calling country clubs "bastions of male privilege." Oldfamily, Rosary, and Suburban have also been mentioned in their local papers: during the 1990s, both gender subordination and racial/ethnic exclusion at local clubs made headlines.

The mayor of a city elsewhere in the region made the news for allegedly extorting a membership in an exclusive private eating club. One newspaper columnist mockingly sympathized with an imaginary club member about the public exposure: "[The member] enjoyed certain boundaries between him and the seedy side of life. He thought those boundaries would always be in place." The club had "held itself above the grubby embarrassments" of the city, but now "its comfortably private confines suffer[ed] the harsh light of public attention."[4]

These criticisms from the media demonstrate that misgivings about exclusive private clubs are, at least sometimes, part of popular discourse. And, my interviewees are aware of it. Some of their comments imply this awareness, and the need to account for their clubs.

A former president of Suburban bemoans the negative stereotype some outsiders have of country clubs. Before he agreed to a taped interview, he told me: "People have preconceived notions about clubs, and usually don't change them regardless of what is read or written. Even some people in Littletown do, like some Jewish people will drive by the club and point it out to their children, saying, 'see that place? We can't belong there.'" I believe he granted the interview partly because he wanted the chance to counter the preconceived notions by providing his account of his club.

A businesswoman transplanted to the area initially declined to join Oldfamily, as she explains:

Theresa: When I mentioned the name Oldfamily to people that I worked with, they'd say, "yeah, I thought you'd go there." Something about that didn't feel right. These are very working class, really good folks. Just didn't feel right to affiliate myself with something that was perceived as so exclusive.

For several reasons she stated, including its diminishing exclusivity, she joined Oldfamily several years later.

Sensitivity to the perception of outsiders is such that another Oldfamily member says she hesitates to announce her membership.

Olivia: I just didn't like that snobby, I didn't want them to think that was me. So people say, "where do you play tennis?" "Oh, I play tennis in [names city]." "Where do you play golf?" "I play golf in [city]." And if they want to pursue it farther, I'll tell them. But I don't say "I play at Oldfamily," unless they ask.

Being interviewed, of course, is an artificial situation especially likely to feel like a call to account. Another Oldfamily member, who belongs to *four* exclusive private clubs, called this revelation in the interview "pathetic" and "embarrassing." And other interviewees announced they expected "tough questions" or "loaded questions" from me.

Again, these examples are cited to show that club members know that some popular sentiment is suspicious of their clubs, and that they need to be able to provide an account. This knowledge is not something that people talk about readily. One social theorist distinguishes between discursive consciousness and practical consciousness, the latter comprising things that people simply know or do without putting into words.[5] The awareness of the need to account for one's clubs is a matter of practical consciousness.

After all, it is theoretically possible for these people to be purely defiant, even self-righteous. But they are not, because one strain of American culture deems exclusion ethically wrong. Club members provide accounts that either deny or justify the exclusion at their clubs in order to counteract that element of the culture. They do it to paper over the ethical dilemmas and feel good about themselves. Their accounts also serve to protect existing arrangements by justifying them. The accounts as a whole help to legitimate the existence of exclusive private clubs and the part they play in reproducing privilege.

Legitimating exclusive clubs is important because of the significance of such institutions to the upper classes. Clubs do not autonomously reproduce inequalities, but they *are* cogs in a more complex machinery. Along with private schools, exclusive neighborhoods, and other voluntary and professional organizations, country clubs provide important opportunities for face-to-face interaction and solidarity building among wealthy people. These experiences foster a consciousness that transcends one's family or firm, a raced and gendered consciousness that inspires class-wide coordinated action. At the same time, clubs provide a context in which to know important people with whom to coordinate. Upper-class policy coordination is enabled by the trust and receptivity that develop in exclusive clubs and other socially cohesive environments.[6] Clubs like those in this sample serve important purposes, so their legitimation is likewise important. I will revisit at the end of this chapter the significance of the legitimating accounts analyzed here.

Even as part of American culture requires accounts from club members, other elements of the culture provide them with the tools they need to develop those accounts. Indeed, accounts always draw upon mainstream culture in order to be effective.[7] As we will see in this chapter, a crucial cultural tool for these interviewees is the American Dream with its "dominant stratification ideology." The American Dream is the promise that upward mobility is possible for everyone, according to their talent and effort. In explaining class issues, most Americans rely on the "dominant stratification ideology," which is

> the age-old notion that individuals are ultimately responsible for their status in systems of social inequality. In capitalism, opportunities are readily available to all who are willing to work hard, and socioeconomic mobility and standing hinge on the possession and expression of acquired personality characteristics such as drives, skills, and motives. Moreover, the logic continues, because virtually all people have the opportunity to acquire and develop these traits, those who do are justly rewarded with wealth.[8]

In this ideology, market forces are seen as neutral and *natural*. Therefore, class divisions are seen as *legitimate*. This is tremendously helpful in accounting for clubs' exclusivity. At the same time, the American emphasis on opportunity for *all* hints at the source of cultural criticism of exclusive clubs.

The cultural climate no longer embraces overt expressions of white supremacy; racial segregation cannot be a useful account for club exclusivity. So, today club members use themes of class and culture more than ever before. Among the justifications discussed below, you will not see anyone express a dislike for a racial-ethnic group; however, you will see references to exclusion based on differences in personal style.[9]

Another cultural tool that club members can use is the legal and cultural support given to their organizations. This is indeed paradoxical, since I just noted that the organizations also receive criticism. But as Jennifer Hochschild writes in *The American Dream*, the analyst's job is not to solve social paradoxes, just to explicate them. Exclusive country clubs do receive some legal and cultural support. Although it is subtly contested, the law does protect the right of incorporated private clubs to do *anything they wish* when it comes to both admissions—which can arguably include racial discrimination—and also club policies—which can arguably include gender discrimination. Cultural support is illustrated when top golf tournaments are played at exclusive clubs, with attendant media coverage, corporate sponsorships, and large audiences.

Now that we have established why club members provide accounts, and some of the cultural tools they use to do so, we may proceed to the accounts themselves. The first group of accounts argues that there is really no exclusion taking place at the clubs. I will discuss variants of this theme, and then move to the larger group of accounts, which justify why exclusion is acceptable. Here, interviewees' talk covers a wide range: sports, family, the "fit" of new members, socializing, tradition, and responsibilities and rights. As I will show, people use—perhaps unconsciously—a variety of rhetorical and cultural tools to de-problematize country clubs' policies and their own membership.

## "THERE ISN'T ANY REAL
## ECONOMIC PLATEAU:" DENYING EXCLUSION

One way that interviewees account for their clubs is to say that there really isn't any exclusion happening. I'll discuss several variations on this theme: from simply denying that there is any screening, to saying that the only filter is social ties, or residence, or affordability, to saying that virtually anyone could afford to belong.

First: when asked about how their club screens potential new members, some people deny that there is a screening process. This denial is supported by their inability to think of many, or any, cases where a candidate was rejected.

Q: What makes someone a good Oldfamily prospect or a hopeless Oldfamily prospect?
   Evan: Hm. I don't, I can't think of anybody who hasn't been admitted, in the time I've been there.

Gloria [*lifelong member*]: I don't know of anyone who has been proposed that hasn't gotten in.

Frank: I don't know of anybody being turned down.

Ralph [*lifelong member*]: It doesn't happen very often. It really doesn't. I've been here a long time. I could if I really thought about it, I could think of maybe three or four or something like that over a long, long period of time.

Reid: It very rarely happens. I only know of three cases in fifteen, eighteen years that I've been here of this happening, so it's not something that happens a lot.

Q: So most applicants get admitted?

Reid: Most *proposed* people get admitted, yeah. [emphasis added]

Being unable to think of any/many cases of rejection isn't exactly compelling evidence for an actual lack of screening. Members may be unlikely to discuss failed candidacies among themselves, because of the discomfort of acknowledging exclusiveness. So, the word wouldn't spread. Also, this account goes hand-in-hand with the argument people make that they themselves are not excluding anyone (see "Governance and Responsibility" below).

This account is also directly related to the particulars of the admissions process, described in the previous chapter. As noted, the issuance of an application to the club is one of the last—not first—steps in the process. Reid, above, who has served on Rosary's board of governors, is making an important clarification. Someone who wants to join, but never receives an application, has not had their candidacy officially proposed and rejected. The procedures of club admission are deliberately set up to facilitate, among other things, this referral to a lack of evidence of screening.

Another variation is to aver that there is no exclusion—*all you need* is to know a couple of people who already belong.

Evan: I get a sense that if, y'know, you know a couple of members, you know a couple of board members, and you want to join, there's nothing, other than the financial obligation, that will hold you back.

Victor: At Shinnecock and National and all those places, that's: who you know, who you are; as opposed to this which is, as you say maybe: if you know someone who's a member there, you can get in if you just get on the [waiting] list.

Among my interviewees, to know a few people at an exclusive local club is a "no-brainer"; most of them could name acquaintances at all four area clubs. This requirement is casually identified as an easy hurdle to clear. But to argue that this hurdle is not exclusionary is to reveal a blindness about the boundaries of their social networks. This sample is so rich in social capital that the people don't see the value and rarity of their network location. The individualism of American culture deflects attention from collective processes like the organizational and personal uses of social networks. And given cultural ideals of equal opportunity, those who benefit most from social capital—club members—might be the most motivated to remain blind to its importance.

Social capital, of course, depends in part on residence.[10] When interviewees contemplate what draws people to a certain club, they often refer to geography. The idea comes up over and over again that club membership is driven by place of residence.

Q: Can you tell me about how you first came to join Suburban?
   Stella: Well, it's right here in Littletown. We did consider joining the Old-family, knew people at both clubs. But we felt that the proximity was good because we had young children.

Ward: I knew it was being built and it was closer to my home, and so I would watch as they were constructing the club, so my wife and I talked about it and we really wanted to be [in a club] closer to home.

Sabrina: You kind of go where your neighbors are.

Roland: I think you'll find the reason most people join a country club is the prox-imity of the club. Well, the facilities first of all, and the proximity of the club.

So if residence drives club membership, what drives residence? None of my interviewees cited a country club as an influence on where they lived, although that was mentioned twice as something other people might con-sider. The quality of local public schools was cited as influencing residence. This was noted only by women, which is understandable given that moth-ers are traditionally more responsible than fathers for parental planning. The public schools in Littletown are better than those serving the Heights, so that is one reason why Littletown—and thus Suburban—attracts fami-lies. It may also be the case that Littletown attracts those families who are not wealthy enough to live in the Heights and send their children to private schools, as the majority of Heights residents do.

While country clubs *might* influence choice of residence a bit, the re-verse influence of residence on club membership comes through more strongly. The idea that club membership is driven by geography is an-other way to say that it's not driven by exclusion. Americans tend to think of residential patterns as the simple accretion of individual preferences.[11] But like club membership, residence is obviously influenced by afford-ability. In 2007, the median sale price of single-family houses was over $425,000 for both Littletown and the Heights. These two areas stand out starkly from the statewide average of about $275,000.

Sometimes people do make note of the financial requirements of coun-try club membership. This variation on the theme is that there is no exclu-sion other than affordability.

Q: So can [your downtown eating club] no longer afford to be too selective as to who could get in?
   John: That's an understatement. I think [it] would be glad to have any member who has two feet and could pay the bill.

This quote aside, statements about affordability being the only criterion are limited to Waterside. Waterside is the newer and pricier club, with an initiation fee in the six figures—an order of magnitude more expensive than Oldfamily, Rosary, and Suburban. Its members suggest that fees are their only filter:

Wendy: If you can afford to pay the price, you can get in.

Q: [*discussing getting the right people to join early on*] What else do you think makes the early people the right people?
Walter: Well, I think a lot of it's affordability, to be honest with you. It's not inexpensive. So I think a lot of it's affordability.
Q: Is there something else though?
Walter: Beyond the economics of it? Uh, I really don't think so.

Relying on the financial barrier takes the onus off of club members. Keeping certain people out of their club becomes an impersonal market force, rather than something that they are doing. The argument that one's club has no restriction other than affordability depends on the dominant stratification ideology, which perceives market forces as neutral and natural.

As I began this project, I expected the fees at Oldfamily, Rosary, and Suburban to be higher than they are. Compared to Waterside, one doesn't hear that affordability is the only criterion at these places, which is telling. They cannot use this account, since their fees are within reach for enough people that they do further screening. Waterside comes closer to the preconception I had of club fees set sky-high as a barrier to entry. (The fees *are* a significant barrier, but I had overestimated them probably because of my own upper-middle-class social location.)

Some club members (other than Watersiders) seize upon the affordability of fees to argue that there is virtually no economic barrier to membership. So not only is economic inequality naturalized, it appears truncated. Club members' vision of socioeconomic stratification—or at least what they verbalize—does not extend too far down. This is due partly to the residential patterns just mentioned: postwar development of housing has isolated the poor away from the affluent.[12] Club members' truncated vision results in an inflated sense of the affordability of country club membership. A former Suburban club president:

Steve: They [some people] may not be happy [at my club] because they feel like they're not as similar to everybody else or maybe there's an economic issue. It's not inexpensive to be a member. By the same token, if you're renting a summer house for a couple of weeks someplace, my guess is it's about the same, not dissimilar from that, plus—
Q: Annually.
Steve: We're talking about $5,000 a year. You rent a nice house someplace, you're talking about $2,000 to $3,000 a week, so probably not much

different than that, so you put your money where you want to get your most pleasure.

[*later*]

We have members that used to caddy, you know. From an economic standpoint you might not think would be members. But they are. Because they like golf and they figured out how to do it. And so *there isn't any real economic plateau that you have to reach to become a member*. People from lots of different areas. Although there are a certain fixed amount of dollars that it costs, so that does bring it to a certain level. But as I said before, a week at the beach, probably about the same. [emphasis added]

In a different interview, we were talking about the financial barrier to membership, and I asked the interviewee if he ever had mixed feelings about it. His reply:

Ward: No. No, it doesn't bother me. I think that people make decisions, I don't come from means that most of these other people at country clubs come from. I sacrificed and I saved a long time to do it, and we have made sacrifices to be able to do this. This is our retirement. We looked at it, my wife and I said this is what we're gonna do for our retirement. We're making an investment in our marriage every time we're at this country club. I don't, I think it's a decision that people have to make. You can own a little bit less of a house to belong to Waterside or if you want the big house, you can have it. I think it's a decision that we made.

A woman from a non-wealthy background first joined Suburban as a teenager under her parents. She says, "economically my family isn't that well off or wasn't that well off, but golf was such a priority for them" that they joined the club. All three of these quotes share the theme that affording country club membership is just a matter of prioritizing: as long as one is willing to live in "a little bit less of a house," or forgo a two-week summer rental, virtually anyone can afford to belong. This truncated vision of stratification serves to keep hidden the depth of our class divisions, and members' privileged economic status.[13]

Interestingly, in denying economic exclusion, these people have effectively chosen to emphasize social exclusion instead. This is a bind for the clubs other than Waterside: they want fees low enough to be comfortable, but then they must perform additional screening as a result, and own up to it. The remainder of this chapter addresses how they do it.

## "IT'S A DAMN GOOD FAMILY CLUB:" JUSTIFYING EXCLUSION

Accounts that justify or excuse exclusion are more common than those that deny or minimize exclusion. Seven such types of accounts emerge from the interviews; I will discuss them in order from most to least common.

## Sports

What is the purpose of these clubs, according to their members? As one might expect, the responses typically include references to friendships and sports, especially golf. When I review the accounts of why clubs exist and why people join them, talk of sports is more than *twice as common* as talk of friendships. And of the sports, golf easily overshadows mentions of swimming, tennis, squash, and so on.

Why golf, of all the possible sports? In the United States, golf and country clubs have intertwined histories. When American elites founded country clubs a hundred years ago, sports with horses were in fashion. Riding in coaches, hunting, cricket, and tennis were popular but became eclipsed by golf for several reasons. These include Anglophilia, anti-modernism, and valuing physical exertion for as many club members as possible. Women (in their turn-of-the-century cultural incarnation), the infirm, and the old were more able to play golf than some of the other sports. The success of country clubs opened them beyond elites to the upper middle class, who found golf more financially manageable than horse sports.[14]

Generally, golf is noted more often than anything else as the reason for joining a country club. A Rosary member talks about his club as follows: "I mean the facilities are there in terms of the house, the pool, the tennis, but truthfully you join that club for its golf. The camaraderie of it is an important part of it too clearly, but it's, the golf is really unparalleled."

A former president of Suburban thinks back to when he joined: "My children were old enough now that I had some time when I could do that. . . . That's the age category where I think people begin to have time anyway for golf, which is the reason why you join Suburban; you join it for the golf course. Everything else is ensuing."

Rosary is in fact the most golf-oriented of the clubs. The membership takes pride in its low average handicap (meaning high average skill). A former president at Rosary notes, "This is a much more serious golf club than Oldfamily." An Oldfamily member concurs: "I think Rosary is a better golf course. It attracts real golfers. A lot of people have quit Oldfamily and joined Rosary for the golf." There is even the suggestion that golf skill factors into how welcome a person is as a member.

> Reid [*about a certain member*]: Some people aren't too happy with him being there. He signs up for the state tournaments, as a Rosary member, he always comes in last. So it's like, "stop dragging us down."
>
> Victor [*on considering joining elsewhere*]: I think one thing that makes a big difference is I'm a good golfer, so I'm welcome anywhere. I think that makes a big difference.

Skill at golf is a valuable component in a high-status cultural "tool kit."[15]

One might expect that friendships would lead people into golfing, but the data include only rare mentions of this progression. (However, it's probable that earlier in life, friendships spurred some people to take up the sport in the first place.) More common is the reverse: golfing leading into friendships. At Rosary, Roland says, "you'd see guys play and it's a place to relax, a place to socialize, and you do have a lot of people that have some of the same interests, you know, golf being one of them and that's where you develop relationships, camaraderie." When friends are made by golfing at private clubs, it strengthens the homogeneity and density of the members' social networks. Developing golfing friendships is promoted as harmless, but it has real patterned consequences.

The emphasis on sports is also impersonal. It is true that a round of golf is more convenient to come by at a private club than a public course, which may require advance tee times and may be crowded with incompetent players. (Golfers proceed through the same sequence of holes, so incompetent players needing more shots per hole can be obstacles for those who proceed more quickly.) It is noncontroversial to claim interest in a country club for sports purposes. This claim avoids the more touchy subject of exclusion and the creation of a homophilous environment. Members of one club in the region are explicit about using this account. The *New York Times* reports that "These days, members like to say, the Orange Lawn and Tennis Club is 'about tennis and not exclusivity.'"[16] But enthusiasts of both golf and tennis are already a socioeconomically select group. And members of clubs in this sample still do considerable work to restrict memberships to those they deem socially acceptable; so proclamations like these deserve skepticism.

## Family

Two-thirds of the interviewees (twenty-three of thirty-five) were country club members as children. They reminisce cheerfully about the sports they learned and the friendships they made growing up there. Also, nearly all of the interviewees (thirty-three of thirty-five) are parents. They talk eagerly about the benefits of club membership for their children. There is distinct (if overlapping) talk both about things children *enjoy* at the club, and about things children *learn or gain* by being members. The former—children's use and enjoyment of the club—was noted by about half of the interviewees as an important reason for their own membership, and/or the reason that people in general join country clubs.

### Children's Enjoyment

There is much for children to enjoy at the clubs in this study. Club members mention the following: golf, tennis, and swimming; lessons and other organized activities around sports; summer day-camp and its various activities; organized social gatherings; and casual meals, often at a poolside snack bar. Children are said to enjoy the "hangout" aspect of being at the club, and enjoy each other's company as facilitated by these activities. This is especially true in the summertime when school is out. However, school can be an important parallel context to the club; club membership and attending the right school can be mutually reinforcing in terms of the ties formed and strengthened. One Oldfamily member admits that his children "did not have friends that were members of the club because they were going to public school, and the kids out there were all going to private school. So they didn't use it very much." What's suggested here is the usefulness of redundant ties. (This applies, of course, to adults as well as children, as seen in interviewees' descriptions of membership helping their careers.) The implication is that parents with fewer resources, who do *one* thing to try to confer advantages to their children, may not succeed as well as those parents whose money allows them to put their children in the same elite circle via club membership *and* school *and* neighborhood.

*Parents' Benefits*

Another thing the children are said to enjoy is some freedom from their parents. This is one of the benefits that club use has for parents as well as children: parents can grant children some independence within an environment that's safe and controlled. This theme is part of a larger pattern wherein the rich withdraw from public spaces in favor of private counterparts.[17] One mother says:

> Theresa: I think that [my kids] also have used it, even though in minor ways, used the pool. With good supervision has allowed them to have a place where they've sort of been able to grow up a little bit. It's a place where at the age of nine they can go by themselves and interact with the lifeguards who monitor their behavior, and I think that's, it's sport, but it's also sort of that little bit of independence that in a safe environment they get to navigate that and figure out how to do it.

Quite a few interviewees (fifteen in all) pointed out that club use benefits parents as well as children. About country clubs in general, one member mused:

> Xavier: I'm not sure it's not more of a place that's sort of a caretaking establishment for children to give the parents some peace: you can take your kids to the pool for the day, and have your own life. It seems to be that, as much as anything for children. More for parents.

Several others echoed this sentiment. Again, the club benefits parents especially in the summertime when school is out, before the children are old enough for other diversions like European travel. Three Oldfamily women separately recalled that when their children were younger (and they were not in the labor force), they spent entire summers with their children by the club pool. Others—Oldfamily men—note that club use can benefit both mothers and fathers; but obviously, it especially helps the "stay-at-home" mother. Given the high incomes the men earn, and the overall gender regime, it is common in this population for women to spend the years of intensive parenting out of the labor force. Gender regimes will receive more attention in chapter 4.

Two more benefits to parents emerge from the interviews. One is the axiom that keeping children busy with activities like sports serves to keep them out of trouble. Two mothers spoke similarly of their sons:

> Olivia: He was one of the ones who picked up golf, and it's a wonderful sport for young boys because it keeps them out of trouble in the summer, they go there every day and they play golf all day long and it kept them out of trouble.

> Suzanne: Golf, music, art, something. I mean you keep them into something. I had him into everything since he was a baby, but keep 'em interested. Don't give 'em spare time to get in trouble.

Indeed, this benefit was said to accrue to sons in particular, without mention of daughters. This reflects the broader culture, where teenage boys are widely assumed to be more prone to "trouble" than teenage girls. Interviewees are also making use of a widely known and accepted axiom in the popular discourse. Popular concern about teenagers' doings has transformed "Idle hands are the Devil's tools" into the bumper sticker, "Do sports not drugs." By drawing on this popular notion, members produce an unassailable account for their club involvement.

The second benefit to parents is that club involvement provides them with opportunities for parent-child bonding through shared activity. Some spoke of golf as a venue for father-child bonding and quality time. There was no parallel talk about mothers, probably because they tend to spend plenty of time with their children as a routine matter of course. This idea of "quality time" is another with popular currency today. It flows in part from the aforementioned concern with keeping kids busy, but also from two more related concerns: one, that today's hardworking parents pay their children too little attention; and two, that children's troubles can be prevented or solved via more involvement from fathers. Both of these claims are of dubious veracity.[18] But still, their currency means that "father-child bonding at the club" can serve as another reasonable account for club involvement.

*Children's Benefits*

Related to what children enjoy about clubs is what they learn or gain through their involvement. This theme is more abstract and reflects the perspective of parents more than children. Although the theme is broader than sports, sports do figure prominently here too.

Parents note two ways in which golf is useful for their children, aside from the enjoyment of the sport. First of all, golf is said to build character. "The game itself teaches discipline. It teaches mental discipline, it teaches decision making, it teaches self control." Another father speaks similarly: "The game of golf teaches a person about integrity, and honesty, and there's a lot to it." Some people may argue that golf does these things better than other sports; but leaving that aside, the idea that "playing sports builds youth character" is a dominant one.

A second way that golf may benefit children is in their own careers as they grow up. One father notes:

> Roland: I've seen a lot of kids that are interested in golf that have become pretty good golfers, it's gotten them scholarships to college, it's gotten them a full or partial scholarship to college. Enables them to play the game well, which is always a good tool to have in a business environment.

Another acknowledges that his son's career as a salesman has been aided by the name he has made for himself as a golfer. It could be mere coincidence, but the virtues of golf in developing character and career were extolled solely by Rosary men. According to interviewees themselves, Rosary consists more heavily of "golf nuts" and self-made businessmen, as opposed to Oldfamily where family money often foots the bill.

However, parents at all clubs agree that even without golfing, club involvement can be beneficial for children. Many concur that time spent at the club can help to improve children's behavior. This is mentioned in about half the interviews, and includes learning what is proper dress, table manners, and interacting respectfully yet comfortably with adults. Clearly, these clubs are useful tools for parents in socializing their children into upper-class lifeways and cultural capital.

Two nonwhite interviewees noted that club involvement has helped their children feel at home in overwhelmingly white environments. These parents point out that this comfort level will be necessary for their children if they maintain affluent lifestyles. It is also a quality likely to help nonwhites achieve affluence in the first place; research shows that an assimilationist identity is required for entry into the power elite.[19]

White parents, too, feel that club involvement can indirectly nurture children's ambitions. Two fathers say:

Ken: One of the major benefits of being a member there is as much for him [*son*] as it's been for me, because . . . he has just been exposed to a lot of successful people as role models that he may otherwise not have been exposed to.

Ward: I think that if you grow up with the country club and those type of ambitions to begin with, you're more likely to try to achieve those things. If they're around everyone who's doing this type of thing, then they'll try to seek that level as well. And I think that's good.

It should be noted that both of these men report modest middle- or working-class origins. Perhaps country club membership is more important to nonwealthy families. Ambition-for-affluence is cultivated throughout an *elite* child's environment by relatives, friends, private schools, and so on. Nonelite families may see country club membership as a crucial boost for their children. Since the notion of doing everything possible to improve your children's standing is quintessentially American, this boost is a culturally agreeable account for country club membership. People striving for privilege in general can explain and excuse themselves by claiming selfless parental goals.

Though wealthy parents do not mention cultivating ambition, they do note the importance of cultivating contacts.

Q: What do you think your kids have gotten out of growing up at the club besides golf?
Richard: Some wonderful friendships. . . . I think as the kids grow, they'll begin to realize too the value of some of the contacts they've made over the years.

Q: What do you think that growing up, going to this sort of place does for a young person?
Suzanne: Gets them one step further into where they need to go in life, into business, get better connections, networking. There really is a lot of networking.

In the previous chapter, I discussed interviewees' acknowledgment that club membership has been useful in their careers. Here we see a parallel (anticipatory) benefit to their children, through the same mechanism of sociable involvement in club activities.

These benefits of membership parents see for their children are all oriented toward the future. One more benefit, which is simple but deserves mention, is that the children are virtually assured membership in their own right as adults. Time after time, members point out that "legacies" receive special consideration. Several, legacies themselves, recount appreciatively how easy it was for them to go from junior membership to full membership.

So, it's evident that beyond the activities children enjoy at the club, there are things parents are eager for them to learn or gain. This talk of benefits to children reveals parents who are mindful of their children's future, and doing what they can to ensure their success. Children's *enjoyment* is often stated as a reason to belong to a country club; and while less often stated (without prompting), children's *benefits* are also an important reason for belonging. This is a useful account because—in a quirk of the American Dream—it is presumed that parents will do whatever they can to help their children succeed. In fact, it is parents' moral imperative to give their children whatever advantages they can.[20] So, the talk of club membership as good for children advances the speakers' own goodness, as parents.

Club members refer to some of these same benefits their children gain when considering golf caddies. Caddies are teenage boys that may or may not be club members. Caddying is described as "a good clean way of earning money," echoing the maxim that teenage boys will stay out of trouble if kept busy. Caddies may also, it is implied, pick up on some of the character lessons of golf through their work. They will also learn discretion, says one:

> Richard: The boys being caddies overhear conversations that teenage boys probably shouldn't overhear. . . . That's something that I suppose is a life lesson that as they grow older and become more worldly, they'll begin to realize that what is said in those surroundings should remain in those surroundings.

I heard no reports of any female caddies. Caddying is physical work; it takes place in the male-dominated space of golf courses; and it gives at least a partial glimpse of men backstage, as Richard says. For all these reasons, it's no surprise that the job is, still, gendered male.

Another man notes that caddies from "the wrong side of the tracks" who are well-liked may earn favors from their regular clients when launching their careers. There are also scholarship funds named for legendary area caddies and subsidized by club members. In this informal and formal way, club members can sponsor the mobility of select young men who show promise and have learned the same lessons about behavior that young club members have. It would probably be an overstatement to call this phenomenon selective recruitment into the elite. Still, this sponsored mobility—also gendered male—serves the important purpose of improving the collective image and self-image of country club members. Others have also documented the image-enhancing significance of charitable acts by the wealthy.[21]

*Using the Word "Family"*

As shown here, interviewees speak extensively about the reasons for club membership for them as parents and for their children. Somewhat less commonly, "Family" is used as a more abstract concept.

As I reviewed the data, I was struck by how often people would refer to the club where they belonged as "a family club."

"The up side of Oldfamily is that it's very family friendly."
"This is a family-oriented club, and people join because they have children."
"[I]t's a real family club, a real young family club."
"The kids at Oldfamily are part of the membership."
"One of the things that I liked about Oldfamily . . . it had a very family sort of feel to it."
"It's a damn good family club."

Two of the above speakers have been president at Oldfamily, and have given considerable thought to what sort of membership the club could draw to ensure its continued health. So for them, the use of the word Family may reflect a sort of marketing decision made by the board of governors.

But aside from that, Family seems to be a buzzword with a positive connotation, which members are eager to conceptually attach to their club. (This is similar to the word "diversity," discussed in the next chapter.) This attachment was impressed upon me early on, as evidenced by my pseudonym "Oldfamily." It is repeated in the discourse around wealthy amateur polo players in the region, who are always portrayed as committed fathers.[22] Some sociologists have noted that "Family" serves as an ideological construct at least as often as it refers to a set of relationships.[23]

One use of attaching Family to one's own club is to make it seem better than a rival club. This is never done by Rosary members, who instead claim superiority through their golf course. But Rosary is the target of these comparisons by members of both Oldfamily and Suburban. Also, Oldfamily members target Suburban in the same way. One pointed out, "There are quite a few people from Littletown that chose to come to Oldfamily, not to Suburban. [Q: What's different about the environment?] The family orientation they found more comfortable." I asked a different Oldfamily member how she would choose between the two clubs, if not via geography. Her answer: "If I lived directly between them? I would choose Oldfamily because of the family feel."

Rosary, as noted, has the reputation of being oriented toward businessmen; but Suburban and Oldfamily seem equally family-oriented. It's uncertain why "Family" is used by Oldfamily to disparage Suburban, but not vice-versa. Perhaps—and this is speculative—Oldfamily needs to refer more to the Family construct to compensate for having more singles and dual-career families among their membership than Suburban. This is parallel to research showing that sometimes mothers with careers talk even more than those without about their emphatic focus on mothering.[24]

In any case, it seems clear that the idea of being "a family club" reflects well on the club and its members. A largely unspoken component of this image is that the men at a family club are involved fathers. As noted above, father involvement is an important value in contemporary culture. Members at both Oldfamily and Suburban feel proud to belong to a club consisting of committed parents. The involvement of Rosary men, as fathers and sometimes as husbands, is criticized implicitly. For example:

> Zach: If someone here [Oldfamily] wanted to come out and play golf, and then after golf, sit around in the men's locker room, and have 4 or 5 card games going, and people smoking cigars and drinking, and hootin' and hollerin,' and their wives—"yeah yeah yeah, tell her I'm not here on the phone"—they would never join this club. Because there's no one else here that wants to do that, you know what I mean? But there are other clubs right here in [this area] that they would join.

Another use of attaching Family to one's club is that it counteracts the popular suspicion that country clubs are actually business places. The idea of family makes exclusivity acceptable, to an extent that would be unacceptable in a business context. The business world now has laws about selection and discrimination. Voluntary connections based on personal preferences are no longer the official standard there, but are still expected—even valued—in the realm of family.

After all, a family is conventionally expected to be ethnically homogeneous. When a country club in Florida came under fire for anti-Semitism, a former club president defended exclusivity by saying that the membership is "like a family."[25] It's possible that Oldfamily members, too, are making the conceptual leap from thinking "families belong to this club" to "this club is one big family."

> Q: About your kids, other than a place to swim, what do you think that they got out of growing up at Oldfamily?
> Marian: Friends. They had their birthday parties there. . . . They had a really tight group of adults and kids and we would see those kids on 4th of July, we would see them wherever we went, so it was a real familial feeling.

There is precedent for feeling familial about one's country club. Historian Richard Moss writes that "tribalism" emerged at American country clubs a hundred years ago: the founders limited admissions, demarcated and romanticized their land, and promoted uniform club attire. Even at their founding, country clubs were in part about creating a community and a sense of belonging.[26] This purpose, which inevitably entails drawing boundaries, continues today. The "family" buzzword helps to cast the boundary-work in a positive light, to the public and to members themselves.

## "Fit" of New Members

Even without using the ideology of family, club members express the desire for fellow members to fit in well socially. In the previous chapter, I briefly described the criteria by which potential new members are screened. Here, I will discuss the issue of "fit" at more length, using examples from interviews of desirable and undesirable club members.

Club members state that any new member should fit in well with them, for their own (the existing members') comfort. Sometimes this guideline is euphemized by reversal: only those who will themselves be comfortable with the members should be admitted. This reversal was acknowledged by a former Oldfamily board member: "It'll be voiced, 'are they going to be comfortable here?' But what that's really a voice for is, 'are we going to be comfortable with them?'"

This maneuver of "euphemism through reversal" is self-serving, in that it changes the speaker from appearing self-interested to appearing concerned for others. So, it was unusual that the member deliberately pointed it out to me. However, I don't take his disclosure to mean that euphemism through reversal is an unimportant tool for board members and other club members. Rather, I think it points to the fact that maneuvers like these exist not just for giving accounts to outsiders, but also for negotiating internally. Polite indirection is characteristic of the WASP style of interacting, which still holds sway especially at Oldfamily. One member says, "The membership application process and all that at all these places is very sensitive, because people's feelings get hurt."

### Comfort = Similarity

Sometimes interviewees state outright that they are most comfortable with people most similar to themselves. (Statements like these can shade into segregationism, which will be addressed in the next chapter.) The aim of attracting new members who are similar is served by the use of already established ties. Social networks are so often homophilous that recruiting new members through existing ties often produces similarity.[27] These ties may be extended family members, neighbors, or schoolmates. Friendships with neighbors can draw someone into a certain club, as in the way the Heights feeds Oldfamily. One man, when asked how he chose Oldfamily to join, said "I felt that the people at Oldfamily were more the kind of people I wanted to be with . . . there was a bunch of people from the Heights that I knew."

Another Oldfamily member notes that, "The people who, at least at Oldfamily, people who are members are much more apt to have gone off to boarding school and college and have a larger circle of friends who you meet." In fact, an Oldfamily board member told me that their membership application was being amended to ask for information about schooling. He also noted that the density of local networks can help with early informal screening:

> Clayton: You see, there's so much to the fabric of a place like [this area], I mean there are opportunities to meet people through the schools, through churches, through social functions, through business, through organizations—nonprofit, for-profit, etc. So that, from time to time, you run into three quarters of the people that are either a member of your club or might want to become a member of your club. And you see them in a different light: y'know anybody can be on their best behavior for a night when they're introduced to the board of governors of a club, but one night is very different from 24/7.

However—at the risk of reading too much into it—the addition of schooling to the application form is a counterpoint. The president's description of dense local networks is accurate; but it is perhaps not as failsafe as it was when Oldfamily membership was limited to WASPs generally from the Heights. Given such trends today as high geographic mobility, and increasing diversity in the upper-middle-class, network density is not as high as in the past. So, signifiers like alma maters must emerge to help with discernment now that candidates are no longer automatically known by most of the membership.

Younger club members don't talk much about the desirability of similarity. But occasionally someone from the old guard will. This former Oldfamily board president is a good example:

> Ian: Oldfamily has changed dramatically in terms of its openness to the point where there are Jewish members and Catholic members and quite a few Black members, which is . . . all to the good. But it has created among those who are, and I don't consider myself a snob, but there are a lot of my contemporaries who are, who find it less pleasant, because it isn't homogeneous.
> [*Later, describing another club where he belongs*] Twin Pines is a happy place, and reasonably homogeneous. I hate to say that, but it does make a difference in your comfort.

Club members and prospective members with successful corporate careers are likely to be familiar with the project of making important others comfortable by projecting similarity to them. A sociological study of corporate managers shows how important this is. To succeed, a manager must be included into "circles of affiliation" that provide important resources; this inclusion depends on whether "one 'can feel comfortable' with another manager . . . if he is 'our kind of guy.'"[28] Youngsters who grow up in exclusive country clubs are well-prepared to make a successful bid for such inclusion and success. Likewise, successful corporate managers are well-prepared for admission to elite country clubs.

## Money Brings Cultural Capital

One dimension of similarity, of course, is the ability to pay the costs of membership. One member notes that one way to join is, "you come just because you're a really nice person and everyone enjoys being with you and you can afford to be a member." But affordability doesn't necessarily yield the sense of similarity and fit. Another interviewee acknowledges that that was the case for him: "Everybody knew everybody [at Oldfamily] and it was hard to break into that. They had set golf games. It was, I mean my wife and I are kind of blue-collar upbringing and we just didn't fit there; just wasn't a good fit." (He joined Waterside instead.) The quote illustrates the popular idea that economic status relates to important matters of style. The following people draw a connection between people's economic status and the cultural capital that would make them a good or bad fit socially.

> Ralph: I mean this is not a working man's golf course. The guy that's driving a truck or something like that is not gonna fit in here socially. He's not gonna—it's a semi-snobby thing for me to say, but it's the truth. He's not gonna be happy here. This place is basically for businessmen.

> Q: Do you know whether there has ever been any talk of if someone who would be a good addition to the club but couldn't afford it, any sort of financial aid?
> Theresa: I'd be really surprised if there has been. I guess the one exception would be affiliated with a firm [IA]. Maybe public sector, I could imagine that happening, but not in [this state], because people really believe either public sector people should have their own money or *they're probably not the people that we want to affiliate with.* [emphasis added]

> Larry [*answering the same question*]: If somebody's not comfortable in a setting that is expensive, then there's discomfort and people who are interested in food, and people that are interested in wine, tend to have gotten there ostensibly because they can afford to be there. It's hard to do those things when you're poor. And so it's almost: who enjoys the kinds of things we enjoy who are also part of what this core is.

There are many more ways that interviewees describe who would, and would not, make a good fit with club members. Many of these also imply the desirability of similarity, even when that is unstated. A prospective member should be a friend, or a potential future friend. Candidates also should be good citizens:

> Richard: I see who's coming in and I think for the most part these are pretty upstanding people that are successful in many different areas of business and commerce, and that's the type of people you want to come in.

> Larry [*describing desirability*]: It's an interesting person, it's somebody that's doing something that's out there and involved, it's somebody who's influential because they are doing things, somebody who could afford to belong.

Richard and Larry are suggesting that clubs seek prospective members with considerable public status; such members can be useful for other members to know, and can also enhance the prestige of the club. Their criteria can be met only by members of the upper-middle and upper classes. Notice that even if people desire to be meritocratic, such class-biased gauges of worth contribute to the reproduction of inequalities.[29]

Candidates should also behave properly. Interviewees sometimes refer to behavior itself, and sometimes to the "character" that presumably drives it. But remember that discernment is done at a cocktail party. One member, when asked about applying to Oldfamily, said that she felt comfortable in the process because her WASPy husband "knew the whole drill, had the right conversation." The ability to interact sociably is important.

Also important is the ability to dress properly. This again is sometimes described as a mark of character. Or at least, proper dress signals that one understands and wants to follow the rules of decorum that are expected at a country club.[30] This signifying purpose of clothing is implied by the following member, recalling her admission to Suburban.

> Samantha: After we sent in our application, we got notice of a new member, potential member cocktail party.
> Q: Was it nerve-wracking at all?
> Samantha: The most nerve-wracking part was what to wear.

The symbolic meaning of clothing is, of course, a more general phenomenon. Clothes are typically "taken as an expression of the individual's intention to act in the same way as others who are similarly attired."[31] Club members are reassured by such a message.

*Undesirable Others*

Proper behavior and dress emerge as components of desirability. But they receive even more frequent mention—over sixty instances—during talk of undesirability. What follows is a brief discussion of what club members say is unacceptable in others. These items are usually mentioned in response to probing, which was needed to get beyond the abstraction of "not a good fit."

> Q: Can you tell me what would make a candidate undesirable?
> Harold: Um, you know, someone whose personal, social, and political views about the world are so different from those of the membership in general that they would have a difficult time functioning in the club.
> Q: Clashing views?
> Harold: Clashing views, clashing values, you know, whether those views be political, cultural, social, economic, you know, these sorts of clubs, whether we

like it or not, these sorts of clubs are not heterogeneous institutions. They're homogenous institutions. . . . Let's take politics. You have Democrats and Republicans. You don't have any Socialists, you don't have any Communists. You see what I'm saying? . . . You put yourself up for membership and say "I'm a member of the Communist Party," you're not getting in. Let's just face it. And it's like that on a lot of other fronts. . . . You go there, whether we like it or not, you tell your, you know, you tell the world that "I'm out of the closet, I'm a gay or a lesbian," you're probably not going to get in.

Harold is, by all appearances, speaking the truth. And yet this quote stands alone in its references to politics and sexuality. (Perhaps his perspective is informed by his work in higher education.) Behavior, dress, and decorum are much more common answers to "what makes someone undesirable." This question was asked about existing members as well as about candidates.

Obviously, part of the answer is just the converse of the desirability of potential friends. Members note that it may be undesirable to admit someone who is only a business contact. One explained Oldfamily's practice of individual rather than couple memberships by noting that, after divorce, a second spouse might be undesirable. The unknown element is not wanted.

To get concrete about what is unwanted, interviewees sometimes cite extreme cases like public drunkenness and criminal records. But the most common (twenty instances) set of responses about undesirability use words like: rude, crude, obnoxious, jackass; "total lack of class." Subcategories of this theme include the following: being mean to staff at the club, having wild children, being a know-it-all, or a chronic complainer, or too loud and flamboyant. An old guard club member opines that inappropriate behavior at Oldfamily includes "being noisy in the dining room or the bar, using inappropriate language. Fifteen years ago I remember being, ten years ago I remember being somewhat horrified when someone came in the clubhouse talking on the cell phone." Another member of the old guard describes memos that remind members of the rules. He laments the fact that these memos are needed more today than in the past.

> Ian: Talking about general members' letters, we remind all members that it is not appropriate to wear a hat in the dining room. Or we remind people that jeans are not to be worn on the golf course, or cutoffs. I mean there's certain, that's dress behavior, but some of it is just boorishness. Do I sound snotty? Yeah. But it's boorishness for people who stride around, big cigars hanging out of their mouth, just acting—not like the refined people we hope we have at the Oldfamily.

Wearing a baseball hat indoors is an example of inappropriateness cited commonly by the old guard of Oldfamily. As noted in the previous chapter on joining clubs, improper clothing can kill an application.

Elsewhere too, but especially here, interviewees have solicited my agreement. For example: "I don't want to be sitting having dinner with my family with a guy at the next table with a baseball hat on backwards and dungarees and a muscle shirt. I think that stinks. Don't you?" This in effect gives me the chance to belong by agreeing, or to make myself foreign by disagreeing.[32] I speculate that interviewees engaged in this practice with me only when they judged my own dress and decorum to be adequately—and comfortably—similar to their own. (I never openly rejected their pleas for agreement, mainly because I felt that an identity of agreeability helped keep the interviews going.)

Comments like these also caricature those who would ruin club members' comfort level. The comments group people into distinctly different types, so as to paint the other as wholly foreign and obscure any commonalities.[33]

Interviewees wanted me to agree with them, which may help explain why decorum is cited more often than—more controversial—politics. Another apparent effort to secure my agreement is when interviewees provide examples that are extreme. For instance:

> Q: What types of things would make the membership chair decline to provide an application?
> Richard: Someone who's a known criminal, someone who's a known philanderer, someone who's a known cheat in business or in golf.

These criteria are fairly bland and hard to argue with. My data show, however, that exclusion is performed on many criteria beyond just these. But taken at face value, they provide an account for excluding that seems benign and completely understandable.

## Socializing

As described in the previous chapter, clubs' official policy is that no business should be conducted on the property. Though this rule is certainly bent by members, it implies that socializing at clubs is primary. And the extensive talk about the "fit" of new members also suggests that socializing is central to club activities. However, this talk of fit is usually in response to my queries about admission; otherwise, many people never mention the social life of club membership, or brush it off when asked as unimportant to them. One says, "Today if I didn't play golf or squash or whatever, I wouldn't belong to Oldfamily. I have no social need there whatsoever." Sometimes, talk of sociability only materializes to deflect the idea that clubs are places where business is conducted. The same Oldfamily member says:

John: There should be no business conducted. It's not a business club. And membership committees are very sensitive to this. Not just at Oldfamily, but most places: you write a letter and you say "I'm writing this letter to support the application of Jessica Sherwood, and Jessica just joined my firm and I don't know her at all and the only reason I'm writing this letter is because she happens to be a partner in my law firm." Well, that is going to send a really strong negative message to the people, because they don't want that. They don't want these places to become the business entertainment places. It's *supposed to be in theory*, and I think it stays that way, it's supposed to be a social or family club, and no business is supposed to be conducted. [emphasis added]

As in the use of the word "family," talk of sociability can serve to distract from the idea that rules against discriminatory selection might appropriately apply at clubs.

There's another way that sociability is used as a deflector. Sometimes, talk of friendships does not appear until the subject of exclusion has come up. It's possible that the social life of a club receives undue emphasis once exclusion comes up, to justify keeping certain people out. After all, the argument that people should be allowed to choose their friends has legitimacy in a culture where social capital, if it is considered at all, is thought of as naturally occurring.

However, I think it's inaccurate to conclude that the social aspect of clubs is truly secondary—say, to golf—based on the rate and circumstances of its mention. Even though golf is mentioned twice as often, it cannot be considered more weighty than the social aspect. Aside from the fact that people generally socialize while playing a round of golf, there are two reasons I make this argument.

First: virtually all interviewees will talk (some after prompting) about the distinctiveness of the members at two, or even eight, different clubs. An in-group/out-group mentality is revealed in their talk of other clubs' members being inferior in some way. Oldfamily is painted as a bunch of snobs; Rosary as run by male chauvinist golf nuts; and Suburban as the provincial nouveau riche.

Second: it could be assumed that if sports facilities were truly the most important consideration, then people would join the club closest to home for convenience—as people argued regarding geography. At least three clubs are equidistant from the Heights (Oldfamily, Rosary, and one other), but there is consensus about which club a person "belongs" at for social reasons. And, there are some Heights residents who belong to the Suburban club instead, and there are some residents of the suburbs who bypass nearer clubs to go to Oldfamily.

So despite the referrals to sports facilities as primary, the social aspect of club membership looms large. Rather than the social life receiving undue emphasis once exclusion comes up, I speculate that sociability might not be mentioned much because it implies exclusion along with it. This silence would follow from the (usually unarticulated) awareness of being called to account, described at the beginning of this chapter. After all, exclusion runs counter to American egalitarianism.

### Stasis and Tradition

Egalitarianism gained cultural strength during the twentieth century; it was less valued back when clubs were institutionalizing. Thus, one response to the implicit questioning of clubs' operations is to justify them by pointing to stasis or to tradition. I'll briefly discuss each of these overlapping themes.

Stasis is merely the condition of remaining the same, and doesn't necessarily have the positive connotation of the concept of tradition. A few interviewees identified the Northeast—or more specifically the site of this study—as a location where stasis has an especially strong hold. One calls the "social connections" in the area "more entrenched" than elsewhere in the country. It's true that this part of the country has been established (by European colonists) for the longest time; perhaps the regional stasis comes partly from "old family" members' consciousness of this heritage and resultant behavior.

Interviewees suggest two more sources of stasis. One is the unquestioning acceptance of the circumstances of one's youth. One such circumstance is the restriction of women from the golf course at certain times. I asked a Suburban legacy how she felt about that, and she replied as follows.

> Sophia: It was one of those things that was accepted by our parents, and then I guess we as kids said "that's the rule." And I think we just learned to live with it and we didn't even talk about it. In those days, women didn't speak up at all. You've got to realize, I'm 65 and I think I was under that guise that: "if that's your rule, that's your rule."

A third source of stasis lies in the governance of the clubs. Occupation of positions of power is said to be circular, even "incestuous." This theme will reappear below under the heading "Governance and Responsibility." For now, suffice it to say that the nondemocratic way in which clubs are governed keeps "real turnover"—change in perspectives and priorities—low, and stasis high.

The regional character, the adoption of childhood customs, and the constancy of internal power combine with a powerful sense of tradition. Like "family" discussed above, "tradition" is an ideological construct with a positive connotation. Oldfamily, Rosary, and Suburban have been around for an average of 100 years, and are lent legitimacy by their longevity and tradition. When the 50th or 100th anniversary of a club's founding is reached, there is usually a self-congratulatory book published to honor the occasion. (I read nine such books from area clubs.) These books reach back into the past, and forward into the future (e.g., "May the next hundred years be as enjoyable as the first."). Reminders of a club's longevity help it be seen as an institution, timeless and permanent. The anniversary books promote timeless tradition by lauding the club as a refuge from the changes of the outside world.

Tradition is enhanced by the presence of legacies. But having grown up at one's club is not crucial; those whose membership tenure is measured in decades rather than years—that is, the majority of members!—are the practical equivalent of legacies in some ways. Having belonged long enough to have a sense of nostalgia about the past, they are motivated to keep their nostalgic vision alive by preventing changes. It is widely common for people to have nostalgia for past environments or relationships; this population is unique not for the nostalgia but because their considerable command of resources enables them to control their environment and preserve it as desired.[34]

The tradition that pleases longtime club members and often attracts new members inheres in the familiarity of the clubhouse, certain club sporting events, and so on. But it also inheres in the membership itself. There is comfort in the sameness of the people one sees at the club, where admission is more controlled than in a neighborhood. Longtime members say that they enjoy the tradition of seeing each other year after year. This is part of the reason that junior members are encouraged to become full members as young adults. It's also part of the reason that bringing in dissimilar new members is frowned upon.

In interviews, "old guard" members (in their late sixties and beyond) lament that the proportion of fellow members that they know has declined. They attribute this decline to turnover rather than to their own use or disuse of the club. On the other hand, interviewees under age sixty gently tease the old guard for clinging to the sameness of the membership. One interviewee lightheartedly acknowledges switching camps:

Ursula: I always couldn't stand it when my mother-in-law said, [*fuddy-duddy voice*] "I don't know anybody at the Oldfamily anymore, I don't even know people who are putting people up anymore." And [now] that's absolutely the case with us. [*Laughs*]

Although the increasing presence of "strangers" is lamented, I'm unaware of a single case in which it prompted a member to resign. Club membership still confers social benefits over, say, golfing at a public course: enough longtime members remain to satisfy each other's nostal-

gia for people as well as for place. This sameness—tradition—is something most members consider a valuable benefit of country club membership. The rhetoric of tradition has been used to justify some horrible social arrangements, of which the composition of country clubs could be considered a case. But, the value members place on tradition helps explain the work that they do to preserve sameness in their club's membership.


## Governance and Responsibility

As noted, country clubs are run nondemocratically. People in positions of power have a hand in choosing who will succeed them; contested elections are virtually unheard of. Members explain:

> Regina: There's a bunch of old guys apparently that run the place. And they're old. They're all in their late seventies and eighties, and the key to power there apparently is the nominating committee. Because the nominating committee picks the next president. And they like, the nominating committee is always trying to pick someone that they can manipulate. So the same people have been on the nominating committee for years.
> Q [*Later*]: So you said that the nominating committee's kind of a clique. And I'm wondering how you get onto that committee in the first place.
> Regina: They all nominate themselves.
> Q: Okay.
> Regina: It's a self-perpetuating, the nominating committee also nominates the nominating committee, which I think is crazy.

> Olivia: The process is as follows: the board appoints a nominating committee. The past presidents and the board see candidates through the nominating committee. The nominating committee sends the slate to the board who present it to the members, and at the annual meeting as long as there's a quorum present, it's kind of a *fait accompli*. There is a procedure if you wanted to raise an opposing slate. Never happens. . . . So yes, it's voted on by the membership, but it's really: the past presidents and the board decide.
> Q: So the nominating committee is put together by the board.
> Olivia: Yes.
> Q: How are the board members chosen?
> Olivia: Board members are chosen by the nominating committee. [*Laughs*]

So, turnover of power is low. This may be true even more at Rosary than at Oldfamily or Suburban. At Rosary, voting privileges are reserved not just for the overwhelmingly male members, but for a subset of those members: voting privileges are extended at the discretion of the board on a case-by-case basis, in an arbitrary process which was never fully explained to me. This unique policy leads Rosary to have even more stasis, an even lower turnover of real power, than the rest of the clubs. A Suburban member says that at Rosary, "It's really a nucleus of about five guys that's running that club. Whether they're on the board or not. They've just been there since day one." This isn't literally true of course, since the club is a hundred years old; but it captures the way members feel about all three clubs.

In one way, this division of labor between members and governors is efficient and common. It's probably true that in many organizations, the majority of participants are glad to have governance taken care of rather than getting involved.

But there is another way in which this division is convenient for the interviewees (twenty-six of thirty-five) who have never served on their club's board of governors. If excluding is controversial, these club members may claim to be innocent of it. They can say that it is other people doing the screening, even if they are happy with the results. They talk of how certain other members have "pull" when it comes to making decisions, thus deflecting any responsibility from themselves.

In fact, some members' comments suggest that they are glad that the dirty work is taken care of by others.

Stella: I was asked to be on the admissions committee and I turned it down recently because . . . admissions wasn't one area that I wanted to get involved in, partly because of the time and partly because I don't like to make those kind of judgment calls on people's character.

John: I have no interest [in committee service]. Ten years ago, twenty years ago I might have been interested. More of an ego thing for me than anything else, but . . . I've seen friends go through it and I've never heard anyone say "gee, what a rewarding experience that was." You'd be amazed at how petty it all is.

Marian: I suppose I'd be upset if some really bad person got in that caused a lot of harm or a mobster or somebody else that I wouldn't want to be there, but I don't know how you play with that. I guess there are ways. The membership committee does all that and I wouldn't want to be on the membership committee.

This division of labor frees most club members to reap the benefits of exclusion while keeping their hands clean. However, it would be an overstatement to say that each act of exclusion has members cheering from the sidelines; most acts are apparently unknown to most members. (This is true for many processes wherein inequalities are reproduced.) As noted at the beginning of this chapter, some interviewees were unable to think of a single instance where an interested prospect was denied membership.

And, the appropriate extent of exclusion is not unanimously agreed-upon. Almost half of interviewees report that they have never objected to a candidate for membership. A few tell stories of proposing someone without success, which demonstrates the lack of total consensus. Some members even go as far as to suggest that if it were up to them, anybody could get in to their club. One Oldfamily member explains: "Your sphere is very much smaller, so you see the people that you like. You sit with the people that you like. But, let them [anyone else] join the club too. They help me keep my dues down so I can enjoy my game." Or as another put it, "I don't go for this blackballing business."

It's impossible to judge the sincerity of these statements, and pointless to try. The point is that once members have established that they themselves are powerless in club governance, they are free to make sweeping pronouncements that sound inclusive—and that make them look like especially good people. But the reality is less clear: the board makes many decisions in secret, and some members confess to turning a blind eye. "If you get too involved with clubs, there's an ugly side to them," says one. The easiest way for club members to feel okay about their membership is to embrace a lack of involvement and awareness; this is the path of least resistance chosen by most interviewees.

### Rights

Once in a while (eight instances), club members resort to invoking their rights. One of two ways this appeared was in the context of my early research, when I asked for more access to the clubs. An Oldfamily board member used the word "privacy" over and over in explaining to me why the board of governors declined to grant me access to club property, or to authorize my research generally.

> Clayton: And, you also have to remember that we have three lawyers on our board. . . . And so, to sanction research at a private club is tantamount to opening yourself up to a potential lawsuit. And the question—and it was raised in a sort of a Socratic fashion: "what if so-and-so were to go to so-and-so and ask them this question," you would never want to put that member under that kind of pressure. And say, particularly in saying that it was sanctioned by the board. It takes the privacy factor out of the private club.

The second and more generic way that rights are invoked is when the topic of exclusivity arises. Another Oldfamily member explains:

> Harold: I think that private institutions should have the right to or should have some say as to who, people in those private institutions should have a lot to say about who it is that they interact with and who it is that they socialize with. And that's why you're paying, that's what you're paying for.

If an organization is considered legally *private* and *social*, then its members have the right to admit and deny people at will. The first criterion, "private," has received scrutiny in recent years. Disgruntled country club members—that is, women chafing at restricted tee times—have success-fully argued in court that their club does enough public business to dis-qualify them from legally private status. This has exposed such clubs to charges of sex discrimination.

This legal development alarmed the country club industry and one of its professional organizations, the National Club Association. Its response has been to issue alerts to club managers and boards advising them to check state rules and to modify their operations, if need be, to avoid dis-qualification from legally private status. Clubs are advised to limit as much as possible the access given to, and money taken from, nonmem-bers; otherwise the club could become subject to laws about public accom-modations. Clubs are also advised to put membership decisions in the hands of current members, who are legally *encouraged* to use subjective social criteria in evaluating candidates.[35]

In talking with a former Suburban president, I mentioned a club whose operations disqualified them from private status. He replied, "That's what the accounting people are for. To make sure we don't" join that category.

This maneuvering reveals the changeable quality of the idea of "pri-vate." Rather than being an agreed-upon status with automatic implica-tions about membership selectivity, it is socially constructed—as all law is—and sometimes contested. However, its problematic nature usually goes unacknowledged (like most social constructions), with club mem-bers instead referring to it as a bedrock principle.

After "private," the second criterion is that a club is social. As already discussed, referring to the social nature of the club serves useful purposes. So when invoking their rights, club members point out that friendships are at the core of the organization.

Parker: A social club is a club, and it is closed in the sense that it's people choosing to be with other people.

Xavier: Should we always be told who we have to associate with?

This parallels other research in which elites discuss exclusive clubs; one woman says flatly: "People have a right to choose their friends."[36]

When pressed about whether the exclusive organization is morally ac-ceptable, socializing is invoked. This stands in stark contrast to members' common acknowledgment that club membership can help careers, even that they themselves have benefited. Interviewees reconcile this discord by arguing that social ties are primary and business ties are derivative of them. This sequence is indeed true much of the time. But the argument is also a *necessary* one to make: to be social and private is the way to receive the law's consent to exclude.

However, it is true that this invocation of rights does not occur frequently. But its rarity should not be mistaken for insignificance. Interestingly, this account that appears last on the list is the one pointing to the critically important legal foundation for country club exclusion. As well-educated people, the club members likely know at some level (of practical rather than discursive consciousness) that laws are socially constructed and can at times be unjust. Referring to legal rights is not the most sophisticated and noble way to respond to the ethical dilemma of exclusivity. It does not do much for one's sense of oneself as a good moral person. This may explain why, aside from club managers and board members, the invocation of rights is a fairly uncommon account.


## SUMMARY

Club members use these various accounts to make their actions, or those of club leaders, seem acceptable. In part, they do this accounting to and for themselves. As noted in the introduction to this chapter, a part of American culture calls into question the morality of exclusion. Thus to feel comfortable with exclusion, club members need a set of intangible tools that guards them against personal moral attack. The foregoing accounts show how those tools are put to use.

As noted, there are several ways in which club members can claim to be innocent of performing exclusion: they can chalk it up to impersonal market forces or pawn it off on club leaders. They can claim that they belong only for the golf course and don't personally care about the composition of the club. In an account that simultaneously provides a pat on the back, they can claim to participate in clubs only as part of their identity as good parents. (Though it wasn't identified in interviews, men's talk of belonging for business purposes can also be construed as connected to their identity as good family providers.) If all else fails, they can appeal to a listener to agree with the reasonableness of exclusion. In all these ways, club members come to feel good about, or at least adequately comfortable with, belonging to an exclusive club. The exclusion at country clubs has met some challenges recently, but overall it is well accounted for: clubs have not lost the legal and cultural support they enjoy. Well accounted for exclusion at clubs is significant for several reasons.

The dominant class in America enjoys quite thorough legitimacy for its power. In other words, most Americans seem to accept the rightness of the arrangements that give the dominant class so much privilege. The American Dream with its dominant stratification ideology dictates that things are fair and just.

Well accounted for country club exclusion makes its own small contribution to legitimating the status quo. Legitimation is, in part, dominance of the belief that unequal distribution of resources is just. In admittedly circular logic, most Americans see wealth as evidence of deservingness of wealth. The more control people have over resources and interactions, the more worthy of power they appear, to themselves and others.[37] Having a beautiful country club and choosing who is and isn't allowed to belong is an impressive show of control over resources and interactions. So it contributes to the legitimation of the power of club members. In studying exclusive volunteer groups, sociologist Diana Kendall similarly notes that the members' ability to exclude and include enhances their social power.[38] These interviewees are privileged in general; their country clubs are sites where their power is solidified and, strangely, legitimated.

In a recent review of cultural capital scholarship, the authors note: "One important area of future investigation is the question of how markets for cultural capital are constructed."[39] In these clubs, privileged people have constructed a market for cultural capital, to their own benefit.

Exclusive country clubs are also sites for nurturing class consciousness. Some sociologists question whether the concept of "class" remains at all useful today, as the universe of occupations is increasingly complex and fragmented. But as noted in the prior chapter, class is much more than a workplace phenomenon: our broader conception must include its cultural components, and its intersections with race and gender. This research shows that class, broadly conceived, remains a very powerful social fact.

The concept of class consciousness has been rightly criticized as hollow when measured via decontextualized answers to survey questions. Rick Fantasia argues that analysts would do better to think in terms of "cultures of solidarity," as "expressed in emergent values, behaviors, and organizational forms."[40] Clearly, the exclusion and its accounts covered here are expressions of solidarity within a socioeconomic group. The extent of such solidarity is of interest because it is presumed to influence behavior that will support (or potentially alter) the status quo. Country clubs, along with other social organizations and activities, improve cohesion in the upper classes and help them coordinate their actions. They are also sites of opportunity hoarding, where privileged people reserve social opportunities for, and pass advantages to, their own children.[41]

Clubs like the ones here help to insulate their members and contribute to the homogeneity of their social lives. One consequence of this lifestyle is that club members see nothing special about their economic and social capital, because everyone around them seems to be similarly situated. Another consequence is that this lifestyle can keep one's belief in the American Dream safe from challenges. In studying the working poor, Katie Hyde describes how their experiences lead them to believe, mostly but not entirely, in the American Dream.[42] My interviewees are like hers in that they are immersed in a world that lacks counter-ideologies with any impact. But Hyde's interviewees also have some experiences that challenge the American Dream: they have participated in actions for workers' rights, they have had trouble making ends meet despite working hard, they have been victims of discrimination, and they are cultural outsiders as immigrants. Four occasions to question the validity of the American Dream, and not a single one occurs in the lives of my interviewees. Paradoxically, people in the dominant class use their power to structure their lives in a way that facilitates belief in egalitarian meritocracy.

More specifically, we can hear the following beliefs in the accounts club members offer: that connections are unimportant in the context of a stratification system that is meritocratic and natural; that residential patterns also occur naturally; that having more money usually entails having more/better cultural capital; and that it's natural and right for parents to do whatever they can to improve their children's lot in life. The belief in meritocracy assists the quest for a sense of moral comfort. If stratification is neutral and natural, then club members deserve everything they have; they need not feel guilty about their privileges, one of which is country club membership. The naturalization of economic stratification excuses exclusion based on affordability; people can sensibly claim not to be responsible for financial obstacles. However, club members also exclude on sociocultural bases; when that is exposed, interviewees sometimes appeal to me as the interviewer to agree with their choices.

The belief in meritocracy is in tension with the assumption that parenting includes doing whatever possible to give a boost to the life chances of one's children. This push is evident when parents talk about the ways in which club involvement can benefit their children. In another interview study, Heather Johnson similarly describes the contradiction between middle-class parents' stated beliefs in merit and their actual attempts to confer advantages for their children.[43]

Regarding community, the following beliefs appear here: that privacy is a right, including for organizations; that longstanding tradition deserves preservation; that people should be allowed to choose with whom they associate; and that our egalitarian ethic demands equal access. Clearly, these last two are in tension. Sometimes members claim that their club hardly excludes at all, or that at least they themselves want no part in it; this affirms the egalitarian ethic. But as noted, the costs of club membership are within the means of enough people that members must own up to performing screening beyond affordability. Then, they draw upon the right of free association to defend themselves.

It is not my intention to portray club members as an unusually conflicted population. Have you ever experienced tension between your principles and your behavior? Virtually everyone must come to terms with some ways in which their behavior fails to match some abstract principles of justice or goodness. Perhaps the considerable privileges these people enjoy make their sense of contradiction especially acute. But then again, they are reflecting conflicts that lie within American culture itself. One journalist points out that the recent public controversies over golf tournaments at exclusive clubs spotlight our cultural tension between "freedom of association versus freedom of access."[44] Some pundits—including some club members!—announce that the era of exclusivity is ending. But exclusive private country clubs still enjoy legal and cultural support, including playing host to major golf tournaments, with their attendant media coverage, corporate sponsorships, and large audiences. These tournaments, and the laws that allow club members free rein to handpick participants, show that exclusion, under the banner of "freedom of association," is still culturally approved.

As I've argued, the consequences of this well accounted for exclusion are to help keep strong both the legitimation of inequality and also socioeconomic solidarity. A final consequence is that the racial and gender regimes in clubs become legitimated too: the ethnic composition of clubs and the ideology surrounding it, and the status of women club members, all come to seem right and normal to participants. We turn, in the next two chapters, to matters of race and then gender.

## NOTES

1. The sociology of people's accounts is built on work by Mills ("Situated Actions and Vocabularies of Motive." *American Sociological Review* 5 (1940): 904) and Scott and Lyman ("Accounts." *American Sociological Review* 33 (1968): 46).

2. Howard, "Shoal Truth: This Is The Same." *Newsday*, 12 April 2003.

3. Anderson, "Woods is Not Obliged to Boycott." *New York Times*, 8 December 2002, 8-1; Araton, "Other Women's Issues Need A Voice." *New York Times*, 8 December 2002, 8-1; Brown, "Augusta Answers Critics on Policy." *New York Times*, 10 July 2002, D-4; Della Cava, "Men Tee Up As Critics Tee Off." *USA Today*, 4 October 2002, A-1; Kuczynski, "It's Still A Man's, Man's, Man's World." *New York Times*, 21 July 2002, 9-1; Litsky, "Women's Group Vows to Pressure Augusta." *New York Times*, 13 July 2002, D-6; Scott, "Debating Which Private Clubs are Acceptable. And Private." *New York Times*, 8 December 2002, W-5.

4. Kerr, "A Casualty of the Trial Suffers Quietly." *Providence Journal*, 3 May 2002, B-1.

5. Giddens, *The Constitution of Society*. Berkeley: University of California Press, 1984.

6. On cohesion leading to coordination, see Domhoff (*Who Rules America Now?: A View for the '80s*. New York: Simon & Schuster, 1986). For more on upper-

class institutions, see also Mills (*The Power Elite.* New York: Oxford University Press, 1956), Baltzell (*The Protestant Establishment: Aristocracy and Caste in America.* Glencoe, IL: Free Press, 1964), Useem (*The Inner Circle: Large Corporations and the Rise of Business Political Activity in the U.S. and U.K.* New York: Oxford University Press, 1984), Ostrander (*Women Of The Upper Class.* Philadelphia: Temple University Press, 1984).

7. "People must account for their experiences in ways that are intelligible and legitimate in their current social context" (Orbuch, "People's Accounts Count: The Sociology of Accounts." *Annual Review of Sociology* 23 (1997), page 460).

8. From Huber and Form (*Income and Ideology: An Analysis of the American Political Formula.* New York: Free Press, 1973, page 6); see also Smith and Stone ("Rags, Riches, and Bootstraps: Beliefs About the Causes of Wealth and Poverty." *Sociological Quarterly* 30 (1989), page 94), and for the above definition of the American Dream, see Hochschild (*Facing Up to the American Dream: Race, Class, and the Soul of the Nation.* Princeton: Princeton University Press, 1995).

9. Lamont and Fournier (*Cultivating Differences: Symbolic Boundaries and the Making of Inequality.* Chicago: University of Chicago Press, 1992) ask, "are boundaries based on moral, cultural, or socioeconomic status increasingly used to euphemistically draw gender, racial, or ethnic boundaries at a time when norms against boundary work based on ascribed characteristics are gaining greater legitimacy?" This study shows support for that proposition.

10. Coleman, "Social Capital in the Creation of Human Capital." *American Journal of Sociology* 94 (1988): 95; Portes, "Social Capital: Its Origins and Applications in Modern Sociology." *Annual Review of Sociology* 24 (1998): 1.

11. Massey and Denton, *American Apartheid: Segregation and the Making of the Underclass.* Cambridge: Harvard University Press, 1993.

12. Harrington, *The Other America: Poverty in the United States.* 2nd ed. New York: Penguin Books, 1981, page 154.

13. Bettie (*Women Without Class: Girls, Race, and Identity.* Berkeley: University of California Press, 2003) and Stuber ("Talk of Class: The Discursive Repertoires of White Working- and Upper-Middle-Class College Students." *Journal of Contemporary Ethnography* 35 (2006): 285) make the same point about their interviewees' vision.

14. On the history of golf clubs in America, see Mayo (*The American Country Club: Its Origins and Development.* New Brunswick, NJ: Rutgers University Press, 1998, chapters 2 and 3); and Moss (*Golf and The American Country Club.* Urbana: University of Illinois Press, 2001, chapters 2 and 3).

15. The metaphor is from Ann Swidler, who "offers an image of culture as a 'tool kit' of symbols, stories, rituals, and world-views, which people may use in varying configurations to solve different kinds of problems" ("Culture in Action: Symbols and Strategies." *American Sociological Review* 51 (1986), page 273).

16. Schumer, "A Peek Inside the Country Club." *New York Times,* 16 March 2003.

17. Lofland, *The Public Realm: Exploring the City's Quintessential Social Territory.* Hawthorne, NY: Aldine de Gruyter, 1998.

18. Sandberg and Hofferth ("Changes in Children's Time with Parents: United States, 1981–1997." *Demography* 38 (2001): 423) note that time spent parenting is

actually higher than in the past, not lower; and the father-as-panacea idea has received extensive criticism, from, e.g., King and Heard ("Nonresident Father Visitation, Parental Conflict, and Mother's Satisfaction: What's Best for Child Well-Being?" *Journal of Marriage and the Family* 61 (1999): 385) and McLanahan ("Family Structure and the Reproduction of Poverty." *American Journal of Sociology* 90 (1985): 873).

19. Zweigenhaft and Domhoff, *Diversity in the Power Elite: How It Happened, Why It Matters*. Lanham, MD: Rowman & Littlefield, 2006.

20. The "ideology of competitive individualism . . . imposes a moral imperative on parents . . . to make sure that their children acquire as much cultural capital as possible" (Schwalbe, Godwin, Holden, Schrock, Thompson, and Wolkomir. "Generic Processes in the Reproduction of Inequality: An Interactionist Analysis." *Social Forces* 79 (2000): 419).

21. See, e.g., Odendahl (*Charity Begins at Home: Generosity and Self-Interest Among the Philanthropic Elite*. New York: Basic Books, 1990) and Kendall (*The Power of Good Deeds: Privileged Women and the Social Reproduction of the Upper Class*. Lanham, MD: Rowman & Littlefield, 2002).

22. Dolgon (*The End of the Hamptons: Scenes from the Class Struggle in America's Paradise*. New York: NYU Press, 2005, chapter 4).

23. See, e.g., Gubrium and Holstein (*What Is Family?* Mountain View, CA: Mayfield, 1990), Osmond and Thorne ("Feminist Theories: The Social Construction of Gender in Families and Society." In *Sourcebook of Family Theories and Methods*, edited by Pauline Boss et al. New York: Plenum Press, 1993).

24. Hays, *The Cultural Contradictions of Motherhood*. New Haven, CT: Yale University Press, 1996, page 150.

25. Bravin, "How A Jewish Man Got Into a Ritzy Club in Palm Beach, Fla." *Wall Street Journal*, 28 February 2001, A-1.

26. Moss (2001).

27. See McPherson, Smith-Lovin, and Cook, "Birds of a Feather: Homophily in Social Networks." *Annual Review of Sociology* 27 (2001): 415.

28. Jackall, *Moral Mazes: The World of Corporate Managers*. New York: Oxford University Press, 1988, page 39.

29. Lamont makes this point in *Money, Morals, and Manners: The Culture of the French and American Upper-Middle Class*. Chicago: University of Chicago Press, 1992.

30. Similarly, Kendall (*Members Only: Elite Clubs and the Process of Exclusion*. Lanham, MD: Rowman & Littlefield, 2008, chapter 4) notes that as new members' dress and comportment conform, they feel and show that they truly fit in, that they embrace upper-class norms and values.

31. Finkelstein, *The Fashioned Self*. Philadelphia: Temple University Press, 1991, page 109.

32. Schwalbe and Wolkomir ("Interviewing Men." In *Handbook of Interviewing*, edited by Jay Gubrium and James Holstein. Thousand Oaks, CA: Sage, 2001) call this a "bonding ploy" with the interviewer.

33. These are social processes known as "boundary heightening" (Kanter, *Men and Women of the Corporation*. New York: Basic Books, 1977) or "othering" (e.g. Schwalbe et al. 2000).

34. Firey (*Land Use in Central Boston*. Cambridge: Harvard University Press, 1947, chapter 3) describes a similar case of elites in this region having a favorite neighborhood whose "lineage" they fight to preserve.

35. For a more thorough review of legal skirmishes around private clubs, see Kendall (2008, chapter 6).

36. Ostrander (1984:103).

37. The circular logic comes from Della Fave ("The Meek Shall Not Inherit the Earth: Self-Evaluation and the Legitimacy of Stratification." *American Sociological Review* 45 (1980), page 961). Also see Della Fave, "Toward an Explication of the Legitimation Process." *Social Forces* 65 (1986): 476.

38. Kendall (2002).

39. Lareau and Weininger, "Cultural Capital in Educational Research: A Critical Assessment." *Theory and Society* 32 (2003), page 598.

40. Fantasia ("From Class Consciousness to Culture, Action, and Social Organization." *American Sociological Review* 21 (1995): 269); criticism also comes from Ostrander ("Class Consciousness as Conduct and Meaning." *The Insurgent Sociologist* 9 (1980): 38).

41. Domhoff (1986), Tilly (*Durable Inequality*. Berkeley: University of California Press, 1998).

42. Hyde, *Holding Disillusionment at Bay: Latino/a Immigrants and Working Class North Carolinians Expose and Reinforce the American Dream's Discrepancies*. Doctoral dissertation, North Carolina State University, 2002.

43. Johnson, *The American Dream and the Power of Wealth: Choosing Schools and Inheriting Inequality in the Land of Opportunity*. New York: Routledge, 2006.

44. Scott (2002).

# 3

# "Similar but Diverse"

## Explaining Race and Ethnicity in the Clubs

I heard a comment that one old longtime female member made that
said, you know, she finds it very distasteful that she has to look at these
Italian guys smoking cigars with their shirts open.

—Harold, Oldfamily member

### INTRODUCTION: AMERICAN RACIAL DISCOURSE

Is it an oxymoron, or can a group of people be both similar and diverse
at the same time? "Similar but diverse" is how an Oldfamily member
described the makeup of his club. It turns out that since these words are
specified in a certain way, the description holds.

In this chapter, we will hear interviewees' accounts for the racial-ethnic
composition of their country clubs. After a brief description of racial ideology, and of the clubs' composition, I will show how club members use
the former to explain the latter. Their accounts are of two types: the first
justifies the homogeneity that still largely characterizes the clubs, and the
second emphasizes what heterogeneity there is. Interviewees make use of
the concept of diversity, which is emerging as an important element of the
dominant American racial ideology.

The United States has recently undergone a shift in the matter of race.
Until the Civil Rights era, racism was explicit and unabashed. In the post–
Civil Rights era, things have changed. Scholars who disagree on the par-
ticulars are at least unanimous that race in America is different now than

it used to be. This system includes both the structure of opportunities and constraints for groups of people, and the ideology about the structures and groups.[1] The racial order is related, usually symbiotically, with those of class and gender.

Biologically based racism still has some subscribers, but it is no longer dominant, as evidenced by its disappearance from indicators of public discourse like the mass media and educational curricula. Instead, the dominant racial ideology of the post–Civil Rights era is characterized as "color blind."[2]

Sociologist Eduardo Bonilla-Silva has studied white Americans' racial talk, and finds a distinct discursive *style*, *stories*, and *frames* of the dominant ideology. The discursive *style* of colorblind racism avoids racial language, uses semantic moves as buffers, and projects motivations and feelings onto minority groups.[3] The *stories* are either generic ones that oppose affirmative action and deny the contemporary significance of racism, or they are testimonials about personal experience. The most useful part of his analytic trilogy is *frames*—"set paths for interpreting information."[4] The four main frames dominant today are naturalizing segregation, cultural arguments, minimizing racism, and especially abstract liberalism. This last one is the most important of the four for this study.

Abstract liberalism means using liberal tenets of individual choice and meritocratic equal opportunity, in a decontextualized way that denies the history and persistence of racism. This frame relies on the "dominant stratification ideology" discussed in the previous chapter, and presumes that the American Dream, of upward mobility based on merit, is a reality for all.[5] The implication is that no social/governmental intervention is necessary to reduce racism, because there is none. The inferior social position of minorities is explained, in this ideology, not by biology but by their moral or cultural deficiencies.

I will refer back to the frames, style, and stories of Bonilla-Silva below as they relate to my own findings and analysis. However, I do not use his term "colorblind racism." I believe that today's dominant racial ideology has colorblindness as one component, but is not wholly captured in that concept.

As you'll see here, racial ideology is sprouting an important new branch that contradicts colorblindness. This new branch is the exaltation of racial-ethnic diversity. To my interviewees, the word "diversity" means the adding-in of some people from different religious, ethnic, and racial groups. This inclusion need not come from any progressive political or ideological impetus. In this chapter, I will use the word as these club members do, but its simple use should not be read as a simplistic acceptance of the dominant definition and frame.

The emergent frame of valuing diversity originated in both the academic and the corporate arenas, with the latter more influential. Businesses reacted to the combination of the shifting post–Civil Rights cultural tide, America's increasingly diverse population, and the increasingly global economy, by embracing racial-ethnic diversity. Searching library catalogs for the keyword "diversity" yields a stack of books on recruiting and, especially, managing a diverse workforce. This change in business was driven more by material necessity than by changed principles.[6]

This is an example of what scholars of elites have shown: that elites will adjust their discourse and actions as needed to serve corporate profits by forestalling criticism.[7] Developments in elite ideology are important because they usually influence—rather than reflect—the broader mainstream discourse.[8] Valuing diversity is now a part of the elite discourse, as shown in the following two sites. One site is in interviews with country club members, which will of course be the focus of the body of this chapter. Another is the discourse surrounding a recent Supreme Court case, which debated the merits and constitutionality of racial preferences in higher education admissions.

*Grutter v. Bollinger et al.*[9] is the case of a white applicant to the University of Michigan's law school, who complained that applicants receive a better chance of admission when they are nonwhite. *Amicus curiae* briefs in support of the school were filed by many different organizations. The Court ruled that the school's admissions practices were acceptable, because it agreed with the argument that education (whites' education, presumably) is so enhanced by diversity as to be a compelling state interest. Following the 1978 *Bakke* decision, this Court agreed that "the nation's future depends upon leaders trained through wide exposure to the ideas and mores of students as diverse as this Nation of many peoples." The text of the ruling cited the briefs filed by major businesses as support. A brief from "65 Leading American Businesses" argued that "an educational environment that ensures participation by diverse people, viewpoints and ideas will help produce the most talented workforce." General Motors filed its own brief, which similarly argued that: "Success in today's business world demands cross-cultural competence and the ability to view problems from multiple perspectives—skills best learned in diverse academic environments."

Academic institutions and social science and other professional organizations joined big business in filing briefs emphasizing the positive value of racial-ethnic diversity; so did the federal government and some U.S. Senators and Representatives. The position that diversity is important was repeated in the ruling of the Court.

Overall, the discourse surrounding this case shows that the dominant racial ideology as developing in elite circles is not just colorblind, but also places value (at least in some contexts) on racial-ethnic diversity. As well as serving corporate profits, this recent valuation of diversity strengthens the power elite via selective admission of minorities, as advocated by E. Digby Baltzell, a scholar of and from the upper class.[10] This plan of selective admission makes a show of meritocratic upward mobility, without at all diminishing elite power. Such a conceptualization of diversity is "safe" for the wealthy because it does not reduce their own privileges.

The new cultural valuation of diversity has some quirks, especially that it is in tension with the concept of colorblindness. As the Michigan law school shows, achieving the prized diversity requires racial consciousness: colorblindness is suspended to yield diversity. This has also been the case at some country clubs, as the talk below will show.

Not surprisingly, it is only wealthy minorities who gain admission to exclusive country clubs, and more men of color than women of color. (One "marked" status may be more surmountable if the person is otherwise privileged; also, one may be motivated by the other privileges to assimilate on the marked dimension.) As the previous chapter made clear, admission depends on more than just money. The proper cultural capital is needed, whatever one's racial-ethnic status. Even if admissions decisions are colorblind, they remain conscious of culture. One white woman mused that when blacks joined Oldfamily, they must have thought, "Okay, yeah, I'll be the well-behaved WASP with dark skin." The cultural conformity—assimilation—required for country club membership points to the shallowness of the diversity that is currently valued.

But these nuances are not part of the dominant American racial ideology. Most white Americans seek to minimize talk about race itself, which is why the dominant ideology has been deemed "colorblind." And yet the importance placed on diversity suggests that the colorblindness is not thoroughgoing.

Overall, what talk there is about race is more subtle than in the past, with animosity hidden between the rhetorical lines or arguably absent. So, some scholars advocate using qualitative methods to capture the complexity of the attitudes, talk, and behavior that impacts racial systems. Typically, researchers find among the people they study a distinct absence of talk explicitly about race.[11]

This discursive absence reflects today's cultural climate. The dominant post–Civil Rights discourse has been to avow colorblindness and avoid the topic of race/racism altogether—both in everyday speech and, when possible, in interviews.

In the interviews conducted for this study, club members account for the racial-ethnic composition of their country clubs. Their several accounts either justify the clubs' homogeneity, or emphasize their heterogeneity. For the most part they avoid talking about race, as we might expect: they justify homogeneity using nonracial frameworks. As they emphasize heterogeneity, they deny the importance of racism; but interviewees' focus on diversity represents an important exception to the silence about race found elsewhere.

And how diverse are the clubs? Before analyzing the accounts, I will describe the racial-ethnic composition of the clubs in this study as best I can, given incomplete information.

Oldfamily, Rosary, and Suburban all have long histories of being exclusively white. Today, all three clubs claim that membership is open to people from every religious, ethnic, and racial group.

Members of all three clubs told me of their openness, but without a census of each club, it's impossible to know their true composition. Oldfamily members were the only ones who actually referred me to minorities in their club. But this could be an artifact of how many more members of Oldfamily I interviewed; I'm told there are also nonwhite members at both Rosary and Suburban.

(Waterside is such a new club that it does not have the local reputation that Oldfamily, Rosary, and Suburban do. Those three clubs are the focus here.)

As well as indicating the openness of their own clubs, interviewees also suggest that other clubs are less diverse. This charge of homogeneity—discussed as an account below—is leveled at *each of the three* clubs by members of the other two clubs. So this also fails to yield systematic information about club composition. Overall, it is safe to say that Oldfamily, Rosary, and Suburban are still prominently WASPy, Catholic, and WASPy respectively, but with some modern-day exceptions.

Now, let's hear the two groups of accounts that members offer for the racial-ethnic composition of their clubs. To *justify homogeneity*, they do the following: perform "othering," say that minorities choose not to apply, argue that people have a natural urge for separatism, and refer to the importance of economic status. On the other hand, members *emphasize* what *heterogeneity* there is in their clubs. They do this by indicating minority presence, noting that their club is more diverse than in the past, and more diverse than rival clubs. Members have various accounts for the increase in heterogeneity. In both types of accounts, people make use of the dominant racial ideology.

## JUSTIFYING HOMOGENEITY

### Othering

In the previous chapter, we saw "othering"—talk that draws distinctions and emphasizes boundaries—based on dress and decorum. Certainly, and perhaps more perniciously, people also perform othering along racial-ethnic lines. These symbolic boundaries no longer rely on biological arguments, as they traditionally have. Instead, racial-ethnic othering relies on culture today, as shown here.

### Othering by Dominants

WASP has traditionally been the unmarked category, and therefore mainly a standpoint from which to other. Most characterizations of this group are similar to how they lightheartedly characterize themselves: stodgy, penny-pinching, uptight Yankees. Mostly, the othering is done in contrast to this reference group: sometimes in a generic "not us" contrast, and sometimes targeting other ethnic groups.

Members of Oldfamily's old guard sometimes lament the looser admissions standards of today. Ironically, they disparage the new diverse membership for caring more about appearances and about maintaining social boundaries:

Ian: But we've now gotten some people—to be honest with you, I'm going to be very frank—some people who for years would not have been allowed in the Oldfamily because of their ethnic background who are now the ones who are creating this bigotry within the club. "We're in, pull up the ladder, don't let anyone else in, and most of all," and this is really true, [*knocks on table with each word*] "do not let the women have authority."

Ursula: It's actually the WASPy people, here I go again, but I don't know how else to describe them, care less about trappings than other groups and as a more diverse group has come in, they want things a little fancier and they want air conditioning and they're not as happy with the rustic charm. They want to, I don't know. The redecorating looked like the Ramada Inn to me . . . the wall-to-wall carpeting comes in and the scrolly wallpaper and stuff. Which just is . . . they're not willing to put up with the, anything rustic.

The old guard also others the nouveau riche, in a pattern visible elsewhere in the northeast and beyond.[12] Suburban members make similar comments to the ones above from Oldfamily members:

Suzanne: I know one in particular . . . his kid flies by me every single night, excellent golfer, flies by me in a cart every night at sixteen years old with either his brother in the cart, or his brother driving another one right behind him. As I'm carrying my bag down the fairway, and I look at 'em. And I'm thinking . . . what are you teaching these kids? . . . And every time they go by me, I get madder and madder. I just wouldn't let my son do it. But he is a nouveau riche and got his money and "oh, I'm gonna show it and flaunt it around."

Sophia: We've got a lot of nouveau riche at our course who want to change everything every other year, get a new decor for the dining room and living rooms. They want to do some grandiose ideas with the rooms upstairs . . .

these new people just want to, they've got some bucks and they're gonna use it. It was never that way before. We have never, never, never had so many projects over so much money. We used to run that club on a shoestring. And everybody was happy. Now *the doors opened* and people just want, it's a gimme, gimme, gimme situation. [emphasis added]

The term "nouveau riche" can sometimes serve to designate non-WASPs, without having to speak about race/ethnicity. Ian and Ursula above are referring to non-WASPs, so it is possible that Suzanne and Sophia are as well. Sophia is hinting at ethnic diversification by tracing the source of problems to when "the doors opened." In today's era, "nouveau riche" can serve as a code for a category of others who may be denigrated less controversially than othering a specific ethnic group.[13] Or even if the dominants have equal ("colorblind") disdain for everyone who flaunts their wealth, non-WASPs are still targets because new money is the only kind of money they have: WASPs have a monopoly on old money.

When interviewees do address Jews as a group, they characterize them as more focused on both the country club as a lifestyle and the appearance of the club. A Jewish member of Oldfamily said that he chose not to join the local Jewish country club partly because he perceived pressure there for families to maximize their involvement. When I asked an old guard Oldfamily member to distinguish between the Jewish club and hers, she called the former "very special in its layout and its looks," where by contrast, at Oldfamily, "there are no marble baths." To point out Jews' materialism as culturally significant is to draw on (and help reproduce) a common anti-Semitic stereotype.

Italians receive even more othering treatment in these interviews than do Jews.[14] They, and their clubs, are characterized as sexist, flamboyant, and criminal.

Harold: I heard a comment that one old longtime female member made that said, you know, she finds it very distasteful that she has to look at these Italian guys smoking cigars with their shirts open.

Ian: We have a few members who want to go out there and play the $1,500 Nassau [a bet on golf], up or down $300 or $400 a day and stride around. And there are clubs where they'd be happier, where the other members do that. Tuscan, Sicillia, Venetian. It's just a different kettle of fish. And that has a lot to do with the tone and the background of the club.

Q: What types of things would make the membership chair decline to provide an application?
　Richard: Someone who's a known criminal, someone who's a known philanderer, someone who's a known cheat in business or in golf. You know, those types of indiscretions would certainly be enough to say maybe you should be interested in joining Fiorenza. [*Laughing*] Or Tuscan.

Reid [*asked about the mix of people at different clubs*]: If you go to Venetian, it's heavy Italian, mafia type of mentality.

Harold: I don't want to really stereotype people, but if you look at the club here in [this state] that's the most notorious in terms of the treatment of women, it's Venetian. And it's all Italian. And I think it's cultural.

These examples echo Kristen Myers' finding that casual discourse includes caricaturing and surveillance of out-group members.[15] Though her work concerns whites' talk about nonwhites, this study shows that her analysis is extendable to talk about white-but-marked ethnic groups, too.

This portrayal of Italian Americans, like that of Jews, echoes the generalizations in popular culture. As noted in the previous chapter (under "Undesirable Others"), this othering may work to secure the listener's agreement that a certain group is undesirable. Bonilla-Silva similarly notes interviewees' testimonials that "portray a negative incident with blacks, usually used to justify a position taken on some issue."[16] The quotes above represent, for members, "evidence" which justifies ethnic exclusion at their clubs.

Actually, the first two quotes above concern Italians who do belong to Oldfamily, which implies that some people see their admission as a mistake. As candidates, was their improper cultural capital judged less harshly because of their white racial membership? We can only speculate in this case, although research does show that whites tend to be judged with a "benefit of the doubt" that is not extended to nonwhites.[17]

Interestingly, Italians are often the target of othering in these interviews, but African Americans are virtually never a target. The one and only instance is a member's comment about the complexion of a (the?) black member at Suburban. Since he is dark-skinned, she says, "I mean when he comes through the door, you know he's coming through the door." Otherwise, African Americans as a group do not receive the explicit othering treatment that Jews and Italians do.

The instances of othering certain ethnic groups reflects their relative proportional size in the population of the area. Jews and Italians are more numerous than African Americans. In this area, Italians have a long history of significant presence and even power, including positions in the state and local governments. The visibility and power of the Italian ethnic group leads it to be a target for othering, whereas African Americans as a group do not have the same status, in this area of the country. (The same goes for Latinos.) Jews, while visible, are less numerous than Italians and seem more atomized. Their smaller numbers might lead WASPs in this area to feel less threatened than they are by the significant Italian presence.[18]

The pattern here also aligns with competition theory, which predicts that dominants will respond to minority groups in proportion to their relative numbers. The response of dominants to another racial-ethnic group is based on the threat that the group is perceived to pose. But that threat is not calculated by sheer numbers alone, as suggested by the distinction between Jews' and Italians' (greater) local power. Race relations depend on people's sense of group position, not just on arithmetic.[19]

As this research shows, financial and cultural requirements for joining country clubs remain quite strict. The assimilationist cultural requirement sheds a new light on competition theory. The nonwhites that are allowed to join are so assimilated that their race-identification is presumed to be weak. It's true that the interviews don't show that explicitly, but given the requirements of conformity and not making waves, I speculate that memberships are only issued to those whose identity promises no race-based activism. These individuals would not trigger a "perceived threat" reaction. In another research study, an upper-class white woman perfectly reveals this preference when screening nonwhite candidates:

> I was in the League when we took in the first black, and I don't think there was a big debate about it. She's an outstanding gal, and there [doesn't] seem to be any more who want to join. The blacks I know wear their black awareness proudly and I don't think they want to join. This woman we admitted is more interested in general welfare than she is about raising the cause of blacks.[20]

Another implication of the strict requirements for membership is that they keep the number of potential minority members very low. Few can clear the financial and cultural hurdles. The cultural requirement is in place for the comfort (-in-homophily) of existing members, as they would say. But it also limits the numbers of minority members, and ensures that those who do join pose no threat. It is uncertain how the dominants would respond if many more minorities could meet the requirements; I would predict that the response would depend on whether minorities' behavior reflects more identification with racial-ethnic group membership or with the class and culture of the club.[21]

It is ironic that Italians and Jews receive more othering treatment here, while blacks receive less and yet do the most for clubs' image as diverse. This may reflect the greater cultural assimilation on the part of the affluent blacks who are "country club material"; perhaps the other groups' more secure social position translates into weaker pressures toward assimilation.

This irony also reflects a gap between the national public discourse and the localized feelings that grow from the specific population and history on the smaller scale. The national public discourse equates diversity with the addition of nonwhite racial minorities; but when club members here think of alien groups, they are likely to caricature white ethnics. For these members, diversification on skin color feels more comfortable than cultural diversification. Time will tell whether this attitude bodes well or ill for reducing racial-ethnic inequalities.

### Othering of Dominants

Though othering is often something the dominant group does to outsiders, there is also "defensive othering by subordinates."[22] Though Rosary members are privileged in many ways, they were traditionally subordinated to Oldfamily, whose members excluded the Irish as undesirable. While Irish-Catholics used to receive the same othering treatment as Italians, this study has no instances of it. Interviewees do characterize the membership of Rosary, as they do for every club; it's hard to tell whether or not that represents veiled Irish-Catholic othering.

In interviews, some Rosary members disparaged the Oldfamily membership as snooty people who have inherited money. Their own membership, by contrast, consists of more friendly, "self-made" people.

> Roland [*describing an inquiry at Oldfamily by someone who later joined Rosary*]: And they had a formal interview and they sat down, he and his wife, and [the Oldfamily representative] described Rosary as a blue collar place. . . . He was, like, he was knocked over by the rudeness.

> Reid: We've had a few Oldfamily, existing Oldfamily members apply to Rosary who have not treated the Rosary members in a proper manner maybe within business or in a cultural event, and they just didn't like their style.
> [*later*] Very rarely do you find at Rosary do you have the silver spoon kids that inherited the money and there's just a trust fund going on. I don't know a lot of them. Almost everybody has been their own person and made the money on their own. Or they've taken over a small business from their father and it's grown and grown . . . and they know how to have a good time.

Othering Oldfamily members as uppity "silver spoon kids" can be considered an instance of subordinated people creating alternative hierarchies of value. These alternative hierarchies place themselves "above people above," which is the title of a research article by Michèle Lamont.[23] It is typical for a group to draw a symbolic boundary against those "above" them, which works to deny the group's own privilege and to erase the underprivileged "below."[24]

The othering here, as in Lamont's research, is gendered, using elements of dominant masculinity to draw distinctions. Lamont's interviewees disdain the rich as cold, shallow, and insincere. In contrast, they take pride in their own manly work ethic and self-reliance, "implicitly drawing boundaries against those above, who have benefited from the help of their parents."[25] While that research focuses on working-class men, the men of Rosary show that these hierarchies are also used to make distinctions at the top of the socioeconomic scale. As with the othering done by dominants, race and ethnicity are unspoken.

Overall, the effectiveness of othering as an account presumes that people prefer to spend time with people similar to themselves. This preference is one that usually goes unstated except by some members of the old guard, who have perhaps incompletely adopted the newer racial ideology. When preference for racial-ethnic similarity is explicitly stated, in our culture, it is disdained as segregationist. Only softer versions of this preference are stated, as in the section "Natural Separatism" below. The presumption that people naturally prefer to spend time with similar others is an invisible prerequisite for "othering" to be an effective account for club homogeneity. At the same time, people's very notions of who is considered dis/similar are shaped by the othering they hear and internalize.

## Other Clubs and Minorities

One account for the composition of one's club is that, while it may not be terribly diverse, it's at least better than others. These boasts and put-downs about composition reflect the new cultural frame valuing racial-ethnic diversity. As noted, accusations of homogeneity are leveled at *each of the three* clubs by members of the other two clubs. Examples: an Old-family member says that his club has the most African Americans of any club in the area; but a Rosary member calls his club "more diverse" than Oldfamily; another Oldfamily member calls Suburban "less diverse than Oldfamily;" but a Suburban member counters that "we probably have a broader spectrum of people." And so on.

This circularity suggests that the accusations of homogeneity do not reflect real knowledge about differences in club composition. Instead, it implies that interviewees know (at the level of practical rather than discursive consciousness) that exclusion may be construed as morally problematic. The finger-pointing represents a strategy to improve the image of one's own club. This strategy aligns nicely with the broader claim, noted in the previous chapter, that one's own club does not practice exclusion in general.

Importantly, accusations of racial-ethnic exclusion are not limited to the dominant exclusive clubs profiled here. In pointing out other clubs worse than their own, interviewees collectively name more than a dozen in this geographic area alone, including Italian and Jewish clubs. They also rhetorically point to clubs in Georgia, Alabama, and Florida to find racial-ethnic discrimination. The Oldfamily manager, on the defensive about my scrutiny of his club, said: "If you wanted to spend the money, would you go down to Atlanta to a predominantly black club, and have the same interview with their manager or their board if they allowed you to, and what would your perspective be after having that interview, I'd be very interested."

Interviewees argue that exclusivity is rampant at Catholic/Italian/Jewish/black clubs. They are suggesting that this other exclusivity is equivalent to that done by dominants. The implication is that a WASP club should not be singled out, either by a researcher to study, or by the public to criticize. But Oldfamily and its peers have traditionally functioned to foster ties that help reproduce the power of WASP elites. Presuming equivalence among ethnic groups is inaccurate, but it's a useful tool for the most powerful of the groups.[26]

When it comes to the racial-ethnic composition at their *own* clubs, members often use individualistic explanations. They point to the choices or the personalities of members of disadvantaged groups in giving accounts.

> Clayton [*former Oldfamily president*]: Now, are we half black? No, because I think that most of the black people who are club-oriented wouldn't necessarily be interested in our club.
> Q: Why not?
> Clayton: I don't know, because there are too many white people there [*chuckles*], y'know I mean it's reverse discrimination.

> Reid: We only have like, I think we have two blacks and maybe five or six Jewish members. We'd like a lot more. . . . But it's just they're not applying.

These quotes can be read as projection, a psychological defense that shifts focus onto the other. Projecting racial motivation onto minorities, a part of the style of today's racial ideology, can be "a way of avoiding responsibility and feeling good about [oneself]."[27] While the above examples indicate that minorities opt out of club membership, this individualistic attribution is also applied to those who do belong.

Non-WASPs who belong to Oldfamily are sometimes deemed to be there because of their personal fortitude. I was told the story of the first Jewish couple at Oldfamily, who were admitted about twenty-five years ago, after the old guard lost a struggle to keep them out. I asked a friend of theirs involved in that fight (described under "Good Deeds" below) if there had been any negative feedback. He says: "You just hear scuttlebutt. That's the way life is. It's uncomfortable. You go out to dinner with them, people'd be kind of looking at you. Fortunately, *they [the Jewish couple] were comfortable enough with who they were, so it worked out*" [emphasis added]. This might be another instance of projection, in part, as the speaker must also be comfortable enough under the pointed gaze of his peers.

Interestingly, this emphasis on personal fortitude also comes from minorities themselves. Here are two nonwhite Oldfamily members:

> Yardley: We usually pick the places that we like, the places we want to be, it doesn't matter who's there and who isn't. Well, y'know, my attitude is one a little bit different, even though I grew up in the South until I was about 15, I had never had a feeling that somebody was discriminating against me. I was never taught that. I was always taught that you set your goals, and that's it: it's up to you to achieve, not somebody else, and *there's no one who can hold you back* if you want to succeed. [emphasis added]

> Q: So does it [being one of the few nonwhites] make you uncomfortable? Do you feel like you're in the spotlight?
> Harold: Nope.
> Q: Okay.
> Harold: Let me say this: because I feel like I belong there. That's the difference. You can find yourself with African American members in clubs who don't feel that they belong there, who don't feel that they have a right to be there, and they will always feel uncomfortable. *I never feel uncomfortable because I feel that I have a right to be there* and I feel that I'm as qualified to be there as anyone else. [emphasis added]

The reports from Yardley and Harold might imply that gender and class privilege make the racial structure recede into irrelevance, at least in a certain context. Hierarchies are never really irrelevant—for any of us—but it may be true that privilege on two fronts motivates people to "go along to get along" on the third front.

These men have self-protective reasons to focus on personality instead of discrimination. Each of these men may be polishing his (manly) self-image and reassuring himself about his place among his fellow club members—and above those members of his ethnic group who have not succeeded. Fortuitously, their WASP fellow members have the same preference to focus on personality instead of discrimination. In another study, interviewees similarly attribute the mostly white composition of their exclusive organizations to "minority women" who "hesitate to step outside their comfort zone."[28]

Attributing club composition to the choices or personalities of the disadvantaged reflects a blindness to the racial character of the recruitment mechanisms and other structures erected by club members. This parallels the broader American emphasis on individuals and blindness to social structure. This emphasis, combined with the very invisibility of the unmarked, makes attributing situations to the *disadvantaged* an effective account. In studying whites' racial talk, it's interesting to note how their responses to racial inequality so rarely implicate whites.[29]

**Natural Separatism**

Another account that justifies club homogeneity is that homophily is natural. Interviewees portray the urge for separatism as natural, drawing on several sources of evidence for support.

One source of support is that even today, most clubs retain their ethnic identities as "the Italian club," "the Jewish club," and so on. Members of the dominant WASP group point out the exclusion performed by subordinate groups. As noted, this serves to make the subordinates themselves responsible for the homogeneity in elite clubs. It also suggests that if all of the groups are participating in separatism, then perhaps it's only natural.

The idea that "birds of a feather flock together" is supported more broadly, too. Some interviewees argue sweepingly that homophily characterizes all civilizations, and that people have always excluded and even hated those who are different. One man denotes Bosnia and Rwanda as examples. He adds, "This is going further a field from what your thing is, but there is no such thing as equality in man. They don't want that. There is a nature of competition, and competition begets exclusivity."

Rhetorically pointing to ethnic war is perhaps a global and extreme version of the finger-pointing mentioned above, excusing one's group by referencing another group whose record is worse.

Separation of the sexes is also used as evidence for the naturalness of homophily. In contemporary American culture, gender segregation is seen as comparatively harmless.

One Oldfamily woman says: "I think there are times when men want to be together, and I know there are times that I'm with my girlfriends and I have a great time. And you know, get over it. Life is short." (Her dismissal echoes the common charge that members of aggrieved groups need to lighten up.) While no interviewee explicitly connects it to ethnic segregation, such mentions of gender segregation suggest that separatism is natural—and in some cases, even beneficial.

This account, that separatism is natural and universal, is one of the main frames in Bonilla-Silva's formulation. My interviewees echo his, who say for example that segregation is "human nature's fault." And: "I don't think it's anybody's fault. Because people tend to group with their own people. . . . Just as animals in the wild, you know."[30]

However, given today's dominant racial ideology, it would be culturally unacceptable for country club members to state an explicit preference for an all-white environment. When it comes to considering their own organizations, club members talk of a separatism based on congeniality (or cultural capital) rather than on ethnic group membership. This confirms the hunch that "boundaries based on moral, cultural, or socioeconomic status [are] increasingly used" in place of inborn statuses.[31]

Steve: That's the premise of a private club, it's where people get together with their common thoughts and common ideals and things they want to do together.

Sophia: [At Oldfamily,] Shorts have to be two inches above the knees and when you go to the dining room, you don't go in your golf clothes. You go in and dress up. . . . A certain segment of our population really appreciates the type of people that are running Oldfamily, and I think that's fine. I would not say that they should diversify any more because I think that's the club that they want, I mean that's the kind of club that they want and that's fine. There's gotta be a certain club for everybody, I think.

Gloria: You don't see too many black polyester pants and gold chains at Old-family. But if, you know . . . someone who was comfortable in that attire may know in advance they may not be comfortable at Oldfamily, and might not apply, so, I don't know. Y'know, birds of a feather, flock together.

As noted, the dominant ideology includes the assumption that preference for homophily—separatism—is natural. If we accept the argument that people want to be with similar others, then exclusivity based on congeniality, rather than race and ethnicity, may be promoted as the best possible state of affairs. It can wear the prized badge of colorblindness. Interviewees avow colorblindness, but also avow that separatism of some sort is natural; the two accounts combine to make contemporary country club exclusion acceptable. But the change in criteria for "doing separatism," from ascribed to achieved characteristics, suggests that homophily is not natural but socially constructed. Social scientists looking across cultures or over time are often able to see differences in phenomena regarded as natural that reveal them to be socially constructed. Such is the case with the separatism club members desire, based formerly on ascribed and now on achieved statuses.

Keep in mind that ascribed racial-ethnic statuses overlap significantly, in this country, with achieved statuses of personal style. So even if exclusion at clubs today truly lacks racial animus, the ascribed-achieved overlap means that it (the exclusion) still has the consequence of contributing to the reproduction of racial inequality. This is also true for financial exclusiveness: given the race-class overlap, even racially innocent financial exclusion has results that reproduce racial inequalities.

## The Role of Money

We saw in the previous chapter that members sometimes refer to finances when accounting for exclusivity. Here, I will revisit those themes and expand on them to include consideration of clubs' racial-ethnic mix.

One account acknowledges that not everyone could afford club membership; it avers that affordability is the only hurdle to belonging. When members must account for the racial-ethnic homogeneity of their clubs, sometimes they do refer to the racialized character of class stratification— without ever acknowledging the racism responsible. They simply point out that nonwhites are, on the whole, less likely to be able to afford to belong. These Oldfamily men agree:

> Evan: You have to think that any country club, by virtue of membership and dollars, limits who belongs there. And so I think to that end, you don't get the broader spectrum of people who can belong, because you're dealing with people who have enough disposable income to belong to the club, or play the games or whatever, so it does limit somewhat the people who belong, and I think . . . so it's not a cross-section of the world we're looking at, that belong there.

> Ian: Hispanics . . . they're very dominant in the [city] community in terms of numbers, but not in terms of achievement, and that's one thing, you know, to join a country club, you've got to have some excess income, and you've got to have achieved in the community and gained the respect of people.

> Larry: It was always a question of: given what the cost structure was, and given that you want to be with interesting people who are influential, and since it's been so difficult for many minorities to get to that position, that the pool that one could pick from was extremely small.

Affordability provides an impersonal account for the overwhelmingly white character of the clubs. As stated in the previous chapter, this account reflects, and relies on, the presumption that economic stratification (of the acuteness found in America) is right and natural. As for the potentially awkward fact that affordability varies by racial-ethnic group, there are ways to explain it. The "dominant stratification ideology" of American culture presumes equal opportunities for all individuals. If opportunities are equal, then everyone is responsible for their own social location. This echoes the frame in colorblind racism of abstract liberalism, which is to argue against racial ameliorations on the grounds that equal opportunity and meritocracy already obtain. This colorblind assessment of affordability neglects the history of institutionalized discrimination that has prevented minorities from accumulating wealth at the rate of their white counterparts.[32]

Among whites, there is a sense that racial discrimination is a thing of the past.[33] And the dominant stratification ideology receives more support from those with gender/race/class privilege[34]—the population of this study. Also, whites tend not to see their fortunes as interdependent with those of the disadvantaged; the benefits of whiteness are rarely noticed by benefactor or beneficiary.[35] So this account can use the racialized character of the class structure without spurring any soul-searching. The race-class link is something the dominant ideology buries, and something that these club members are motivated not to ponder.

During one discussion with an Oldfamily member about racial-ethnic diversification, I asked whether the club today was "equally welcoming to people of all different backgrounds." She replied: "I think it's equally welcoming to all very senior executives in large companies that have, that know how to act at country clubs. [*chuckles*] And that's a much more diverse group today than it was in 1990." So while symbolic boundaries are still being drawn, they are no longer drawn simply on the basis of race. Rather, club members would say they draw boundaries along cultural lines in a colorblind manner (though in present-day America, claims to true color blindness are dubious).

This leads us to another account mentioned previously: that money brings cultural capital. A sense of similarity and "fit," interviewees say, depends on the stylistic trappings that tend to go with economic privilege. Like the hurdle of affordability, the hurdle of proper cultural capital often ends up excluding nonwhites. In musing about the dearth of African American Oldfamily members, one member—himself nonwhite—says: "I don't know if barriers are the right words or not because if you've got all of these criteria you need to possess in order to be a member, I'm not sure how many African Americans possess those sorts of things." Note the narrow definition of "barriers": he would consider an explicit bar on blacks a barrier, but his definition does *not* include other screens that, while neutral on their face, have race-based consequences and origins shaped by racism. This is an important element of the contemporary racialized social system: using rules that seem neutral is a common way to facilitate accounting for racially unequal outcomes.[36] In the case of country clubs, the reliance on matching members according to cultural and economic capital provides an account for homogeneity that's colorblind on its face.

All of the foregoing accounts have justified the clubs' homogeneity; but given the cultural trend to "celebrate diversity," interviewees use a second set of accounts to shine a light on what heterogeneity exists in their clubs.

## EMPHASIZING HETEROGENEITY

In emphasizing the heterogeneity at their clubs, members make extensive use of the concept of racial-ethnic diversity. They point to the presence of minorities at their clubs. And, they provide a multifaceted explanation for the recent changes in club composition. Let's consider each of these three themes in turn.

**The Frame of Diversity**

Though the racial-ethnic composition of their clubs was not announced as a topic of the interviews, people seemed aware of its importance. I checked the transcripts for instances of the word "diverse" (or diversity, diversification, etc.), and found two things. First, even though it reflects a research interest of mine, the interviewee uses the word before I do in just over half the cases. (It's possible they were adjusting their talk to their understanding of sociological research.) Second, the word is used more often than not to reflect well on oneself or one's club. Examples:

> Larry: Clubs have rediscovered themselves. I think the emphasis on recreation, on children's programs, on teaching golf, teaching tennis, having programs with the schools where they bring people in on the off-times, and creating a more diverse, both economically diverse, racially diverse, gender diverse, age diverse, most of the clubs have been trying hard to find a balance.

> Richard: I think Oldfamily still kind of holds on to their old roots. It still matters to some extent what your last name is and what your pedigree is. Rosary is a far more diverse club in that regard.

> Zach: Put it this way, given the population and demographics of [this state], I would bet that this club is more balanced and diversified, or closer to the percentages that mirror the population, than any other club in the state.

It seems unanimously understood that diversity is a positive quality for a club. As with the word "family" discussed previously, "diverse" has a positive connotation that interviewees are eager to conceptually attach to their clubs or themselves. This talk of diversity, then, is an important exception to the colorblind discourse discussed above, as it is color-conscious and front-stage.

And, this talk goes beyond the "testimonials" of Bonilla-Silva's formulation.[37] Rather than just rhetorically pointing to any minority presence in their lives, as his interviewees do, some of these people have acted to ensure that they do have minority presence in their clubs to point to. Club leaders have accepted or even recruited nonwhites as members, and this has not happened because of colorblindness. It happened because the newest element of the public discourse about race is to value racial-ethnic diversity as an end in itself.

The cultural valuation of diversity came from both the academic and the corporate arenas, with the latter more influential. Corporate concern for diversity springs from concern for profits, as discussed at the start of this chapter. It is a case of people at the top of the class order strategically adjusting the racial order.

The membership committees of the clubs in this study could be considered analogous to the hiring offices of corporations.[38] Both groups know, given the new cultural climate, that they need to include some nonwhites among their recruits. To do so helps with the organization's public image. It also helps the self-image of those organization members who believe in the importance of diversity. So, people on the membership committee and people in the hiring office hand-pick nonwhites that fill the bill.

While members are eager for their clubs to be known as diverse, the concept is in tension with the homogeneity they account for in the first half of this chapter. Club homogeneity is more or less a practical reality, but it's also a preference that must be defended by those who argue for the right to free association. This tension is exemplified in the interview with Steve, a former president of Suburban.

When Steve was talking about the formation and composition of private clubs, he talked of homogeneity, in that a private club is a collection of people with similar interests and values. But a little later in the interview, he was talking about the diversity of the membership, and the idea of homogeneity never reappeared. He said that the club is ethnically diverse, and made a point of naming two Jewish members that he plays golf and tennis with. He said that the membership is diverse economically, after a certain point, arguing that club membership isn't unaffordable. (He compared it to the cost of renting a vacation house for two weeks in the summer.) And, when I asked him about the trials of club management, he used the word "diverse" to describe the opinions and personalities of the members.

An Oldfamily member characterized the membership of his club as "similar but diverse," and this phrase reflects people's tensions around the issue. Homogeneity is a fact of club composition, and some recognize that they want to preserve the right of homophily. But stating a preference for racial-ethnic homogeneity is culturally unacceptable today. So, most interviewees are clear in telling me that their club membership is diverse. However paltry the diversity, it is useful to point out; and—as in the case of Steve above—it may be a *remedy* for the admission of some homogeneity. In an ironic development, the admission of nonwhites serves to make the remaining homophilous exclusion more palatable.

## Indicating Minority Presence

It is very common for club members to cite minorities who are also members. Four out of every five interviewees point to the presence of non-WASPs in their clubs. This is comparable to the cliché of "I have black friends." Part of the style of racial ideology in Bonilla-Silva's formulation, such semantic moves can serve as a conversational buffer for more objectionable racial statements. But even if today's club members are truly color-blind, they remain cognizant of the importance of the "fit" of prospective members. Candidates for membership may be admitted no matter what their religion or race, as long as they possess the requisite cultural capital. (See the section on "Fit" in the previous chapter for details.)

"Now we've got United Nations over there," says one Suburban member. The presence of non-WASPs is proof, of a sort, of the enlightenment of the modern club. I suspect that sometimes this minority presence is overestimated.[39] I've heard estimates of the number of blacks at Oldfamily that are double the number given me by an African American member, whom I consider a reliable source in this matter. (He names four African American men as members, out of a total of over 600.) Being able to point to minority members says that a club's exclusiveness is acceptable because it is no longer taking place on discriminatory bases. And given the dominant narrow definition of racism (as inhering in hostile bigoted white individuals), mixing with minorities can be presented as proof of nonracism. These accounts of minority presence are testimonials that assist in positive self-presentation.

However, given the logic of tokenism, the slightest minority presence is all that is required. Tokenism is the practice of visibly including a few different others in a group to forestall criticism about homogeneity. Tokenism is practically promoted by organizations like the United States Golf Association. In 1990, the golf world was publicly embarrassed by the discovery that Shoal Creek, a club hosting a PGA tournament, was defiantly all-white. As a result, the USGA and other organizations now encourage clubs to have a black member in order to qualify to host sanctioned tournaments. In discussing Suburban's composition, one member says, "And we actually have a Black. We have to, if we have a USGA tournament." Proportional representation is never discussed. Nobody ever spoke to me about limiting the presence of minorities, although such limits can be enacted in many unspoken ways. A journalist reports: "Although few managers will speak publicly on the subject, most agree that clubs that would not or did not admit people from certain racial or ethnic groups in the past now probably do, although *not in large enough numbers to affect their profile.*"[40]

This practice at country clubs is similar to that found in some exclusive volunteer organizations. Sociologist Diana Kendall writes: "In elite white women's organizations, highlighting the few members who are from diverse racial, ethnic, or religious categories . . . makes it possible for the group to convey the appearance of diversity while maintaining the elitist, essentially all-white prestigious organization that controls privileged ties and rituals."[41] That effort to highlight diversity reveals the same cultural pressure and response that are seen here.

Rarely is there any reflection about tokenism. The sole instance in these interviews comes from a disillusioned Oldfamily member. She says of her peers: "they always say oh, so-and-so is Jewish, therefore we're open-minded; but they always have to use the same name."

## Accounting for Change

The recent diversification at clubs is explained, oddly, both as something that occurred naturally and as something that was arrived at deliberately. The three accounts below move from the organic to the deliberate.

### A Colorblind Generation

When asked to explain the modern-day diversification of country clubs, several interviewees point to the broader horizons of younger people. In this context, "younger" includes people into their fifties.

> Wendy [*barred from Oldfamily as a child for being Italian*]: Then all of a sudden there were a lot of young people and they began to expand their horizons. So now it's a very active young, people your age or older. It's a good club. And if I told some of those people what the club was like before, they would never understand or believe.

> Evan: I think, like a lot of clubs, the more younger people they bring in, the more that barrier and [WASPy] reputation kind of changes itself.

Given the cultural trend to disapprove of segregationist sentiments, people want to include themselves among this enlightened younger generation. A member of the Oldfamily old guard says:

> Ian: Through the Vietnam war era, which was a great changing point in our society, became more liberal, opened up [IA] and through the 70s and into the 80s and even into the early 90s, I believe that people who were in leadership in that club, including myself and a lot of my friends, people became increasingly open minded in terms of equality for women and in terms of ethnic diversity.

Ian wants himself and his friends included among the colorblind generation. But this is the same man who expressed regrets that Oldfamily is heterogeneous today, and calls another of his clubs "a happy place, and reasonably homogeneous." I mention this not to incriminate him, but simply to show that colorblind thinking does not pervade his interview. Lapses like this are evident primarily among the old guard.

Young and old alike agree that today's generation lacks the racism that preceded it. This conviction depends on a reassuringly narrow and individual definition of racism, as several scholars have pointed out.[42] The presumed lack of racism bodes well for racial harmony, which interviewees believe is happening virtually automatically. As one member of Suburban's old guard advises: "wait for time to pass and things will happen." This account fits with the ideological frame (noted, again, by Bonilla-Silva) of denying the significance of racism, and with the stories that say that "the past is past."

This generation is said to be colorblind, an important concept in today's dominant racial ideology. Interviewees herald colorblindness as a welcome and recently achieved state of affairs. They note that it has been made possible by the way interaction has evolved in school, in business, and in friendships.

> Parker: Simply people's friendships through schools and everything else is just a much more diverse, you know, much more diverse and integrated world.

> Q: Can you identify a catalyst to this diversification?
> Clayton: It's business, and sociability, today, period. It's . . . we make friends with lots of different people in business who become our social friends, or social friends who become our business friends, and it's all intertwined.

In this population, part of colorblind ideology is the idea that WASPs no longer reign. Nine of the thirty-five interviewees argue that the social hierarchy topped by Oldfamily is obsolete. For example:

> Q: What would you say is the top club in the state?
> Olivia: In terms of what?
> Q: Well,—
> Olivia [interrupts]: The top kitchen is at the [Jewish club].
> Q: How about most prestigious?
> Olivia: I don't think there's such a thing.

> John [regarding facilities and amenities]: Rosary or Suburban or whatever, they were, and still are frankly, getting a much better product for their dollar. And so Oldfamily used to sort of get around that by saying "yeah, but we're Oldfamily."
> Q: An intangible part of the product?
> John: Yeah, right. "We're socially better than," you know. But I think most people were saying, "no you're not. Why do you say that?" And I think the demand has been to upgrade the place a lot.

John sums up a theme that many agree with: "Anything about what used to be a racial or socialization structure between these different clubs has been replaced, in some part at least, by money." The implication is that what made Oldfamily distinct is now irrelevant, but I disagree that Oldfamily is no longer distinct. Leaving ethnic exclusivity aside, Oldfamily has a unique analytic place because of its tradition as a site for the concentration of power. The demise of the power elite has been announced periodically throughout American history; so today's announcement should also be greeted skeptically, perhaps especially when it comes from elites themselves.[43]

During these interviews, colorblindness is announced with notable frequency. This makes sense in the context of interview-as-call-to-account, as opposed to the context of everyday speech. But the avowals of colorblindness are so numerous that it smacks of "protesting too much." The refrain is matched by the majority of corporate managers interviewed in another study. They stand in contrast to "the few employers who explicitly support multicultural policies. . . . Such managers need not say that they do not discriminate, nor that they hire all colors, and so on. In multicultural discourse this is simply presupposed and need not be asserted."[44]

Club members' announcements of colorblindness might also signal a change in the response to challenges about clubs' composition. In 1990, when the Shoal Creek golf club of Alabama was challenged for racial homogeneity, its president responded simply: "The country club is our home, and we pick and choose who we want. We have the right to associate or not associate with whoever we choose."[45] While similar arguments about the right to selectivity appear in the previous chapter, when members are questioned about race specifically, they show more sophistication than the blunt Shoal Creek president: they claim to be colorblind personally, exaggerate their clubs' heterogeneity, and attribute their clubs' homogeneity to various external factors beyond their control.

### Oldfamily's Membership Drive

Oldfamily members provide further explanation for their club's diversification. The club was threatened with declining membership about twenty-five years ago. Oldfamily leaders cite multiple causes for this, many of which apply beyond their own club. (In fact, elite clubs in Texas have also experienced a decline in membership and resultant diversification.[46]) The Oldfamily members note that country clubs were shrinking in importance in individual lives. Golf courses and good restaurants, each an alternative to the club, were proliferating locally. The club's standing as the social center for the affluent community weakened. This is partly because the social density (the proportion of members each member knows) dropped. This, in turn, is a result of a confluence of factors. Geographic mobility raised turnover in club membership, reducing the core of lifelong members. The WASP community has become "diluted," as one Oldfamily board member put it. He cited as evidence his own marriage, between someone from a prominent old local family and someone from a tiny town in Iowa. As more and more of their class peers are non-WASPs, WASP marriages are increasingly "mixed." Social power has also become

decentralized: another interviewee points out that the social power formerly concentrated in the Heights and its city is now spread among the
city and suburbs like Littletown.

In Oldfamily's recent history, the combination of a weak economy and
an aging membership posed a new threat of decline. This prompted the
board to promote the idea of drawing new members from beyond the
traditional pool. At around the same time, leaders became conscious that
their membership in a homogeneous exclusive club posed a potential
problem for their self-image and their public image. Larry sums up the
sentiment emerging then: "[clubs] were thought of as being elite, snobby,
Anglo Saxon White, and I just, that's not me. In the first place my corporation is diverse, my corporation's going after the diverse marketplace, and
I don't want to see my name on the front page of the paper that says I
belong to Oldfamily."

So, the Oldfamily club needed new members' money, for a variety of
reasons; and Oldfamily leaders wanted to add some diversity to their
ranks. As Larry's comment makes clear, this desire stemmed less from
principled goodwill than from a realization of a potential image problem,
and a "trickle-down" from business concerns. As with the national scale
mentioned above, locally people at the top of the class order can make
strategic adjustments to the racial order.

Oldfamily did diversify, perhaps because of this potent combination of
material and social pressures. The social pressure is mentioned only by
leaders who were involved in planning for the club; it shows that the
catalyst for change was not exactly colorblindness, but color-conscious
and class-conscious attention to diversifying.

### Good Deeds

In talking about their club's racial-ethnic composition, members often
point out to me the things that they, or club leaders, have done on behalf
of diversification. These stories may be read as testimonials with "a positive self-presentation rhetorical goal."[47] However, as noted, some club
members do deserve credit for going beyond rhetoric and taking action.
The good deeds themselves take several forms.

Eight members said—without prompting—that they have sponsored the
memberships of non-WASPs. A ninth tells of breaking "the color line" by
bringing her African American foster child to the club swimming pool.

John: I proposed one and seconded another Jewish member at Oldfamily
right now.

Ursula: [My husband] never would have been on the board in the old days
because we were putting up Black members, we were putting up Jewish

members, we were putting up you know, whomever we liked. And so we were I guess considered a little rebellious.

Walter: I know in Venetian's case, I was, I had the honor I guess, I was distinguished by being the first person to nominate a Black person.

Having sponsored a non-WASP candidate for membership seems to be a point of pride, whether or not the candidate was admitted. Since actions speak louder than words, these nine members are sharing with me significant evidence that they are "good on race," so to speak.

There are more ways to convey this same point. There are stories from the recent past wherein members fought the board to allow the admission of a non-WASP. Here is an example from Oldfamily:

Parker: I think it was in the early 80s, I can remember one specific instance of—people who have been members of the club now, twenty years, but when we first proposed them, there was a lot of objection. And the objection was because one of them was Jewish. . . . [T]hey happened to be very good friends with about eight or ten of us, and I think part of the influence was also that those eight or ten, four or five families also represented families that had been members of the club forever . . . that had this tradition of clubs: fathers were presidents, all that type of stuff; so it was, and we basically demanded to meet with the board. . . . And it was a group of people that they could not have refused to meet with, and we basically just said, "this is ridiculous. These are our good friends, our children play together, they are among our best friends, the club has to change because if you don't, we're all gonna resign." And a lot of grumbling and grumbling and negotiating afterwards—"you wouldn't do that." And so I mean I think we just pushed, I think they tested our resolve, and I think finally concluded that maybe we actually would resign; which of course they'd be better off with—so, you know, our friends got in.

In the polite WASP world, this was a memorable confrontation. I heard this same story repeatedly, including from someone who was not yet a member at the time; so it has entered the Oldfamily lore to some extent.

In telling the story, Parker acknowledges the nondemocratic nature of clubs, where certain families are more influential than others. But he and the others who "pushed" can be unapologetic about their privilege, in this case, because they used it for a progressive purpose.

Such stories of the privilege of disproportionate social power give the lie to the meritocratic "dominant stratification ideology." The interviews include no mention of the contradiction between the two. This finding is similar to others who report that whites, curiously, believe in meritocracy while acknowledging the boosts they have received or given to those close to them.[48]

From the other side of the board meeting table, there are also stories of using one's leadership position to press for more inclusiveness. The same man did this when, years after the confrontation, he was asked to join the board of governors. He agreed because, he says: "It was at a time when I felt pretty strongly that the club needed to change its attitudes about membership." Another board member reports: "We've worked hard at it, too: I think that people generally don't take credit for saying, 'look, I've worked hard at making diversification work.'"

However, accounts of changing the rules are typically less compelling than accounts (like the one above) of fighting the rules. This is because the rule-changing stories are tempered by the acknowledgment of outside influences. At Oldfamily, leaders take credit for the racial-ethnic broadening of the recent past, but they also acknowledge that the change was a response to declining membership numbers. At Rosary, change was inspired by a somewhat different threat:

> Roland: Rosary's changed a lot. Years ago it used to be very old fashioned. They were all WASPy type people there. No Catholics, certainly no Jewish people, no black people, so that's all changed quite a bit. Partially because they've had to.
> Q: What do you mean by "had to"?
> Roland: Well, they've had to. You certainly can't be a country club as prestigious as Rosary is now without having people of all different denominations. It's just a matter of time before somebody makes an issue out of that. So I think some of the guys that were on the board took a look at that and now they really have all denominations, colors.

Elsewhere as well, statements supporting diversity have this hint of being pressured into it. The cultural sea change that the Rosary board reacted to is the same one that now demands accounting from members of exclusive private clubs, and guides the content of those accounts.

## SUMMARY

Country club members are proud of the recent diversification of their membership. Where possible, they portray themselves as heroes of a new, colorblind era of racial harmony. Some even christen this era "post-racial" in the wake of President Obama's election; but pronouncements of a fully integrated and truly colorblind society are premature.

The members do deserve some credit for the changes. But let's remember that the diversity that now exists at these clubs is of the most limited kind.[49] It remains homophilous by class, and arguably by culture, as the term "WASP with dark skin" implies. By admitting a couple of affluent, prominent black men who like to play golf—minorities with gender and class privilege—these clubs are *just* complying with the "letter of the law" in the current cultural climate. They have achieved racial-ethnic diversity without becoming at all multicultural—never mind a "strong multiculturalism" that seeks to redress inequalities.[50]

Waterside lacks the hundred-year history of the other three clubs, but here too the diversity is only skin deep. Some Watersiders might hope that their club escapes racism via its recent founding; but the quality of Waterside's diversity is severely limited by its six-figure initiation fee.

This development, of "WASPs with dark skin" at country clubs, exposes the limitations of the new public valuation of diversity. The presence of blacks and other minorities at the most exclusive country clubs might appear as a significant sign of racial progress. But the public goal of creating racial-ethnic diversity in organizations can be misleading in its usual guise. Its vision is one of one-way integration: "of people of color assimilating to a white or White Anglo Protestant culture, [which] will not heal the racial divide."[51] The dominant diversity discourse ignores racism, and can distract attention from power differences and inequalities that remain to exclude most Americans from "the good life." As such, contemporary efforts to create diversity at exclusive clubs, schools, and so on are superficial measures that fail to address the original reasons why the remedies are necessary. Worse, the legitimacy lent by token diversity can help to preserve intact the social structures that reproduce inequalities.[52]

After all, the diversification of country clubs (and other organizations) does not spell the end of exclusion. As noted, the map of boundary lines has shifted—from ascribed to achieved statuses—while leaving intact the practice of drawing and defending boundaries. Club members have indeed acted to diversify their clubs, and that is to their credit; but at the same time, their actions still accomplish exclusionary social closure. Admitting a few minorities into elite circles is not a new idea. Elite sociologist Baltzell advocated fifty years ago for an American aristocracy that selected the best "outsiders" for admission into the upper class.[53] He would probably be pleased: today, "diversity has given the power elite buffers, ambassadors, tokens, and legitimacy."[54] Racial-ethnic diversification has done nothing about the power of the elite, and is likely doing nothing about the opportunity hoarding at exclusive clubs. This selective inclusion amounts to sharing a bit more of the pie, without yielding any control of the kitchen.[55]

The talk of diversity is part of a group of accounts that emphasize the heterogeneity at the clubs. A second group of accounts justifies the considerable homogeneity that remains. This two-pronged approach makes sense given the social and historical context: these clubs have indeed diversified in the last twenty-five years, and are eager to point out their progress. However, they do still need to account for some homogeneity, for the following three reasons. First, the clubs' diversity is so short-lived, following nearly a century of segregation, that they have a lingering public image problem. Second, their composition still does not mirror the diversity of area residents (even affluent ones), with WASPs remaining overrepresented. Third, they must account for conducting exclusion in general, as I argued in the previous chapter. Combined with a relatively recent cultural valuation of diversity, all of this represents a call to account for racial-ethnic homogeneity.

Members' overall accounting for club composition reveals some internal tensions, and not just because of their two-pronged approach. One tension is that between separatism and an evolutionary understanding of race relations. Interviewees argue that the urge to segregate is natural; but they also argue that racial integration and equality is naturally evolving. Obviously both accounts cannot hold. The conflict here mirrors a larger cultural tension about race. On the one hand, there is the currency of the term "colorblind" to signify the dominant ideology of racial progress: that as time passes and colorblindness becomes the norm, racial harmony will naturally follow. But on the other hand, the persistence of the concept that "birds of a feather flock together" calls into question the inevitability of evolution toward integration.

"Diverse" is even more of a buzzword than "colorblind." (Indeed, the work done to promote diversity is color-conscious, showing that colorblind society is not the reality.) As stated, interviewees portray themselves and their clubs as proponents of diversity. But this buzzword is in tension with "family," which members also apply to their clubs—a tension between heterogeneity and homogeneity. As we have seen, the composition of clubs has become less homogeneous, with lower social density, in the past twenty-five years or so. So, as the old guard sometimes laments, the "family feel" is *losing out to* diversity. This fact suggests that "family" may become a less effective account for excluding in the future. It also reflects a loss, perhaps, in terms of the country club's function as a community that fosters a sense of belonging. However, it is possible—probable, according to the accounts offered here—that future generations will feel familial even about a heterogeneous group of people, thus reconciling the buzzwords that seem conflicting today.

One more conflict is between the proclamations of progressive ideology and the acknowledgment of being pushed by outside influences. Wanting to present a positive image to themselves and others (as we all do), these people paint themselves as "good on race," and their clubs as peopled with similarly enlightened others who do not discriminate. But as interviewees discuss the addition of non-WASPs to their clubs, one can hear an undertone of having been pressured to become more inclusive. This pressure has come from the cultural sea change away from approving of segregation. Manifestations of this cultural pressure include the following:

fear of social disapproval from nonmembers for belonging; fear of legal action from members of excluded groups; fear of negative publicity for high-profile club members[56]; and if exposed as discriminatory, fears of losing legal/tax advantages and of missing opportunities to host golf and tennis tournaments.

In considering catalysts for change, this cultural and structural pressure emerges as significant. It's probably accidental that this pressure comes through in interviews as a stronger force than ideology, since the latter would reflect better on people than the former. This is not to say that the accounts described here are inaccurate and only self-serving. There is truth to them, but they are incomplete without consideration of the larger social forces and class interests that propel change.

Though their class privilege sets them apart, these club members represent white America in the following ways. Like most white Americans, they are proud of the progress made in recent decades; they proudly proclaim to be colorblind; but they are much more blind to their own advantages and to the indirect ways in which racial inequality is reproduced. They are proud of racial-ethnic diversity in a token way, though it was achieved through color-consciousness rather than colorblindness. Most of all, they resist thinking about racial inequality, especially their own role in maintaining it.

If these interviewees would be among the chorus announcing a post-racial America in the wake of President Obama's election, count me among the chorus of social scientists pointing to counter evidence.

## NOTES

1. "Ideology" means here the public's framework for understanding the social order, following Hochschild (*Facing Up to the American Dream: Race, Class, and the Soul of the Nation.* Princeton: Princeton University Press, 1995) and Bonilla-Silva (*White Supremacy and Racism in the Post–Civil Rights Era.* Boulder, CO: Rienner, 2001).

2. "Color-blind racism" was coined by Carr (*"Color-Blind" Racism.* Thousand Oaks, CA: Sage, 1997) and is used by Bonilla-Silva (2001; *Racism Without Racists: Color-Blind Racism & Racial Inequality in Contemporary America,* 3rd ed. Lanham, MD: Rowman & Littlefield, 2010) among others. For a critical review of analyses of racial ideology, see Bonilla-Silva (2010, chapter 1), and also Carr (1997) and Gould (*The Mismeasure of Man.* New York: W. W. Norton, 1981).

3. I am aware of the problematic nature of the word "minority" (see Wilkinson, "The Clinical Irrelevance and Scientific Invalidity of the 'Minority' Notion: Deleting It from the Social Science Vocabulary." *Journal of Sociology and Social Welfare* 29 (2002): 21). Despite that, I will use the word (as does Bonilla-Silva) for convenience to mean here—for my respondents—the collection of non-dominant

racial-ethnic groups including Jews, Italians, and African Americans. The question of which groups "register" for my subjects as minorities will be addressed in the text below.

4. Bonilla-Silva (2010:26).

5. Smith and Stone ("Rags, Riches, and Bootstraps: Beliefs About the Causes of Wealth and Poverty." *Sociological Quarterly* 30 (1989): 93), Hochschild (1995).

6. Gordon and Newfield cite "the imperatives of 'global competition' and 'changing demographics'" (*Mapping Multiculturalism*. Minneapolis: University of Minnesota Press, 1996, page 6).

7. Carr (1997), van Dijk (*Elite Discourse and Racism*. Newbury Park, CA: Sage, 1993).

8. van Dijk (1993), Feagin and O'Brien (*White Men on Race: Power, Privilege, and the Shaping of Cultural Consciousness*. Boston: Beacon Press, 2003).

9. This discussion relies upon the ruling and briefs surrounding the case, all of which were accessed at http://supreme.lp.findlaw.com/supreme_court/docket/2002/april.html, on 8/21/03.

10. Baltzell, *The Protestant Establishment: Aristocracy and Caste in America*. Glencoe, IL: Free Press, 1964.

11. On subtlety, see Van Dijk (1993) and Wellman (*Portraits of White Racism*, 2nd ed. Cambridge: Cambridge University Press, 1993). For qualitative studies showing a lack of talk about race, see e.g. Bonilla-Silva (2001) and Eliasoph ("'Everyday Racism' in a Culture of Political Avoidance: Civil Society, Speech, and Taboo." *Social Problems* 46 (1999): 479).

12. Kendall (*The Power of Good Deeds: Privileged Women and the Social Reproduction of the Upper Class*. Lanham, MD: Rowman & Littlefield, 2002; *Members Only: Elite Clubs and the Process of Exclusion*. Lanham, MD: Rowman & Littlefield, 2008), Ostrander (*Women Of The Upper Class*. Philadelphia: Temple University Press, 1984), Satow ("New Yorkers in the Countryside: Status Conflict and Social Change." *Journal of Contemporary Ethnography* 22 (1993): 227).

13. Similarly, Satow's (1993) subjects, in their othering, commingle the categories of nouveau riche and Jewish, sometimes erroneously.

14. It's possible that subjects' othering of Jews was suppressed by my own Jewishness. But most subjects do not know me personally, and I doubt that that label followed me throughout the interviewing process.

15. Myers (*Racetalk: Racism Hiding in Plain Sight*. Lanham, MD: Rowman & Littlefield, 2005).

16. Bonilla-Silva (2010:87).

17. For workplace research, see Neckerman and Kirschenman, "Hiring Strategies, Racial Bias, and Inner-City Workers." *Social Problems* 38 (1991): 433; Tomaskovic-Devey, *Gender and Racial Inequality at Work: The Sources and Consequences of Job Segregation*. Ithaca, NY: ILR Press, 1993.

18. This is an example of Horowitz's point that "barriers and bridges [to mobility] . . . vary with the cultural and socioeconomic mix of the particular community" ("Barriers and Bridges to Class Mobility and Formation: Ethnographies of Stratification." *Sociological Methods and Research* 25 (1997), page 524).

19. Competition theory is from Blalock, *Toward A Theory of Minority-Group Relations*. New York: Wiley, 1967; the "sense of group position" insight is from Blumer,

"Race Prejudice as a Sense of Group Position." *Pacific Sociological Review* 1 (1958): 3.

20. Ostrander (1984:101).

21. This prediction is guided by Blumer (1958).

22. Schwalbe, Godwin, Holden, Schrock, Thompson, and Wolkomir. "Generic Processes in the Reproduction of Inequality: An Interactionist Analysis." *Social Forces* 79 (2000): 419 .

23. Lamont, "Above 'People Above'? Status and Worth among White and Black Workers." In *The Cultural Territories of Race: Black and White Boundaries*, edited by Michele Lamont. Chicago: University of Chicago Press, 1999.

24. Stuber, "Talk of Class: The Discursive Repertoires of White Working- and Upper-Middle-Class College Students." *Journal of Contemporary Ethnography* 35 (2006): 285; Wilkins, *Wannabes, Goths, and Christians: The Boundaries of Sex, Style, and Status*. Chicago: University of Chicago Press, 2008, page 250.

25. Lamont (1999:135).

26. Bonilla-Silva (2010:36) calls it the "fallacy of racial pluralism."

27. Bonilla-Silva (2010:64).

28. Kendall (2002:165).

29. Wellman (1993).

30. Bonilla-Silva (2010:38-39).

31. Lamont and Fournier, eds. *Cultivating Differences: Symbolic Boundaries and the Making of Inequality*. Chicago: University of Chicago Press, 1992, page 14.

32. On wealth accumulation, see Oliver and Shapiro (*Black Wealth/White Wealth: A New Perspective on Racial Inequality*. 2nd ed. New York: Routledge, 2006); on the frame of abstract liberalism, see Bonilla-Silva (2010, chapter 2).

33. See e.g. Schuman, Steeh, Bobo, and Krysan, *Racial Attitudes in America: Trends and Interpretations*. Cambridge: Harvard University Press, 1997.

34. Kluegel and Smith, *Beliefs About Inequality: Americans' View of What Is and What Ought to Be*. Hawthorne, NY: Aldine de Gruyter, 1986.

35. DiTomaso, Parks-Yancy, and Post, "White Views of Civil Rights: Color Blindness and Equal Opportunity." In *White Out: The Continuing Significance of Racism*, edited by Ashley W. Doane and Eduardo Bonilla-Silva. New York: Routledge, 2003; Wise, "Breaking the Cycle of White Dependence: A Call for Majority Self-Sufficiency." *ZNet*, 19 May 2001, "Whites Swim in Racial Preference." *Alternet*, 23 February 2003.

36. Carr (1997), van Dijk (1993).

37. Bonilla-Silva (2010:87).

38. For analysis of comparable talk from corporate managers, see Van Dijk (1993, chapter 4).

39. See e.g. Labovitz ("Immigration—Just the Facts." *New York Times*, 25 March 1996, A-15) on white Americans' tendency to overestimate nonwhite presence.

40. Schumer ("A Peek Inside the Country Club." *New York Times*, 16 March 2003) reporting on the Northeast, emphasis added. Kendall (2008:66) reports similar tokenism in Texas clubs.

41. Kendall (2002:162).

42. Bonilla-Silva ("Rethinking Racism: Toward a Structural Interpretation." *American Sociological Review* 62 (1997): 465), Carr (1997), Feagin and Vera (*White Rac-*

*ism: The Basics*. New York: Routledge, 1995), Frankenberg (*White Women, Race Matters: The Social Construction of Whiteness*. Minneapolis: University of Minnesota Press, 1993). Doane shows how "the claim that racism is a characteristic of individuals . . . obscures the existence of institutional racism" ("What Is Racism? Racial Discourse and Racial Politics." *Critical Sociology* 32 (2006), page 269).

43. This point is from Zweigenhaft and Domhoff (*Diversity in the Power Elite: How It Happened, Why It Matters*. Lanham, MD: Rowman & Littlefield, 2006), skeptics who note that the demise of the power elite was trumpeted in the 1830s, 1920s, and 1950s, and "a diverse meritocratic elite" heralded by, e.g., Aldrich (*Old Money: The Mythology of America's Upper Class*. New York: A. A. Knopf, 1988) and Christopher (*Crashing the Gates: The De-WASPing of America's Power Elite*. New York: Simon and Schuster, 1989), who echo my interviewees.

44. van Dijk (1993:148).

45. Quoted in Howard, "Shoal Truth: This Is The Same." *Newsday*, 12 April 2003.

46. Kendall (2008:67).

47. Bonilla-Silva (2010:90).

48. DiTomaso et al. (2003), Johnson, *The American Dream and the Power of Wealth: Choosing Schools and Inheriting Inequality in the Land of Opportunity*. New York: Routledge, 2006.

49. Highly limited diversity is also characteristic of many corporations. See Neckerman and Kirschenman (1991) and Moss and Tilly, "'Soft' Skills and Race: An Investigation of Black Men's Employment Problems." *Work and Occupations* 23 (1996): 252.

50. Gordon and Lubiano, "The Statement of the Black Faculty Caucus." In *Debating P.C.: The Controversy Over Political Correctness on Campuses*, edited by Paul Berman. New York: Dell, 1992.

51. Feagin and Vera (1995:165).

52. Bonilla-Silva ("'New Racism,' Color-Blind Racism, and the Future of Whiteness in America." In *White Out: The Continuing Significance of Racism*, edited by Ashley W. Doane and Eduardo Bonilla-Silva. New York: Routledge, 2003, page 272) similarly argues that incorporating some "safe minorities" is a central tenet of "new racism."

53. Baltzell (1964).

54. Zweigenhaft and Domhoff (2006:245).

55. The phrase "opportunity hoarding" is from Tilly, *Durable Inequality*. Berkeley: University of California Press, 1998; the pie metaphor is from Schwalbe (personal communication).

56. This pressure on high-profile club members applies especially to candidates for elected office. Politicians around the country have resigned their memberships in clubs that remain all-WASP or all-male, because of the image problem those memberships pose. Corporate executives are also vulnerable: recall Larry's comment that "I don't want to see my name on the front page of the paper that says I belong to Oldfamily" if it were to remain all WASP.

# 4

✣

# Gender Accounts, Or Why the Golf Course is the Dads' Domain

I never sat around and talked about WASPs the way I am today, but I think WASPs are better about giving women equality than some other ethnic groups are, who like to assert their masculine right. I truly think that's the case.

—Ursula, Oldfamily member

This chapter is not about club members' accounts for country club admission and exclusion. Women have always been a part of country clubs. This chapter covers the explanations for the status of the women within the clubs.

Before I turn to those accounts, I will describe the circumstances at the clubs. Each club has a "gender regime:" an institutionally specific set of gendered expectations and practices under the larger societal "gender order."[1] Given the situation of the clubs within the larger culture and social structure, these clubs are more alike than different. But we do see somewhat more variation here than we did with racial-ethnic composition.

We'll find out where women are second-class citizens and where they are equal, which may be counterintuitive. After a brief discussion of the modern American gender order, I will describe the gender regimes at each of the clubs. Then we will turn to the explanations for women's status, both in sociological terms and in terms of club members' accounts. We will hear some echoes of accounts offered for race, but also some important differences. By and large, both men and women shrug off the gender inequality in country clubs as sensible and unproblematic.

## GENDER ORDER, GENDER REGIMES

The "gender order" may be considered analogous to race and ethnicity as introduced in the previous chapter. As with race, gender is a system including both the structure of opportunities and constraints for groups of people, and the ideology about the structures and groups. It is related, usually symbiotically, with race and class systems. The gender order is complex and reproduced via mechanisms at multiple sites (families, workplaces) and multiple analytic levels (individual, interactional, and institutional).[2] We certainly won't cover it all here. However, one crucial foundation for the gender order is the dominance of the typically imbalanced marriage. This will receive some attention in the "Marriage and Money" section below.

The public discourse surrounding gender relations is not quite parallel to the racial discourse. My interviewees, and most Americans, seem to enthusiastically embrace a racial rhetoric that acknowledges past wrongs and seeks to right them. Overt racial hierarchy and exclusionary segregation are seen as illegitimate. With gender, however, there is less consensus. While it is no longer popular to say so about "the races," there is legitimacy to the idea that "the sexes" are naturally different at their core. The dominant gender ideology includes support both for some gender segregation and for some subordination of women to men.

However, a counter-current in public discourse challenges these ideas. The call for women's legal and social equality with men is audible, if not as well-established as the call for racial equality. So as I weigh the accounts offered for the status of women at country clubs, I see that members do more accounting for women's subordination than they do for women's equality. But the subordination of women has been a constant fact in the history of country clubs (to say nothing of more broadly), so it does not logically need as much explanation as the egalitarian anomaly. The extensive accounting for women's subordination is a historically specific reaction to the American cultural climate, where the call for gender equality is heard, though not dominant. But unlike the racial accounts of the previous chapter, the accounting for gender inequality is comparatively humdrum and emotionally neutral. These people feel less disturbed about gender inequality/exclusion than about racial inequality/exclusion. The accounts below will show why they accept men's dominance. But first, I will describe the gender regimes at each club; they are not all the same, though they all are influenced by the same societal gender order.

One additional club is considered in this chapter: Northern. It is geographically removed from the rest of the clubs, belonging to a separate constellation of country clubs in a different area. In this constellation,

Northern does not have a reputation as being particularly exclusive or prestigious, though it too offers membership by invitation only.

I sought out Northern because it is a battleground of women's status. The women at Northern chafed at being barred from the golf course at certain times of the week; they agitated for change, and eventually sued the club for gender discrimination. Northern figures prominently in this chapter, but is excluded from the rest because it does not fit with the other four clubs in most ways.

Table 4.1, a condensation of this section of the chapter, provides an overview of the gender regimes at each of the five sample clubs. The column headed "Policy Today" serves as a quick indicator of the extent of sexism at each club. In all clubs, any gender conflict revolves primarily around fees and golfing times, and secondarily around the facilities of locker rooms and "Men's Grills."

Oldfamily takes institutional pride, today, in the fact that the club was founded by and for men and women equally. Like virtually all clubs, Oldfamily has both Individual and Family memberships; but Oldfamily Family memberships are explicitly defined as including two individuals, paying equal costs and each casting a vote. This distinguishes it from most other clubs (including Rosary, Suburban, and Northern), whose family memberships presume one dominant individual.

This legacy of equality is helpful, if imperfect. Oldfamily also carries, like every country club its age, a history of barring women from seats on the board of governors and from its grill room. ("Men's Grills" are traditional at area clubs: they are usually small, casual eating areas, sometimes with their own bars, that are separate from the main dining rooms.) While Oldfamily never had formal rules restricting women's tee times for golf, there was an unwritten expectation that women would not tee off on weekend mornings. In recent years, that unwritten rule was explicitly rejected: women golf whenever they please, the grill room is no longer reserved for men, and women serve alongside men on the board of governors.

Oldfamily women have, of course, agitated for such improvements in their status, and also to improve their once-inferior locker rooms. When they have voiced complaints, they have pointedly mentioned their explicitly equal status. For example, Ursula recounts a skirmish over entering the grill room:

> I said, "I'm a member of this club. I pay exactly the same amount of dues my husband does, and if you'd like to build up a room just like this for women with cable television in it, I'm happy to go use it. But until you do, I'm using this one."

Another indicator of the climate for women at Oldfamily is the number of individual women's memberships. The overwhelming majority of

**Table 4.1.   Gender Regimes at the Five Clubs**

| Club | Founding History | Recent History | Composition | Policy Today | Norms Today |
|---|---|---|---|---|---|
| Oldfamily | founded by both men and women individuals | unwritten expectation that women defer to men; women members informally protested, and Grill and tee times for men were eliminated. | breadwinner-homemaker families, but also more dual-earner marriages and more individual women members than most clubs | gender equality; each adult individual has a vote | gender equality in sports and clubhouse; board of governors is mostly but not entirely men |
| Rosary* | traditional men-dominated founding | Men's Grill; policy restricts women's tee times | overwhelmingly breadwinner-homemaker families | limited tee times for "Restricted" members; voting privileges given to selected Heads of Family | with just one exception, men are Principals and women are Restricteds; all-men board of governors |
| Suburban* | traditional men-dominated founding | policy restricts women's tee times | overwhelmingly breadwinner-homemaker families | policy restricts women's tee times | [no different from policy] |
| Waterside* | founded only recently, not member-operated | gender equality | overwhelmingly breadwinner-homemaker families | gender equality | [no different from policy] |
| Northern* | traditional men-dominated founding | Men's Grill; women members sued over restrictive tee times | breadwinner-homemaker families and many dual-earner marriages | limited tee times for "Restricted" members; club found guilty of discrimination | a few women are Principals; most members eschew activism and ostracize litigants and their supporters |

*: Recall while reading that members of these clubs are identified by pseudonyms that begin with the same letter as the pseudonym of their club.

women at country clubs (and in this study) are there as wives, as part of a Family membership. This is the most common mode at Oldfamily too, but there are also over forty women with individual memberships. This is an order of magnitude more than Rosary or Suburban has. In sum, Old-family is viewed rather unanimously as one of the most "woman-friendly" clubs in the area.

Rosary has a more traditional, male-dominated history. Its reputation centers on golf, rather than club social life or a combination of recreational sports. Traditionally, women at Rosary were there as *wives of members*, and were not to tee off during prime times like weekend mornings. Voting privileges are reserved not just for the overwhelmingly male members, but for a subset of those members chosen by the board. This unique policy leads Rosary to have even more inertia, an even lower turnover of real power, than the rest of the clubs.

A tiny minority of Rosary women—including one judge—complained about the tee time restrictions. This came in the aftermath of lawsuits at Northern and other area clubs, so the Rosary board of governors recognized the gravity of the threat. The board canceled explicit restrictions on women in the mid-1990s. Instead, the rule became that every Family membership included one "Principal member" and one "Restricted member."[3] Principal members were to have unlimited use of the golf course, while Restricted members had the same restrictions that had applied to women. All members were notified that they were to designate who was Principal and who was Restricted in their family; or, both could be Principals at an additional cost.

Interviewees report that, out of around three-hundred family memberships, just one wife became the Principal member with her husband as Restricted; not a single family chose to "upgrade" to two Principals. So, they acknowledge that adopting a facially gender-neutral policy has hardly changed things for Rosary women. They still may not tee off until after noon on Saturdays and Sundays. However, hardly any of the wives at Rosary have careers—more on that below—and so there is apparently little discontent. Interviewees could think of only about four women who have individual memberships, and even they have chosen to remain in the default Restricted category rather than pay extra to become Principals. In sum, Rosary's reputation remains "a real men's club," as members say over and over.

Suburban's history is similar to that of Rosary. It was founded on the assumption that families would belong, and that the breadwinning men would have priority on the golf course over the homemaker wives. Steve, a former Suburban president, told me that in recent years, the idea of instituting Principal and Restricted memberships was proposed, but then discarded. He pointed out that if men's and women's patterns became

Principal and Restricted patterns, then social events like Ladies' Thursdays would die. Imagining such a change, Steve said, "then you destroy all these other operations and everything is now open, and that sort of destroys the fabric of a private club, doesn't it?" Apparently, his argument was persuasive: restrictions on women remain. They may not tee off before eleven or twelve on the weekends. Like Rosary, Suburban's individual women memberships could be counted on one hand. But also like Rosary, discontent at Suburban seems minimal.

Northern is the most notorious of all the clubs when it comes to women's status. Like Rosary and Suburban, Northern has a traditional history of restrictions on women. Women were not to tee off until after two p.m. on weekends. In the late 1980s, Northern switched to a Principal and Restricted member system. Restricted members could not tee off until after 12:30. Several women members wanted to "upgrade" to Principal, which was initially allowed. But before long, the board of governors decided that existing women members upgrading to Principal needed to pay an additional initiation fee—a fee whose amount kept on increasing. Depending on who is telling the story, the fee climbed up to $4,000 either because 1) it was only fair to the club and to other Principals that the new Principals pay the same freight, or 2) because the club leadership wanted to prevent too many women from becoming Principals. On the suspicion that it was the latter, combined with other slights and wrongdoings, a group of women Northern members filed a discrimination lawsuit.

The litigants won their suit and the club was ordered to pay damages. The actual number of Principal women was never higher than ten, and is lower now due to attrition. For the social life of the club, the ramifications of the lawsuit have been disastrous. As shown below, members describe considerable hostility between those who support the discrimination complaints and the more numerous members who oppose them.

Members of all four of these clubs point out that elsewhere in the country, struggles over women's status are nonexistent. Several people note that when they play golf in Florida, there is no distinction made between men and women. Some attribute the troubles here in the Northeast to the long sexist history of these local clubs. This hypothesis brings us to a fifth club in the area.

**Table 4.2.  Interviewees re: Gender Discrimination Lawsuit at Northern**

| Litigants | Supporter | Opponents |
|---|---|---|
| Nadine | Nick | Nathan |
| Nell | | Noreen |
| Nina | | Norman |

The newcomer of this sample is Waterside. Unlike the others, Waterside's age is only a few years rather than several decades. It appears to make all the difference. Like the clubs in other parts of the country that interviewees speak of, Waterside has no distinctions between men and women. It is egalitarian.

Two other qualities of Waterside should be noted. The other four clubs here are member owned and operated. Waterside is a corporate venture; there is no member-elected board of governors. Members may make their wishes known to the staff, of course; but members have no official decision-making powers.

Waterside is also at less than full capacity in terms of its number of members. Members at Rosary, Suburban, and Northern argue that it's easier to be egalitarian when the golf course is not crowded even at prime times. Subjects at all clubs explain the unfettered access of women at Oldfamily, in part, by noting that Oldfamily's golf course is used significantly less than most.

This is not to imply that the status of women at Waterside, or Oldfamily, would be in jeopardy if the golf courses got more crowded. But, the utilization of the course is one of the many accounts given for women's varying statuses at the different clubs. The most important explanations are discussed here.

## EXPLAINING THE LOCAL REGIMES

### Marriage and Money

The accounts about women at country clubs rest on an important principle that is at once obvious and very consequential. The talk presumes that nearly everyone involved is part of a heterosexual, procreative marriage where the woman assumes the majority of the domestic duties. This is "compulsory heterosexuality"[4]: people are automatically thought of within this framework. This is especially true in the context of the club. As noted previously, subjects think of their clubs as "family places"; so it follows that women in clubs are viewed in terms of their domestic identities. The existence of nontraditional women—without children, without husbands, with high-powered careers—barely registers in members' minds. While this may not exactly be "elite think," it is myopia that suggests race and class privilege.

In the clubs in this sample, the majority of members are not only married couples, but *the majority are breadwinner-homemaker marriages.* This is an inversion of the national pattern, where wives are more likely than not to be in the paid labor force.

Homemakers are considered to be lower-status adults, by these club members and in mainstream culture. Money is indeed a source of power, and there is some scorn aimed at those who do not directly earn any money. Homemakers are simply not the equals of their (often wealthy) breadwinning husbands, and this sentiment is reflected in the restrictions on women at many clubs. A few feminist-sounding members protest this attitude in interviews, noting that the homemaker contributes to her husband's career, as the law recognizes. But the protests are distinctly in the minority.

Homemaker wives are subordinated and sometimes disparaged. This disparagement can be self-serving othering that by contrast reflects well on one's own group.

> Q: Why do you think the women at these other clubs haven't made an issue out of their limits?
> Olivia: Because I think it's the makeup of the women also. They're happy to be stay at home wives. They're happy for that. They're happy to stand in the reflected lights of their husbands, so to speak, where I don't think the Oldfamily women are.

The litigants at Northern indulge in some of this talk, when discussing the more traditional women in their club.

> Nell: He makes the real money, he's the breadwinner, and you're just this sub–and they grew up like that. I've heard the women talking how lucky they are. It's sad.

> Nina: They currently, I think, have five women on the board. They're all bought and paid for in different ways.

Perhaps men are too savvy today to so bluntly disparage homemakers. But their talk—and club policies—show that they consider them subordinate.

> Ralph: Most of all the women in this club are nonworking females.
> Q: The majority?
> Ralph: The vast majority are women who are married to men who are successful men and the women don't work. And they play golf all the time. I can tell you right now there isn't a woman at that table [gestures across the club veranda] doesn't play a lot more golf than I do. And I can also tell you that there probably isn't a woman at that table that gives a damn about playing Saturday or Sunday morning either. They play with their husbands Saturday or Sunday afternoon and they play all week, all week.

The implication is that the homemaker is, or at least should be, grateful and uncomplaining. This popular sentiment prevents equality in marriages, and thus in country clubs.

There is yet more evidence of conceptual subordination of women. Sometimes, unprompted, men lump women in with minorities:

Reid: We only have like, I think, we have two blacks and maybe five or six Jewish members. We'd like a lot more. We'd like to have some Principal women members too. But it's just they're not applying.

Q: Well when it comes to diversity, how do you think Oldfamily's doing?

Yardley: Well I presume, they're probably doing as good as any other club, and probably better, as far as I can see. There're a number of African American members there; as I mentioned to you, a fairly large contingent of professional women there.

Or, they lump women in with children:

Q: Your kids use it?

Reid: Absolutely. They've got a great kid's program over there. Plus the pool and the golf. Not so much tennis, but a lot of activities going on with the kids.

Q: Golf lessons?

Reid: Great golf school for the kids. And for the women. They have a women's assistant pro now which they never had before, and they do, they try to promote women's golf, but there's still not a lot of activity over there. They've got a great program for them over there. If you can get them interested.

Ken: The up side of Oldfamily is that it's very family friendly, it's very woman friendly which is not the case in a lot of places. We just had a good friend of mine join, I just sponsored him, who was a member of Suburban. . . . They left and came to Oldfamily because it's more woman friendly, see more kids around, and then there are other clubs in the area that, y'know, don't even let women play at certain times of the day. Don't encourage kids at all to play. So everybody's different.

Social theorists point out that much is revealed in the conceptual categories people use when they talk.[5] These examples suggest that country club women, despite their race and class privilege, are still viewed as "other" by their male counterparts.

Gender equality is especially unlikely to spring from the breadwinner-homemaker marriages that populate these clubs. Much research documents the elusiveness of marital equality, and the material and ideological reasons why most husbands retain the upper hand. For one thing, the norm of asymmetrical pairing leads to couples where the man has an edge not only in physical size and age, but also in education and earnings. Even in dual-earner couples, primacy is generally granted to the husband's career, while the majority of domestic responsibilities are assigned to the wife.[6] After all, family arrangements aren't made just by two individuals in a vacuum, but in the context of a culture where gender still matters a lot.

Sociologist Pepper Schwartz studied the unusual marriages that do achieve gender equality. Among other factors, she writes that "it seems to be easier to create an egalitarian relationship . . . if both partners make similar amounts of money." This is because money is a well-documented source of marital power.[7] Given that the men of these country clubs earn incomes in the very top tier nationally, their wives are especially unlikely to approach matching them in income. In this way, country club wives with jobs are still much like their homemaker counterparts, and are (on this criterion) further from gender equality than wives in most dual-earner marriages.

Wives in such asymmetrical marriages are unlikely to have the power to decide which club the family will join, or to call for resigning if conditions are unsatisfactory.

A question I had during interviewing was why gender struggle exploded at Northern and not elsewhere. Interviewees on the whole give the impression that men at Northern, a less elite club, have smaller incomes than men at the other clubs in the sample. Northern wives are more likely than Rosary and Suburban wives to work for pay. And where the husbands are not very wealthy, the wives' paycheck is more likely to make a weighty contribution to the household, and thus add to women's clout.[8]

Women at Oldfamily have also successfully advocated for change at their club. The interviews suggest that Oldfamily has a higher proportion of career women than at Rosary and Suburban. By contrast, Richard points out that "many of the members at Rosary are very successful guys. Their wives don't work, don't have to work." So, while Rosary (and Suburban) women may be discontented at their second-class status, they lack the power to do much about it.

But many Oldfamily women have power beyond their earnings, which, as noted, are unlikely to match their husbands'. This independent power is one reason that women at Oldfamily are better off than their counterparts at other clubs. It can include both the social power of being influential in relationships,[9] and also the power that comes from (usually inherited) wealth. Two examples come from my interviews, of women who were vocal in improving women's status at Oldfamily in recent history. One has held a prominent statewide elected office; another has the name of a Fortune 100 company in her family tree. Ken assesses Oldfamily's women as follows: "There are a handful of women who have been there a long time, who came from money, who are good golfers, who are not timid, who make a stink when they think they're being discriminated against in any way." Later, he adds: "They just bring some clout because of who they are." Let's remember that women's activism is more possible and more accepted when the women are wealthy and white.

Some marriages at Northern and at Oldfamily are at least partial exceptions to the typical marital asymmetry. But most country club marriages are male-dominated. The wives in such marriages—often, even if they have jobs—are in a deal called "trading power for patronage." This is one of several adaptations that people may make to their subordinate status. In this case, women enter into relationships that "allow immediate psychic and material needs to be met—at the cost, however, of perpetuating a larger system of inequality."[10] In a 1984 study of upper-class women, Susan Ostrander showed how their actions have a payoff in their marriages, but serve to reproduce gender and class inequalities.[11] This is just as true today, decades later.

Part of the patronage deal is that women are not to antagonize powerful men. Some women police each other about staying loyal to the deal of trading power for patronage. A Northern member describes one such "policewoman" at Northern:

> Nick: There's a lot of women up there, I can think of one in particular who never has worked, she's a homemaker, played golf in the afternoons, all her life. She's a woman that's probably in her seventies now, husband's been a golf pro there, and it's like, quote, "knows her place." I mean she always played on a Saturday or Sunday afternoon, so if you say to her, "do you think women are discriminated against at Northern Country Club," "No, I've never been discriminated." Because that's what she always knew, that's what she grew up with, so that's not discrimination to her. And there's quite a few women that are in that group. . . . She just absolutely supports the board, she doesn't see anything wrong with what they've done, "there's never been any discrimination, I don't know what's the matter with these litigants," things like that.

Northern members report that women as well as men have partaken in ostracizing those members who support the complaint of gender discrimination. Part of the patronage deal is that subordinate women want to ensure their peers are participating, rather than inciting anti-women hostility that might spread to them too. So, women who opt out of the deal are punished not just by men, but by women too. Northern women on both sides of the lawsuit confirm this phenomenon.

## Feminine Civility

Country club members' expectations of their women are influenced by norms about femininity. Though femininity takes varied appearances, the dominant version is "emphasized femininity": "organized as an adaptation to men's power, and emphasizing compliance, nurturance, and empathy as womanly virtues."[12] It is easy to see how these expectations fit in with the aforementioned deal of trading power for men's patronage.

Sociologist Kristen Myers studied an upper-class women's organization and found its members more concerned with preserving their status as "ladies" than with the organization's stated social mission. Following the expectations for emphasized femininity, the members excused their limited activity by saying that "they did not want to offend people in the community by being controversial."[13]

Another study showed how women who displayed such disagreeability at an elite college were punished. Wellesley students protested the choice of Barbara Bush as commencement speaker, and hundreds of letters to the school reprimanded the young women as "ill-bred" and lacking in the "manners" suitable to "real [upper-class] women."[14]

Similarly, club members here consider the struggle for women's equality at clubs in terms of manners. Marian, an Oldfamily woman who did lobby for improvements in the women's locker room, insisted: "I'm not a strident person and I'm not, I'm really not a Bella Abzug type or whoever they were afraid I was gonna be." She may have been trying to frame herself as not disagreeable, but she and her husband still felt punished by the club leadership. However, Marian points out that the improvements she wanted actually happened, and that most of the Oldfamily women were glad, though too timid to lead the way. Marian adds: "There were a lot of people who would come up to me afterwards and say, 'will you please do something about the snack bar, but please don't tell anybody I told you.'"

Marian is exceptional in her assertiveness. (It may have helped that Marian did not grow up attending Oldfamily and that she is one of the women mentioned above with an unusually massive share of social power.) I spoke to Suburban women and asked them how they felt about the restrictions on their golfing. Suzanne, a serious golfer, expressed dissatisfaction about the weekend restrictions and said she mentioned it repeatedly to club leaders.

Q: You keep bringing it up, but have you organized other women members?
    Suzanne: Oh, no. I wouldn't do it because I've been a member since the day I've been born.

Though her standing as a legacy might add to her clout at the club, Suzanne sees it instead as entrenching her in mannerly social obligations.

Sabrina is an athletic career woman, younger than Suzanne and never married. I expected her to be a candidate for lobbying for change at Suburban. When she noted that she didn't get to golf much, I asked:

Q: Did you speak up about the tee time restrictions?
    Sabrina: Oh, yeah. I mean all the women did, but it was not like they're going to do much about it, so I just ended up quitting.
    [*later*]

Q: So when you resigned, did you let them know: "I'm resigning because I'm unhappy about these things?"

Sabrina: No. Basically I told them that I was going to be working in [another city] and that since there were no times that I was going to be able to play, what was the use. So I don't think I was particularly belligerent about it or anything. It's been so long I can't remember. No, I don't think so. I don't think I was obnoxious or anything.

Note how Sabrina equates this simple truth-telling—a far cry from circulating a petition or bringing a lawsuit—with being "belligerent" and "obnoxious." Given the constraints of emphasized femininity, there is very little cultural space for women to speak up on their own behalf.

Like Suzanne, Sophia grew up at Suburban. She admits, "I just wasn't a person that stood up for women's rights," and attributes her complacency to growing up amidst sexism. Familiar with the case at Northern, she blames the litigants for their agitation:

Sophia: They have a terrible reputation at the course. And *they've ruined it for themselves*. . . . Terrible. Even their husbands are blackballed. That's the awful thing. [emphasis added]

Instead of a lawsuit, Sophia advocates adjustment and patience in the face of club sexism. Even with her career, she notes that she simply doesn't mind waiting until afternoon to play on weekends. Sophia adheres to "the genteel code that expects women, especially elite women, to suffer in silence when they disagree or are offended."[15]

Most interviewees seem to share Sophia's disapproval of lawsuits like the one at Northern. Northern members who oppose the suit characterize the litigants as devious, money-grubbing, and full of hate. Both sides agree that litigants and their supporters have been ostracized. In an instance of "blaming the victim," this is seen as the logical result of litigants' troublemaking, rather than as a reprisal tactic by those who opposed them. Even a litigant herself (Nell) admits, "we've ruined the club" socially. Nathan, who led the opposition to the suit, notes with a hint of Schadenfreude: "they've had health problems, marriages breaking up, there's just an awful lot of unhappiness, and it's funny how that stuff works."

Olivia, in considering women's predicament, notes, "So you bring a lawsuit. Who's gonna play [golf] with you?" Women at sexist country clubs are indeed in a bind, and their bind is tightened both by the expectations of femininity, and also by the implicit deals they have in marriages to wealthy men.

The expectations of femininity are, in a way, a constituent part of the power-for-patronage deal that women make when marrying wealthy men. Susan Ostrander showed this in relating how her interviewees see their wifely role. They report that their duties include "showing solidarity, giving help, rewarding, agreeing, understanding, and passively accepting."[16] The wives accommodate largely because they believe in the importance of the husband's career—and wealth accumulation—and know that their behavior will further it. Only one of Ostrander's thirty-six subjects had a career herself: the remainder had husbands who disapproved of their working for pay, and they also recognized that a career would be a burden in the face of unchanged domestic duties. Ostrander's portrait of feminine subordination at home is compelling, and it makes the lack of women's activism at country clubs even more understandable.

### Individualist Thinking, Problematic Personalities

The accounts offered for women's status at clubs are strikingly individualistic: though the imbalanced marriage is an important underlying factor, it is hardly ever voiced as conferring systematic privilege or constraint.

A main manifestation of individualistic thinking is to emphasize people's personalities. In many accounts for women's subordination and for women's equality, subjects spotlight the personalities of people in the clubs. My usual question (in some form) was to ask members to explain why women were quite equal at Oldfamily and quite unequal at Northern, Rosary, and Suburban.[17] They say that Oldfamily has a different sort of membership, where the men are more liberal. Or they say (as does Ken, above) that Oldfamily's women are different from most, given their social power and their experience with golf.

Sexism at other clubs is explained similarly, by invoking either the character of the membership in general, or singling out certain people within it. People see more conventional couples in breadwinner-homemaker marriages as responsible for sexism, because they are old-fashioned. This might include one's own marriage, as in the case of Richard.

> Richard: I think for the most part, many of the people have traditional families where their wives are at home on Saturday mornings, the guys want to go out and play and that's just the way it is. Like it or not.

Or, these characterizations may reflect well by contrast on one's own group. Here, an Oldfamily member praises Oldfamily men by contrasting them to those at both Rosary and Suburban.

> Q: How would you explain the difference between the places?
> Olivia: Well, Oldfamily's a family membership as opposed to the man just belonging, so that the members have a totally different outlook. I find, now I shouldn't say this, but I find the men at Suburban, not so much as the men at Rosary, but they are very, they are chauvinistic. They expect their wives to

stay home and cook and stay pregnant and all that stuff. I don't think the Oldfamily men expect their wives to do that. I think it's a whole different kind of person who's a member.

Another Oldfamily member, Ken, chalks up the policies at Suburban to the way people with "new money" tend to "get carried away."

Just as common as characterizations of a whole membership—and perhaps more accurate—is the account that singles out certain personalities within the club as responsible for sexism. Especially at Northern, people on both sides of the fight acknowledge that some "bad apples" have fostered an attitude of stubbornness. Bad apples are often old-fashioned people, "male chauvinist pigs" and their wives. Nadine, Nell, and Nina all told me the same story, which exemplifies the Northern male chauvinist.

Nadine: One of the women who was involved in the meetings, her husband was president for one year after this whole thing began, but this is a woman who raised six children and when she put in her application to apply for [Principal] membership, she was up in the ladies locker room one day, she was sitting at the table. I did not witness this, but many of my friends did. She was just so upset and she was crying because when she went home and told her husband that she had put in the application for [Principal] membership because all her friends were, who was she gonna play with, and they kept cutting the hours, etc., etc., he said, "Well, where are you gonna get the money to pay for a [Principal] membership?" I mean after she raised, it's like she was totally worthless staying home and raising six children for him was really worth nothing, I guess.

Aside from the chauvinist, another problematic personality is the follower. Followers have several forms: they may go along with club leadership (i.e. to fight the lawsuit rather than to settle) simply because they want to avoid any controversial involvement. For example:

Nick: In reality I think, if you take the total membership, they [the leaders fighting the lawsuit] probably have 25 percent that support them. I would say there's probably 25 percent that are dead against them, then you've got 50 percent that stay in the middle. This 50 percent are in the middle because they either don't know; two, they don't want to get involved, they're only there for golf; three, they've elected the officers to represent them; and four, they're cheap. Okay. And I say four is probably the major thing. Because at this point, it would technically cost them out of pocket maybe directly $400 in assessments.

Nick's neutral fifty percent may include two more types of followers. One type is the one who succumbs to pressure, either from his male peers who demand conformity, or from her husband. The woman in Nadine's story above succumbed to her husband's coercion, and Nina reports that "now she's one of the worst against the women." Another woman at Northern also reports marital pressure:

> Nick: One of the wives is a member out there. When she's interviewed and the question was put to her, the case had already been taken to court, "What would happen, how do you people relate to the litigants now? Would you people play golf with them?" [She said,] "Our husbands would kick our asses if we ever played with them."

The final type of follower is one whose material interests lie in avoiding controversy. Nell tells the story, combining husband pressure with material interests, of a friend who joined another exclusive club:

> Nell: A friend of mine, they waited a long time, they got in, and she's very outspoken, and her husband told her in no uncertain terms to keep her mouth shut because he has joined there for business connections, and if her mouth starts flapping, he'll get frozen out. . . . Because really he's there, he's not there to play golf. He's there to make contacts for his financial standing.

Nick, a supporter of the litigants, later refines his typology of the people at Northern.

> Nick: Other than the reasons I've already said, some people are in business in the city.
> Q: They don't want to make enemies?
> Nick: They don't want to make enemies and they don't want them turned against them. There's an insurance guy up there that writes business, and I don't have any business. My business is all in [other states]. . . . I have no problem. But if you're a doctor or a dentist or a banker or real estate agent, someone in the city that depends on your name in the area, it's difficult to make a stand. I mean these people, my eye doctor, he said to me, "you know, I give you credit for what you're doing, I really respect what you're doing because I can't get involved."

Note that those who support women's efforts at change are the ones taking a social and financial risk. Club members who do and say nothing are tacitly supporting the leadership fighting the suit; but this is construed not as support, but as neutrality.

There may be some truth to the reductionist accounts that attribute a club's gender regime to the personalities of members. But I think it would be misleading to accept, say, a generalization that men at Rosary are old-fashioned male chauvinist pigs. There are probably just a sprinkling of them, at Rosary and at most every private club. I believe it's more fitting to think of the average Rosary man as a golf nut who chose to join there, at least in part, because of its stellar golf course. A few may feel a thrill at their superior status to women, and a few may feel guilty about it; I suspect that most are glad to have access to the course, but otherwise don't care very much. As noted in chapter 2, the majority of club members follow a detached path of least resistance.

Beyond attributing arrangements to the personalities of club members, another manifestation of individualistic thinking is to attribute things to the personal choices made by members of the disadvantaged group. (This parallels one of the accounts for the scarcity of racial-ethnic minorities at clubs, described in the previous chapter.) As one might expect, this is an account for women's subordination in particular, rather than for equality. Sometimes this ties in with the disparagement of homemakers mentioned above. Their being "happy to stand in the reflected light of their husbands" is analyzed as a matter of choice, rather than a response to cultural and structural constraints that lead many women to make the "power for patronage" deal of an imbalanced marriage.

Rosary men are fond of using this account. Since they switched to the Principal member/ Restricted member system a few years ago, they can now point to the lack of much change as the women's own doing.

> Ralph: We have, I believe, only one case where the female is the Principal member and the male is the Restricted member. We have no cases where there are two Principals, but if they want to be, they would be.
> [*later*]
> Q: So with the one exception, the women are still the same place where they were five years ago?
> Ralph: Except for their—yes, they are. But *at their own choice.* [emphasis added]

This type of talk reveals a blindness to the remaining barriers to women's equality. It oversimplifies things to argue that the mere switch to Principal and Restricted designations would rid Rosary of sexism. (I doubt the men themselves even believe it, though it's difficult to know.) Choosing those designations is not just, as Richard calls it, "an individual family decision." At least three barriers remain around women's "choices." For one, a woman who upgrades to Principal would face an all-male climate.

> Roland: If you [a woman] want to be a Principal member, that's fine. You can be a Principal member. You can pay the additional money and you can tee off on Saturday mornings at 9:00 with all the boys if you can find someone to play with.
> Q: So does anyone do that?
> Roland: So there's nobody to play with.

Another barrier is articulated by Suzanne, a serious golfer. (Suburban considered a rule whereby any one family member could be designated the Principal.)

Suzanne: Everybody thought I would go for the Principal status so I could play anytime. I said "I wouldn't do that to my husband." He couldn't play on Saturday mornings. Why would I do that to him?

And finally there is the example of the Northern member who sarcastically asked his wife where she would get the money—about $4,000—to upgrade. Though more blunt than most, this example serves as a reminder that some wives have very little financial control. Given the imbalanced marriages typical at the clubs, these dynamics are significant impediments to women simply choosing Principal memberships.

While the club fees are comfortable for the couples who belong, a homemaker-wife without her husband's backing quickly becomes uncomfortable. We can see here how class privilege helps these husbands maintain their gender privilege.

### Genteel Masculine Dominance

When I began this project, I thought that perhaps the women at Oldfamily would be worse off than others. I assumed a correspondence between eliteness and conservatism; I was wrong. Women at Oldfamily are better off than their counterparts at Rosary, Suburban, and Northern. This is partly because of Oldfamily women, whose power was discussed above. But it is also because of Oldfamily men.

Traditionally, the men at Oldfamily have been some of the most powerful in the state. Their privilege has been so unshakable that they have not needed to make a display of superiority over their wives. Research on gender relations usually supports this rule via its converse: that men who *lack* social/economic/institutional power are more prone to making exaggerated masculine displays of dominance. These masculine displays are seen both in public settings of "the street" and the workplace, and in domestic arenas of housework and violence.[18] In the case of elite clubs, the dramatic displays are absent because the men's power is so certain. The term "quiet control" conveys how men with race and class privilege rule their families.[19]

The combination of powerful women and more-powerful men leads to a better outcome for WASP women like those at Oldfamily. The liberalism is reflected in Oldfamily's gender-neutral founding and is part of the club culture. For example, the members' directory gives each member of a couple their own entry, repeating many phone numbers in pairs rather than combining couples into a single listing.

Conversely, stronger sexism is part of the culture at other clubs, which lack Oldfamily's mitigating composition. Because the men elsewhere are less elite, they may be more motivated to enforce masculine privileges at their clubs. Where men benefit from dominance over women, they also act to ensure that no man gets too far out of step. (This is similar to the aforementioned phenomenon of women punishing their peers who buck the implicit deal of asymmetrical marriage.) Research on masculinity has shown how, as part of the project of maintaining dominance, men police and sanction those few men who are "too" sympathetic to women's issues.[20] This policing is reported by women at both Northern and Rosary.

Nadine: Some of the men could care less who's playing in their foursome. My husband could care less. . . . But then I think a lot of them, even if they really don't care, if you want to be accepted by the crew that's running the club now and . . . you won't act as if you don't care. You go along up there or you're ostracized.

Q: So men like your husband get ostracized?

Nadine: Oh, yeah, definitely. Any of the husbands of women involved in the suit.

Regina: [My husband] just thinks it's ridiculous that women have no voice. . . . He's kind of known as being, [*chuckling*] soft on the issues, I guess. They tease him. He just thinks they're all juvenile about it.

Q: So does he get ostracized socially from other men?

Regina: Probably. He doesn't care. He's not a good golfer. I mean you know, he has a couple of friends that are macho that kind of protect him, I guess.

The husbands of Nadine and Regina are more visibly sympathetic to women's issues than most men at their clubs. But they are informally reined in by their peers; and less bold men are likely prevented from voicing any anti-sexist dissent. Thus men police each other into conformity, and gender-progressive change is impeded.

Oldfamily members are proud of their egalitarianism, and both men and women in the club give the men rhetorical pats on the back for their progressiveness. It works well for Oldfamily members to attribute women's status at clubs to the enlightenment of Oldfamily men and the backwardness of men elsewhere. (Though to be fair, some Oldfamily members supplement this account with other ones too.) As noted above, one Oldfamily member attributed the difference to "new money" at Suburban. But more often, the reason given for the difference is ethnicity. (In fact, as mentioned in the previous chapter, "new money" is sometimes a veiled reference to Jewish or other non-WASP people.)

Ursula: I also think that WASPs are, I never sat around and talked about WASPs the way I am today, but I think WASPs are better about giving women equality than some other ethnic groups are, who like to assert their masculine right. I truly think that's the case.

Many subjects, when considering sexism at country clubs, invoke Italians as the prime example.

Harold: I don't want to really stereotype people, but if you look at the club here in [this state] that's the most notorious in terms of the treatment of women, it's Venetian. And it's all Italian. And I think it's cultural.

Gloria: Venetian, that was a big one because I remember it being in the paper. I don't know how it was resolved, but I remember thinking, "I'm glad I belong to the Oldfamily, where we're so progressive, I can play golf when I want."

The masculinity at the elite clubs of this sample is sanitized in comparison to the "others" who are backwards. Subjects are extolling masculinity of a certain culturally ethnic sort.[21] This is also a class-specific masculinity: as noted, men with the most power have the least need for overtly sexist displays.

Some scholars critique the apparent gender liberalism of powerful men as shallow.[22] Michael Messner writes that the praise given to "the [sensitive] displays of the (mostly white, professional, and upper class) 'New Man'" deserve skepticism. Rather than heralding real change,

> these gender displays may serve as signs that, in fact, serve to divert the feminist critique of masculinity on to less powerful groups of men, who supposedly embody the atavistic traits of "traditional masculinity." A structural analysis of power reveals how a focus on men's personal styles and gender displays shifts attention away from a critical scrutiny of men's institutional power, thus helping to re-stabilize hegemonic masculinity, and the positions of power held by upper class, white, heterosexual men.[23]

Club members' veneration of elite, WASP masculinity is an example of the very phenomenon Messner identifies. Their talk shows how racism can be used in the service of men's dominance. Also, Messner's argument serves to remind observers that the apparent liberalism at Oldfamily and similar sites should not be confused with real anti-sexist social movement.

It is no surprise that Oldfamily members pat themselves on the back. However, it is notable that members at *all five* clubs use the strategy of pointing out how another club is worse than their own.

Nell: If a private club's really trying to be truly, truly private, they have now gone out of their way to make sure they're truly private so they will not.
    Q: Because of Northern.
    Nell: That's right. Instead of possibly addressing the women issue. They've ensured that that can't, they can't be sued for it, but they continue [laughing] the way they are.

Richard [about the Northern leaders]: The idiots running the joint didn't learn the first time. I mean that to me is industrial strength stupidity. But you can't protect stupid people from themselves. They're gonna do that, it's mind-boggling why they did what they did, but they're paying for it now.

Roland: There's a club in [the South] that a friend of mine who actually belonged to . . . asked me to go down with a bunch of those guys, and this club, there's no women allowed on the, not only can they not be in the club, they can't be on the property. . . . I don't know how they get away with it. Unbelievable!

Q: Well, that sort of brings me to tee times for men and women, because isn't it true that women's tee times are restricted?

Sophia: Right. I think less and less however. You could find some clubs, I can mention a couple to you. Rosary is the prime one where women don't have much of a, they don't have much say in the doings of the club. Suburban is more family oriented and I think women have a lot more say.

Walter: I think again some, maybe some of the problems or shortcomings with some of the older clubs is that they are, they're probably a little more male-driven and I think the game of golf has become so popular and so international now, it's crossing all kinds of barriers that I think clubs are doing themselves an injustice to be that restrictive and think that only thirty-five to fifty-five-year-old males can play the game. That's just not true. And I think you might see that approach, the approach at Waterside to be a little bit more inclusive.

These put-downs are like the finger-pointing about racial-ethnic exclusivity discussed in the previous chapter. They are best interpreted not as gauges of the gender regimes at different clubs, but as examples of a useful account that serves the speaker and his/her own club well. Putting down another group is a common way to make a status distinction while simultaneously minimizing or excusing the flaws in one's own group.

## Gender Evolution and Stasis

In explaining women's status, club members sometimes refer, accurately, to the history of women's subordination. (They do not refer much to the history of men's dominance; as is typical in inequalities, the trouble appears to lie with the disadvantaged group, leaving the dominating group unmarked and invisible.) As in racial-ethnic matters discussed previously, subjects discuss the history and future of gender relations as naturally evolving.

The first aspect of the evolutionary account is to point out that sexism is written into the history of golf and country clubs in this country. Therefore, old clubs—that is, most of those in the Northeast—still have a case of it. New clubs—Waterside and exemplary clubs elsewhere in the country—were founded with gender equality and will presumably not backslide. Men's dominance is, in this narrative, analogous to a chronic health condition that, once in a body, may be ameliorated but not eliminated. This, of course, excuses the modern-day men who are still actively cultivating domination over their women counterparts.

On a more positive note, interviewees sometimes point to the importance of the surge in women's workforce participation in the last few decades. Sometimes they confess that this societal change demands changes
in country clubs that have not yet completely occurred. But more often,
members point to the fact that only a small minority of country club
women have careers, to suggest that that major societal change is irrelevant to club operations.

However, this is not to suggest that they are embracing a 1950s-era
doctrine of women's status. Careers or not, interviewees avow that today's generation lacks the sexism of those that preceded it. (This is the
same as the account denying racism among today's generation.) Wives
are participating more than before.

> Sophia: Whereas before if John and Jean Doe came in, John played golf, Jean
> didn't have any interest, she had to bring up the kids. Now the kids and the
> mother are over there playing golf, take lessons and they're on the courses.

> Regina: All the young husbands come out and play golf, and they come back
> and maybe spend ten minutes with the kids. And a lot of these young
> women are getting sick of it. They don't play golf, they don't see their hus-
> bands, every vacation day is a golf day, and it was, we accepted it but these
> girls are not accepting it.
>     Q: But it sounds like now maybe with these young couples maybe it would
> change?
>     Regina: We never even, as far as, looking back we think about it. They're
> talking about it now and saying, "this is unacceptable."

Though Regina's quote suggests that dissatisfied wives are demanding
change, some men also report that wives are now seen as social friends in
a way that used to be unusual.

> Norman: You had people of our age and our generation coming in which was
> different from say Noreen's father's generation that had been there for forty-
> something years, right, and it was basically understood that, like Noreen
> said, it wasn't written, but it was almost like it was off grounds for the
> women. And then we came in and we said, "we're doing so much together
> as couples" and stuff like that, you know, and we spoke up and said "I want
> my wife in here" and whatever else.

> Richard: People want to come in as couples and enjoy the atmosphere of the
> club. There continues to be this feeling among some of the gray beards at the
> club that their grill room is sacrosanct and should not be, you know, utilized
> by anyone other than men. There's a growing number of people who happen
> to believe otherwise and don't share that same feeling. And some of the
> changes recently at the club evidence that there is a growing desire for a
> mixed environment.

The implication of this talk is that gender inequality will simply die along with the "gray beards" who now belong to clubs. Like parallel talk about racial inequality, this strikes me as either wishful thinking, and/or an account designed to absolve oneself and one's peers from any responsibility.

The ones who do embrace their own role in the history of gender relations are the litigants in the Northern lawsuit.

> Nadine: She [a friend at another club] was telling me, *as a result of our case*, and this was before we went to court, and her husband was the president and some of the women were complaining about the restrictions they had at the club, and so they wrote a letter to them and they sat down and said they were going to file . . . and her husband sat down and said, "just give me a month before you do anything, if you'll just give me a month and I'll meet with the board and let's see if we can't work this out." So he met with the board and from that day on, *everything they asked for, you want a Principal membership, you get Principal membership*. They just simply said they were going to file with the state Civil Rights Agency and they said "no, don't do this" because they didn't want to ruin the reputation of their club. [emphasis added]

> Nina: Our old club down in [another state], we went there last year, just got there and were talking to people there and they said "when this came down, we changed a lot of things to make sure that we don't get involved in something like that."

> Nick: These other clubs are learning. They're watching this. There's no doubt about it. I'll bet you if you called [the suing attorney] she could tell you how many different clubs have called for her advice. . . . They know that they're next on the list. I think a lot of clubs are kind of in limbo, they're probably changing slightly. Some of them may be changing greatly. If they're anything like Northern, they're gonna lose, they really are. They're not gonna lick this so they might as well be aware of it.

Even the men at Rosary took note of the troubles at clubs like Northern, which is why they switched to an officially neutral "Principal-Restricted" system a few years ago. The evolutionary account of progress toward equality denies due credit to the impact of lawsuits and other activism.

The women who complained at Northern, and a few activist women at Oldfamily, expressed their outrage at being treated like second-class citizens. They backed up their talk with action: lobbying the club board, circulating a petition, filing a legal complaint.

But these women are in the minority. Virtually all of the club members *speak* approvingly of equality for women. But at the same time, most of them are complacent about the gender inequality in their own clubs. Given the imbalances in the average marriage at the club, and given a cultural milieu that still embraces explicit segregation by gender (unlike race), many are unworried about the status of women in country clubs.

The narrative goes like this: since most of the women are homemakers, and uninterested in competitive golf, some bad apples at the club can prevent egalitarian change; but the women, who golf socially throughout the week, really aren't bothered by the current rules.

Some men are bold enough to dismiss the idea of gender-neutrality as a bad idea. Recall Steve's argument that going gender-neutral would "destroy the fabric of a private club." Rosary did go officially gender-neutral, and Reid argues that the women did themselves a disservice.

> Reid: No single women, no Principal women at all in the club. They fought for it and yet nobody took advantage of it.
>
> Q: What's your guess as to why?
>
> Reid: Because unless a lot of women join as Principal members, there's no advantage to it because they'd rather play with just women. They don't want to play with guys. So if they're just stuck with two or three of them or four of them, they're the only four that can play. Then they can't be in the ladies' tournaments because they're now "Restricted tournaments," they're not "women's tournaments."
>
> Q: I see.
>
> Reid: And it really lost an awful lot by forcing an issue. They should have left it alone. They would have enjoyed it a lot more, had a lot more advantage out there.

He says that men and women, as a general rule, belong in different golf games:[24]

> Reid: The women want to go out there and be able to talk and have fun and go at their own pace. The men are very, very competitive and they want to move fast . . . the majority of people, it's two different styles of golf out there.

This boldness highlights a way in which gender justice lags behind racial justice in the public discourse, since nobody was brazen enough to dismiss the idea of racial integration as a bad idea. At the same time, the common and premature belief that racial inequalities have been "solved" puts racial justice, paradoxically, behind the more contested gender justice.

## SUMMARY

In their complacency about gender inequality, club members are reflecting the state of contemporary mainstream culture. As in the case of race, most people think of "discrimination" as a workplace issue; outside the workplace, women as a whole are not widely considered to be an oppressed group.

Interviewees' talk also reflects the state of their marriages, or at least of the average marriage among club members. Women are presumed to be homemaker wives, whose duty it is to support their husbands. One small piece of this support is to stay off the golf course so men may use it at certain prime times. Note that in many clubs, these prime times are reserved for "men," not for "people with careers," a designation that would include working women and exclude retired men. Such a lack of clarity shows that the account about careers is, at least partly, a smokescreen for sexism.

Club members use and reproduce the presumption that asymmetrical (heterosexual, procreative) marriage is the starting point for gender relations. The presumed domestic starting point has ramifications to other arenas, like workplaces and private clubs. At these exclusive clubs, the members' wealth generally means that the marriages are especially weighted in men's favor. Though they are rarely blunt enough to say so, members imply (in both word and deed) that husbands who provide particularly cushy lives for their wives can expect more deference in return. This replicates other research findings on upper-class marriages.

Country club women in general have made a deal in marriage of "trading power for patronage," which is one option for adapting to subordinate status.[25] This deal restricts their opportunity to advocate on their own behalf, as does the related set of expectations for upper-class femininity. The women in this population are thus in a bind, which makes their seeming complacency more understandable.

Conversely, the men in this population are cultivating a discourse that sanitizes their class and race specific brand of masculinity. By replacing displays of male dominance with gender-equal displays, such men hope to escape feminist critique. But these privileged men have and use the power to keep themselves at the top of gender, class, and race hierarchies.

It might be surprising that gender inequality remains so persistent, even among women with the privileges and resources to put up a fight. If the persistence of inequality is the question, an intersectional approach helps improve our answers. Once we analyze the contexts of gender and class and race—for both the women and the men in their lives—the persistent inequalities seem sensible rather than surprising.

The dominance of asymmetrical marriage and the images of dominant femininity and masculinity are some of the components of the societal gender order. As noted, this order is intertwined with class and race hierarchies and is reproduced at multiple sites. The country club should be viewed as one of many interlocking contexts, rather than as a crucial causal agent in its own right. As long as the broader gender order has legitimacy, little real change will take place at exclusive clubs.

There are serious consequences of the second-class status of women at many clubs and the lack of will to ameliorate it. For one thing, it teaches a subliminal lesson to all club members about women's inferiority. There are consequences to situations wherein people of different groups also have differing access to resources: that makes the two groups "doubly dissimilar."[26] When such situations accumulate with consistency, it inspires the perception that one group is superior to the other, which diffuses into widely held cultural beliefs. This is exactly the situation at country clubs with rules restricting women. The experiences of the men, women, and children at the club reinforce the idea, for all involved, that women are subordinate to men. Thus, country clubs can serve as an opposing force to the formation of a gender-egalitarian outlook.

A second and related consequence is what the clubs teach the next generation. Children are absorbing the above phenomenon just as adults are. They also experience segregation in which gender sometimes (though not always) trumps generation. Interviewees paint the picture of children spending their club time with their mothers at the swimming pool and with their fathers on the golf course. As they become teenagers, they emulate the adults' spatial segregation: girls can earn money by watching over other children at the pool, and boys can caddy. (I didn't hear of a single female caddy or male babysitter at these clubs, though they may exist.) Since the spaces of the pool and the golf course remain somewhat gendered, it follows that the opportunities to baby-sit and caddy also remained gendered. Also, the talk analyzed here—including, perhaps, among their own parents—tells children that the second-class status of women is sensible and normal, rather than anything that requires rectifying. While official policies at some clubs are now gender-neutral on their face, this represents the barest compliance with the letter of the law. To children and adults alike, the newly sanitized policies do not speak as loudly as the still-sexist norms.

Club members might protest that sexism is a historical remnant that will die along with the club elders. And it is true that some progress has been made for women in recent years. But the actions that do the most to spur change—circulating a petition, filing a complaint—are scorned by the majority of club members. Their position is contradictory: they see gender equality as progressing naturally, but they dislike the "growing pains" associated with actual change.

Members point to egalitarian clubs like Waterside, and new clubs across the country, as heartening evidence. But building new clubs does not solve the problem of the many existing clubs that persist in subordinating women. And, while attributing sexism to history is partly accurate, it is also partly a smokescreen. At least two new clubs, one near Phoenix and one near Chicago, are opening their doors to men only.[27] These clubs show that men's dominance, contrary to some accounts, is not a dying echo from the past; but rather, it remains very much alive.


## NOTES

1. Connell, *Gender and Power*. Palo Alto, CA: Stanford University Press, 1987, page 98.

2. Risman, "Gender as a Social Structure: Theory Wrestling With Activism." *Gender & Society* 18 (2004): 429. For alternate theorizations of gender in society, see Andersen ("Thinking About Women: A Quarter Century's View." *Gender & Society* 19 (2005): 437), Connell (1987), Lorber (*Breaking the Bowls: Degendering and Feminist Change*. New York: W. W. Norton, 2005), and Martin ("Gender as a Social Institution." *Social Forces* 82 (2004): 1249).

3. I use "principal" and "restricted" for all such arrangements, although in reality different clubs give different names to these gradations.

4. Rubin, "The Traffic in Women: Notes on the 'Political Economy' of Sex." In *Toward an Anthropology of Women*, edited by Reyna Reiter. New York: Monthly Review Press, 1975; Rich, "Compulsory Heterosexuality and Lesbian Existence." In *Powers of Desire: The Politics of Sexuality*, edited by Ann Snitow, Christine Stansell, and Sharon Thompson. New York: Monthly Review Press, 1983.

5. Eliasoph, "'Everyday Racism' in a Culture of Political Avoidance: Civil Society, Speech, and Taboo." *Social Problems* 46 (1999): 479; Zerubavel, *The Fine Line: Making Distinctions in Everyday Life*. New York: Free Press, 1991.

6. Baca Zinn and Eitzen (*Diversity in Families*. 5th ed. New York: Longman, 1999, pages 224, 264); West and Zimmerman ("Doing Gender." *Gender & Society* 1 (1987), page 138); Deutsch (*Halving It All: How Equally Shared Parenting Works*. Cambridge: Harvard University Press, 1999); Hochschild (*The Second Shift: Working Parents and the Revolution at Home*. New York: Viking Penguin, 1989); Schwartz (*Peer Marriage: How Love Between Equals Really Works*. New York: Free Press, 1994).

7. See, e.g., Blumstein and Schwartz (*American Couples: Money, Work, Sex*. New York: William Morrow, 1983); the quote is from Schwartz (1994:6).

8. Deutsch (1999 chapter 9), Schwartz (1994).

9. Kendall, *The Power of Good Deeds: Privileged Women and the Social Reproduction of the Upper Class*. Lanham, MD: Rowman & Littlefield, 2002, page 4.

10. Schwalbe, Godwin, Holden, Schrock, Thompson, and Wolkomir. "Generic Processes in the Reproduction of Inequality: An Interactionist Analysis." *Social Forces* 79 (2000), page 427.

11. Ostrander, *Women Of The Upper Class*. Philadelphia: Temple University Press, 1984.

12. Connell (1987:188).

13. Myers, "Ladies First: Race, Class, and the Contradictions of a Powerful Femininity." *Sociological Spectrum* 24 (2004), page 23.

14. Hertz and Reverby, "Gender, Gentility, and Political Protest: The Barbara Bush Controversy at Wellesley College." *Gender & Society* 9 (1995): 594.

15. Hertz and Reverby (1995:602).

16. Ostrander (1984:39).

17. Waterside received much less attention—it doesn't appear to be part of people's schema of the local cluster of clubs. When addressed, its equality is attributed unanimously to its newness.

18. On public settings, see Baca Zinn ("Chicano Men and Masculinity." *Journal of Ethnic Studies* 10 (1982): 29), Bourgois (*In Search of Respect: Selling Crack in El Barrio*. New York: Cambridge University Press, 1996), Connell ("Live Fast and Die Young: The Construction of Masculinity Among Young Working-Class Men on the Margin of the Labour Market." *Australian & New Zealand Journal of Sociology* 27 (1991): 141), Majors and Billson (*Cool Pose: The Dilemmas of Black Manhood in America*. New York: Lexington Books, 1992), and Willis (*Learning to Labour: How Working Class Kids Get Working Class Jobs*. New York: Columbia University Press, 1977).

On housework, see Brines ("Economic Dependency and the Division of Labor." *American Journal of Sociology* 100 (1994): 652) and Hochschild (*The Second Shift: Working Parents and the Revolution at Home*. New York: Viking Penguin, 1989); and on violence, Anderson ("Gender, Status, and Domestic Violence: An Integration of Feminist and Family Violence Approaches." *Journal of Marriage and the Family* 59 (1997): 655), McCloskey ("Socioeconomic and Coercive Power Within the Family." *Gender & Society* 10 (1996): 449), and Szinovacz ("Family Power." In *Handbook of Marriage and the Family*, edited by Marvin B. Sussman and Susan K. Steinmetz. New York: Plenum Press, 1987).

19. Hondagneu-Sotelo and Messner, "Gender Displays and Men's Power: The 'New Man' and the Mexican Immigrant Man." In *Theorizing Masculinities*, edited by Harry Brod and Michael Kaufman. Thousand Oaks, CA: Sage, 1994, page 214.

20. Cockburn, *In The Way of Women: Men's Resistance to Sex Equality in Organizations*. Ithaca, NY: ILR Press, 1991; Connell, 1987; Mac an Ghaill, *The Making of Men: Masculinities, Sexualities, and Schooling*. Philadelphia: Open University Press, 1994.

21. Choo and Ferree ("Practicing Intersectionality in Sociological Research: A Critical Analysis of Inclusions, Interactions and Institutions in the Study of Inequalities." *Social Forces* 28 [2010], 129) call this "gendered racialization," and show how it appears in the data, but not always the analysis, of ethnographies like Lamont's *The Dignity of Working Men: Morality and the Boundaries of Race, Class, and Immigration*. New York: Russell Sage, 2000.

22. Hondagneu-Sotelo and Messner, 1994; Messner, "Men as Superordinates: Challenges for Gender Scholarship." In *Privilege: A Reader*, edited by Michael S. Kimmel and Abby S. Ferber. Boulder, CO: Westview Press, 2003; Pyke, "Class-Based Masculinities: The Interdependence of Gender, Class, and Interpersonal Power." *Gender & Society* 10 (1996): 527.

23. Messner (2003:293).

24. The idea that women and men should play sports separately is a dominant one and probably has some validity. But of all sports, golf is not one that requires segregation. People playing golf together do not go "head to head" physically in any consequential way; golfers agree that the game is played against oneself and

the course. Handicaps are designed to equalize competition, as are "ladies' tees" which make each hole of the course somewhat shorter.

25. Schwalbe et al. (2000).

26. Ridgeway ("The Social Construction of Status Value: Gender and Other Nominal Characteristics." *Social Forces* 70 (1991): 367), using Blau (*Inequality and Heterogeneity: A Primitive Theory of Social Structure*. New York: Free Press, 1977).

27. See *Business Week*, "Rule No.1 at This New Club: No Dames." *Business Week*, 21 January 2002, p. 10; and Vanderpool, "Lawsuits Tee Off Against Male Golf Clubs." *Christian Science Monitor*, 16 October 2001, p. 3.

# 5

# Conclusion

In the end, what is really going on at exclusive country clubs, and why should anyone care? This final chapter addresses that two-part question. In its first half, we review the accounts that club members give: both about exclusion and about the dominant inequality ideology. For both of these points, I discuss similarities and differences among the class, race, and gender axes. Beyond the content of the accounts, I also address the reasons for their use.

The second half of the chapter concerns the broader significance of the site: first, what the consequences are of the effective accounting seen here; and second, additional aspects of country clubs that contribute to the reproduction of the status quo. Here, I link the processes found at clubs with some seen elsewhere in social life.

A metaphor of camera work is apt here: in reviewing accounts, we're zooming up close to study the things people say; then we zoom out to see macrostructures. We also pan across society to see the larger context of the country club, and the two ways it connects with other sites. First of all, we see the influential connections between sites like clubs, neighborhoods, marriages, and workplaces. Second and more abstract, as we pan we can see generic processes in the reproduction of inequalities, to better understand how they work and how to effectively intervene.[1]

By now, we have seen how social structure can influence culture: at exclusive country clubs, protective laws and participants' considerable financial resources (the structural) enable them to draw and maintain exclusionary social boundaries (the cultural). But social structure and culture are in a reciprocal rather than a one-way relationship. In this final chapter, we pan to the other side of the two-way street: how culture influences social structure. The first half of the chapter, on accounts, covers the cultural elements that guide the practices and policies covered in the chapter's second half—the social structure, which is reproduced through people's talk and coordinated action. There are *material consequences to patterned ideological talk*, which is why the study of talk, especially the talk of the powerful, is so important. At the same time, we should remember that the talk of the powerful supports the dominant ideology not by happenstance, but precisely because it is this ideology that confers material and other advantages to those doing the talking.

## UP CLOSE: A REVIEW OF ACCOUNTING

Accounts are always, inevitably, culturally located rather than idiosyncratic. It is when a dominant cultural ideal has been violated that an account is called for. The results of this research are distinctly American in that interviewees have extensive accounts for behaviors that would be entirely unremarkable in some other societies. The exclusive character of country clubs requires explanation because of the American ideal of egalitarian freedom of access.

Accounts are also cultural in another way: to be effective, accounts must make use of some elements of the dominant culture. Only then can they be convincing and thus useful. So here, people's accounts draw on dominant cultural explanations for class/race/gender inequality, as well as more specific cultural elements like the ideal that parents should be highly involved and give their children whatever advantages they can.

### Talk About Exclusion

The interviews—and implicitly the lives of club members—show the "norm of exclusivity" in action. As Diana Kendall writes, the norm of exclusivity is the presumption that excluding certain people from one's social life (neighborhood, school, voluntary organizations) is a right and normal practice.[2] This research shows that the norm and related behaviors that she reports extend beyond her sample of upper-class Texas women. However, it does call for one adjustment: while Kendall calls the norm of exclusivity taken-for-granted, my research suggests that it is somewhat problematic. If it were not at all problematic, then the interviewees would not do so much accounting for it. But they do so, by denying or minimizing the exclusion of their clubs, or justifying why excluding is an acceptable or even worthy practice in this case. Even Kendall's interviewees offer accounts for their exclusion, for example:

> Invitations are sent to major contributors and people who've attended the parties in previous years, so we don't have too large a list of minorities because very few have been interested in attending. Invitations and reservations never have *anything* to do with race, but they do reflect friendships.[3]

Even in the reputedly less-progressive South, exclusivity is no longer a norm that the upper class may take entirely for granted.

Members of upper-class voluntary organizations report that a main reason they exclude is so that they feel socially comfortable in their organizations; it is a comfort predicated on homogeneity.[4] If the club or volunteer group is defined as social, then participants feel more justified stating a desire to include only those people whose personal style matches their own.

Sorting people by personal style is inevitably part of social life: it is, in part, how we choose our friends. The cultural ideals of privacy and the right to free association in social life are important rhetorical tools for club members. By discursively emphasizing the social nature of their clubs, and minimizing the consequences of their exclusive gatherings, club members lay claim to these ideals of privacy and free association. Americans view social life, even when institutionalized as an exclusive private club, as a realm where the concept of discrimination does not apply. The dominant cultural definition of discrimination is related to business and finances, so emphasizing club social life is a (mostly) effective shield against charges of discrimination. In these ways, club members contend that the exclusion they do is inoffensive. This is despite the fact that the financial and cultural requirements for membership do serve as barriers to belonging.

However, club members' accounts concerning gender are necessarily different from the ones addressing class and race exclusivity. Women have always been part of country clubs. While not (in most cases) kept off the club property, women have typically been kept off the golf course at certain prime times, off the board of governors, and out of the men's grill room. As Patricia Hill Collins points out, gender is different from the other two main axes of domination in that, while class and race depend on various distancing mechanisms, gender hierarchy depends on a close symbiosis between men and women.[5] We have seen the impact patriarchal marriage has on the gender regimes at clubs. These marriages are an important reason for the persistent subordination of women/wives in clubs even today.

Gender segregation is more culturally accepted than explicit racial segregation. Some club members speak approvingly of separating the sexes, in a way that they would not, today, of separating "the races." This may be because gender subordinates are in many ways closer to their dominators than class and race subordinates. While class, race, and gender hierarchies are important organizing principles of American society, each axis works somewhat differently. However, there are some overlaps too, which we will discuss next.

## The Dominant Inequality Ideology

Ideologies justifying economic stratification and racial stratification are related, since class is raced and race is classed. The two artificially separated ideologies could be conceptually combined into a dominant inequality ideology, with the word "inequality" implying complexity beyond the conventionally class-focused term "stratification."

According to the dominant inequality ideology, the American Dream of meritocratic equal opportunity is a reality.[6] Since opportunities for advancement are equally available to everyone, people's station in life thus depends simply on their talent and work ethic. This equal opportunity is characterized by colorblindness rather than any racial discrimination. As I've shown, the talk of club members reflects complete support for this ideology. This talk of meritocracy contributes to keeping privilege invisible; and among such affluent people like this, it has a hint of self-congratulation.[7]

The dominant inequality ideology is thoroughly individualistic. On all three axes of inequality, interviewees display individualist thinking and other shared discursive styles, stories, and frames.

The individualism of the American Dream is evident in some of the accounts given regarding both race and gender. On one hand, the situation at any given club for minorities and women is sometimes attributed to the character, be it progressive or chauvinist, of certain club leaders. On the other hand, the situation is sometimes attributed to members of disadvantaged groups themselves. Minorities are said to be scarce at the sample clubs because they haven't succeeded financially, and/or their personalities or lifestyles would be mismatched to club members. Women are said to be content as second-class club members, and to choose not to pursue equality.

Beyond individualistic thinking, more styles, stories, and frames are shared among the accounts for race, class, and gender. These include othering those who are deemed outsiders; pointing out the good deeds done at one's club and that other clubs have even worse situations; using evolutionary and generational accounts for change and its pace; and hinting, perhaps accidentally, that some changes have been made in response to outside societal pressures.

On the other hand, the dominant ideology of equal opportunity changes its tune when considering gender, as reflected here. The dominant, though not unanimous, position is that men and women are "just different." Even many people who support legal and social equality for women prefer the dubious prospect of discarding inequality while maintaining a firm grasp on essential gender difference. This is implausible because most gender difference is actually produced by inequality: the differing social location of men and women incline them to divergent behaviors and identities.[8] These differences are seen as prior, as evidence of intrinsic gender dichotomy, and as justification for segregation and unequal opportunities. In other words, "differences are inequality's post hoc excuse."[9]

Club members seem to think of their women in terms of their domestic identities, in keeping with their view of the club as a family place. But the notion that men and women are just different extends beyond home and family, helping to maintain men's privilege.

The country club is one of several sites where the dominant inequality ideology, about gender and class and race, is reproduced. These three axes all share some discursive elements, such as individualistic thinking. But they differ in that gender is the only axis that still relies on an ideology of intrinsic difference to justify inequality. Class and race inequalities are thought to be the outcome of a meritocratic free society. But the site of the country club is influenced by non-meritocratic practices from other contexts, as I discuss below. At the same time, it tends to reproduce and strengthen the conservative cultural strains found elsewhere.

### Reasons for Accounting

Our society is not one in which whole categories of people are regularly held accountable for their actions—especially unmarked categories like the upper classes, whites, and men. In fact, the literature on accounts conceives of them as responses to behavior that violates a norm. Since country club members are operating mainly within accepted norms, their accounting has a more subtle inspiration: it is in response to tensions within American culture and the ideology that legitimates our social structure. Country club members are rarely "called to account" as it's traditionally conceived.[10] This is one of their privileges.

And yet, the interviews show that these members have quite an extensive repertoire of accounts and other rhetorical tools for explaining how clubs operate and why they are involved. Rarely did people seem taken aback by my inquiries, or comment that I was bringing up issues they had never thought about before. Rather, there was considerable consistency in the explanations given by women and men, white and nonwhite, from all of the five clubs. I doubt that people prepared much for their interviews. Instead, they have accounts at the ready for their own reasons, even though their daily interactions rarely demand it.

People have accounts at the ready because they need to make themselves feel comfortable about their club memberships. One part of American culture promotes inclusive egalitarianism. This calling elitism into moral question is the primary motivator for developing a set of accounts for club membership. Interviewees need these accounts in order to feel like good and moral people.[11]

Membership in these exclusive clubs is, among other things, a marker of especially high socioeconomic status. So as they account for their club memberships, interviewees also account for inequality generally. They use the dominant inequality ideology because they believe in it. They are motivated to believe in it because disbelieving it would be an implicit critique of their social location. Believing in the dominant inequality ideology absolves privileged people from feeling guilty about their privileges. Indeed it goes further, suggesting that richer people are better people. All of us want to feel like good people, and we all have accounts that "explain ourselves to ourselves" or to others. These accounts vary systematically by social location. The beliefs and actions of this population are especially important because of the disproportionate power their social location affords them; I do not intend to impute any extra selfishness to these people.

Club members' beliefs and actions can serve inequitable ends, even if they are not scheming to accomplish that. In fact, their exclusive clubs, and their promulgation of the dominant inequality ideology, do serve to preserve their own advantages. They are doing their part to legitimate existing inequalities, hoard opportunities to pass to their own children, and develop the consciousness and social power of their class. The macro consequences implicit in this work make it a significant topic for research. But the motivation of feeling good about oneself is, I argue, just as important as the motivation of preserving advantages. Both reasons apply. Legitimating the status quo that rewards them, and assisting their children and their peers, are activities that help people feel good. At the same time, people like these interviewees, who disproportionately benefit from a certain social structure, have a (generally unconscious) material motivation for being loyal to that structure.

## WIDE ANGLE: REPRODUCING THE MATRIX OF PRIVILEGE

We have now reviewed the accounts used by club members, and why they use them. The motivations for accounting hint at the consequences of an effective set of accounts for reproducing the status quo. In this second half of the chapter, I discuss the significance of the accounting on both the micro and macro levels. I also discuss four more ways that country club members participate, deliberately or accidentally, in the unobtrusive reproduction of class, race, and gender inequalities. The site of the club, including the accounts surrounding it, will be compared with social processes in other contexts.

## Consequences of the Effective Accounting

### Micro Consequences for the Self

Though the discussion of why club members give accounts focused on class, it can be extended to race and gender. Individuals' racial and gender categories figure prominently into their sense of identity. Whites and men are aware, to some extent, of their dominance, but they do not want to embrace an identity of oppressor. Or in the sexist verbiage of yesteryear, "No one [wants to think] of himself as a son of a bitch."[12] We have seen here that white men account for their dominance in ways that absolve themselves of responsibility for it. Their adherence to exculpatory dominant racial and gender ideologies is perhaps especially strong because of their class privilege: since the three axes interlock, supporting racial and gender inequalities helps support the class structure that advantages them (and vice-versa).

But curiously, we have also seen here that nonwhites and women subscribe to the dominant ideologies too. Nonwhite members of Oldfamily agree with the dominant inequality ideology, and with the individualistic account that attributes the club's composition to people's character. This is self-serving because it paints the speaker as a man of unusual fortitude. And, women largely subscribe to the dominant inequality ideology and the tradition of pairing men of high power with women of lesser power and greater domestic responsibility. This too is self-serving, in a way, because the women gain from it the patronage of wealthy men as husbands, raising their own status as a result. Entering into this deal is helpful in constructing an appropriately upper-class lady's identity.[13] Again, the subscription of these people to the dominant ideologies may be especially strong because of their high socioeconomic status. Nonwhites must demonstrate cultural assimilation to gain membership in the upper class; and the payoff to women for their compliance is at its highest here.

So in this case, there is more similarity than difference among the three axes of inequality. For every axis, legitimating accounts are used both because they help the speaker feel like a good person, and in service to a presumed material payoff. This is true for nonwhites and women as well as for those people who are privileged on all three axes, which may well be an artifact of the selectivity of only interviewing members of exclusive clubs. All of the accounts use tools of the dominant culture; and in recirculating the beliefs, the speakers make a small contribution to reproducing their dominance.

*Macro Consequences for Ideology*

Belief in the dominant inequality ideology is certainly not limited to those who benefit economically from its dominance. It is hegemonically embraced across classes and races. Other researchers have demonstrated that in the working classes, adherence to the American Dream is still considerable, if more conflicted than it is in this population.[14]

Working class people must come to terms with the inequality ideology, despite personal experience. Their coming to terms represents an emotional exercise in "holding disillusionment at bay" to salve the "hidden injuries" common to their class.[15] Affluent people, on the other hand, are motivated to support the inequality ideology because it confers on them both material benefits and the psychological bonus of feeling successful on their own merits. Their standpoints and motivations are different, but both groups end up reproducing the legitimacy of the ideology.

The dominant inequality ideology extends beyond class to race, if only to suggest that race makes no difference at all in contemporary America. All racial-ethnic groups are presumed equal, but this presumption of equivalence is premature given our national history (and persistence) of institutionalized racism. It is the fallacy of racial pluralism, and can lead people to draw false parallels.[16] Club members draw false parallels when they suggest I study the exclusive Italian, Jewish, and African American country clubs; and other whites do it when, for example, they complain about affirmative action. This study corroborates the finding of whites' discursive use of false parallels, and shows it in a higher socioeconomic stratum than most previous research.

In the dominant inequality ideology, socioeconomic status practically becomes a marker of moral worth, since the rich must be deserving and poorer people have nothing but personal flaws to blame. Many scholars have noted this American phenomenon of translating economic hierarchy into moral hierarchy.[17] For many sociological reasons, the American economic hierarchy is raced: whites are overrepresented near the top and minorities overrepresented near the bottom. Since most Americans lack a historical and social-structural understanding of the underlying forces, this class-race overlap appears to be evidence of white superiority. Lillian Rubin discusses how the belief in equality and the belief in white superiority can ideologically coexist:

> The myth that we are a nation of equals lives side-by-side in these United States with the belief in white supremacy. And, unlikely as it seems, it's quite

possible to believe both at the same time. Sometimes we manage the conflict by shifting from one side to the other. More often, we simply redefine reality. The inequality of condition between whites and blacks isn't born in prejudice and discrimination, we insist; it's black inferiority that's the problem. Class distinctions have nothing to do with privilege, we say; it's merit that makes the difference.[18]

In this way, the dominant inequality ideology that claims colorblindness is actually racist, because of its implication of black inferiority. But the racism of today has gone underground and is largely invisible, as are the forces behind class inequality. As noted above, individualist thinking fills the void. In the contemporary cultural climate opposed to explicit racism, the individualist dominant inequality ideology is a useful tool for the preservation of white privilege and class privilege.

## Other Ways the Status Quo Gets Reproduced

We have seen that effective accounting by club members is significant for its contribution to reproducing the status quo, both by reinforcing people's classed/raced/gendered identities, and also by helping to reproduce the dominant ideology that supports the hierarchies. Beyond these consequences of effective accounting, there are four more ways that country clubs subtly contribute to the reproduction of inequalities. Clubs are sites where class consciousness is developed; they help their members accumulate (further) advantages; they make some reforms without any restructuring, and they show a mismatch between official policy and norms. We'll pan across each of the four in turn.

### Class Consciousness and Selfhood

Country clubs like the ones in this study are sites where class consciousness flourishes. In complex late-industrial societies like ours, workplaces are atomized, and people's class location in the traditional sense (of production or market position) can be blurry or even contradictory.[19] Organizations outside the workplace serve important class-cohesion purposes. Exclusive clubs send important messages about the in-group and out-groups, to both participants and onlookers.

As well as building a sense of "us" which transcends any one family or firm, country clubs also send messages about "how things are done."[20] The consciousness that is developed includes absorbing and embracing the dominant inequality ideology—it includes legitimation. Country clubs teach that exclusion on subjective criteria, extreme economic inequality with whites on top, and the subordination of women to men are all right and natural. The class consciousness nurtured here is raced and gendered. These lessons have conservative consequences as the "movers and shakers" at the club, and their youngsters, go out into the world of neighborhoods, schools, workplaces, and governance. The lessons of country clubs can be a countervailing force against progressive ideas available elsewhere.

This development of (raced and gendered) class consciousness is not unique to exclusive clubs. It occurs similarly at private schools, in philanthropic circles, and in exclusive places to vacation or live.[21] By carefully choosing where to live, elites minimize their children's interactions with out-groups.[22] Homogeneity among neighbors, schoolmates, and voluntary group members tends to foster homogeneity in consciousness.

Elite or not, people's self-concepts are influenced by the social structure and their place in it. One learns who one is by looking around: literally, at the people one routinely encounters at home and in organizations; and metaphorically, sizing up hierarchies of class, race, and gender. Social structure influences self-concept.[23] In turn, one's self-concept guides one's talk and other action. These actions often work to help reproduce the social structure, structure that appears prior to the individual but in fact stays alive only through ongoing human behavior. Members of exclusive country clubs have self-concepts that are heavily class-based, probably more so than members of other classes.[24] The more that a person's self-concept hinges on their place near the top of the socioeconomic hierarchy, the more we can expect (with the occasional exception) that their actions will help reproduce rather than alter that structure. Together with parallel sites such as private schools and elite neighborhoods, country clubs contribute to developing self-concepts around class privilege and, usually, whiteness. Clubs condition their members to uphold the status quo.

### Capitals and the Accumulation of Advantage

The members themselves know that exclusive country clubs help them pass their advantages on to their children. The club is a valuable tool for developing social capital, a.k.a. the "networking" so important to career success.[25] This is opportunity hoarding: reserving resources only for members of one's own group.[26] As one of several examples of successful opportunity hoarding in America, this is also one of several examples that refute the meritocratic ideal.

In this case, "one's own group" refers to those people in the community who have sufficient social—and financial and cultural—capital to have been invited to join the club. By definition, they already knew at least a few club members; they already had the advantage of high-status social capital. Given severe residential segregation, and the under-representation of people of color in the club—that is, admission likely requires knowing some white members—the initial capital requirement for joining is raced as well as classed.

Once in, club membership allows each family to develop its social capital further, by making valuable new contacts through involvement in club activities. In other words, the initial advantage accrues into further advantage. Country clubs are incubators not just for social capital, but also for cultural capital: they are the perfect context for youngsters to learn the leisure activities and personal style that will serve them well in adulthood.

This process, of advantages accumulating, obtains in several contexts in America.[27] One prime example is wealthy families, where the process plays out in the following ways. First, growing up in a wealthy home affords children the opportunity to gain high-status cultural capital, like appreciation of fine arts and international travel. This cultural capital often translates into advantages in their education, partly by impressing teachers.[28] This is in addition to the more direct way family wealth can build children's human capital through education.

Second, the social capital that goes with growing up wealthy, among wealthy friends and neighbors, also assists careers. This occurs especially when launching a career, as some parents in this study acknowledge for their own children; but it also occurs in the course of careers that rely on networks, including the financial advisors, realtors, and attorneys of this study.

Though the foregoing primarily concerns class, families are also an important site where advantage, and disadvantage, accumulate based on gender. Indeed, marriage is a cornerstone of American gender inequality.[29] Most club members endorse and enact the pairing of a husband with a less-powerful wife, in keeping with an ideology of essential gender difference. Given his initial social and economic (and physical, as a last resort) advantages, the man generally comes out ahead in marital power as measured in domestic responsibilities, financial control, and other decision-making.

Men's dominance in the home is maintained reciprocally with men's dominance in the workplace. As with country clubs and families, workplaces often operate on the assumption that men and women are just essentially different. This gender ideology can do damage both at the point of hiring decisions and also when workers are selectively sponsored for advancement. An ideology of gender differences also drives such phenomena as occupational segregation, comparable worth discrimination, the very definitions of firms and workers, and employers' use of gender to divide, distract, and profit.[30] At country clubs, members spend years absorbing and enacting a regime of gender difference and men's dominance. Many elite club members are corporate managers and/or board members, and they are very unlikely to leave the sexism behind when they go to work.

All of the phenomena just mentioned combine, along with women's caregiving breaks from the labor force, to put women at an economic disadvantage relative to men. In other words, the workplace is—like the home—a site where men leverage the gender order to their further advantage.

In these several ways, an initial advantage leads to further and further advantage; country club involvement is just one of many similar examples. Conversely, a lack of money is an initial disadvantage that, especially in America, leads to further and further disadvantage in housing, health, and education. This cumulative disadvantage is studied more often, although the accumulation of intersecting privileges deserves attention too.[31]

It is important to remember that, despite what the dominant ideology would suggest, there is nothing *natural* about this accumulation of advantage or disadvantage. The phenomenon is especially strong in America, where self-reliance looms culturally large. And yet, people with privilege have worked to reproduce a social structure that enables the hoarding of opportunities and the intergenerational passing of advantages. This work contradicts the American myth of meritocratic individualism.

One reason that these non-meritocratic processes seem legitimate is because of the use of cultural capital as a tool of mystification. "Because it can be hard to see how cultural capital is transmitted in families and schools, and even harder to see how it is 'cashed in' in closed circles, the unequal distribution of wealth, power, and status can come to look as if it corresponds to a natural distribution of ability."[32] In the case of country clubs, the use of cultural capital as a screening device combines with the official emphasis on the social-and-not-business nature of the clubs to produce an accepted account for the clubs' existence and operations. After all, the logic goes, these clubs are simply a gathering of friends, and everyone may choose their friends on any criteria, including cultural capital. But cultural capital is an insidious tool, as its importance at school and work makes clear. Country clubs legitimate the pernicious drawing of social boundaries according to cultural capital at these other sites.

## Reform Without Restructuring

Some people might argue that social boundaries based on cultural capital are a welcome development. It is true that cultural criteria appear less bigoted than the rules of the past, since—for example—this development has allowed minorities into the formerly all-white clubs in this study. The American Dream that "anyone can become anything" rang false when elite circles barred entry to people based on an ascribed status. Now that the color bar has been removed from the most exclusive doors, isn't that cause for celebration?

This recent change among these clubs, from ascribed to achieved criteria for belonging, is important as far as the message it sends onlookers about racial-ethnic matters. As club leaders hoped, the message it sends is one of reassuring colorblindness. This is indeed progress of a sort. But unfortunately, the recent change in criteria may be less important than it initially appears. It represents reform without restructuring: a change in a few of the rules of admission, but no change at all in the balance of power or in the many subtle ways in which privilege is reproduced at the clubs. As I have noted, the clubs are still sites where a conservative consciousness is nurtured, the status quo is relegitimated, and privileges are passed to the next generation. In some cases, they are also sites where gender inequality persists despite the reform from Men's and Women's memberships to Principal and Restricted memberships.

Nonwhite club members are now full participants in nurturing a conservative consciousness, legitimating the status quo, and passing privileges to their children. Any restructuring to lessen inequalities is not inevitable from here, if it is even on the horizon. In fact, some analysts believe that changes like this one make restructuring *less* likely, because selective inclusion appeases members of formerly excluded groups and strengthens the legitimacy of the current arrangements. By replacing ascriptive boundaries with cultural capital, club members have responded effectively to the present cultural challenge, averting a threat to their clubs' existence.[33]

Such reform without restructuring is also seen in other social contexts; one example is the role of class in higher education. The egalitarian American impulse spurred some reforms in education in the twentieth century. Seen as the "great equalizer," opportunity for education plays an important part in the American Dream. But there has been only superficial reform in access to top schools. The introduction of the Scholastic Aptitude Test (SAT) was hailed as meritocratic, an improvement over Ivy League admissions that drew overwhelmingly from prep schools. This standardized test is in fact biased rather than meritocratic.[34] But even aside from that criticism, elite schools still admit students from elite backgrounds preferentially, sometimes despite their SAT scores.[35] This pattern—also an accumulation of advantage for prep school students—shows how a reform in one building block of class inequality can leave the structure unchanged.

The present study shows the limits of thinking and reforming along just one axis. As Ostrander noted in the classic *Women of the Upper Class*, such women tend to reproduce class hierarchy even when they work to reform gender hierarchy. Recall that the reformers here—Marian and Ursula in chapter 4—are women with race and class privilege. Similarly, Amy Wilkins found in her ethnography that "stability on one boundary legitimates the challenge to another boundary, and each project's boundary challenge is blunted by its dependence on the stability of other boundaries."[36] I would paraphrase Wilkins to say that "privilege on two axes legitimates the challenge to a third axis."

Here is a possible parallel (speculative given the paucity of cases) between the nonwhite men discussed in chapter 3 and the Oldfamily reformers discussed in chapter 4. Perhaps the people at the center of the matrix of privilege are most receptive to people who are privileged in every way except one. This is good news for wealthy (heterosexual, able-bodied, and so on with unmarked statuses) people who *either* are nonwhite or are women. But phrasing it that way makes clear how paltry this good news is, and shows the limits of single-axis reforms like the ones discussed in this study.

### Mismatch of Policy and Norms

Organizational policies, and especially changes to them, can reflect cultural imperatives in the same way that accounts do. As I've shown, one account members offer for their clubs is that they are strictly social organizations. So, the policies of clubs forbid the conduct of business—and its markers like mobile phones and exchanging paperwork—on club property. When considering their clubs' racial-ethnic composition, interviewees use a rhetoric of embracing diversity. So, especially at Oldfamily, club leaders decided officially to pursue non-WASP new members. And, explicit sexism is now under some cultural attack, so the cultural response is evident in (for example) Northern's and Rosary's switch to a policy of "Principal and Restricted" memberships. It is as though some urgent accounts have become institutionalized in changes to club policy.

However, in any organization, actual norms do not always match the language and spirit of its constitution and bylaws. So, in this study: despite the no-business policy, club members report an unwritten code of acceptable business conduct, and admit that their club membership advances their careers. And despite the stated celebration of diversity, the clubs remain exclusive and monocultural. And despite officially gender-neutral rules of membership, members continue to keep women inferior. While club members' *policies and accounts* are exculpatory, the *norms and behavior* they (accidentally?) report tell a different and more accurate story.

This difference is illustrated by the discussion of obstacles, both for nonwhites (see chapter 3) and for women (see chapter 4). Policies have been changed to remove official race and gender barriers; the accounts point proudly to this. But in both cases, interviewees define barriers narrowly and fail to see that raced and gendered obstacles remain entrenched in norms. The more ensconced people are in the matrix of privilege, the more obstructed is their view of the workings of inequalities.

There are plenty of comparable examples of norms that give the lie to organizational statements. (Indeed, if the two always matched, then "norms" would not be the powerful concept that it is.) Some examples appear in research on inequalities in the workplace. For instance, many large companies have adopted "equal opportunity" policies in an attempt to redress discrimination against women and minorities. The official principle at these companies is to combat the routines that have historically advantaged white men workers by changing those routines. But all too often, norms continue to confer these unearned privileges, despite official directives. Opportunity hoarding and status processes still operate to produce gender and racial segregation and inequality in the workplace. These can include actions by men or white employees, who resist integration in an attempt to uphold the quality of their pay and working conditions. Managers and employers often tolerate the discriminatory actions of their supervisees, and add their own obstacles by, for instance, making discriminatory assumptions about the fit between jobs and certain people.[37] All of this occurs even at companies with policies designed to avoid creating racial and gender inequality. The language of policy is clearly insufficient, as one researcher notes: "it is quite common for top managers to have a relatively strong public commitment to equal opportunity, but have difficulty acting on it."[38]

Like these corporations, the country clubs' stated philosophies promote the colorblind socializing of club members, and gender-neutral operations. But I have argued that the actual action at clubs preserves white privilege and male privilege. The former is because of both the raced financial barriers to club membership, and also the "comfort factor" requirement of cultural homogeneity, which is also often raced. The latter matter of continuing male privilege is due to the gender asymmetry in club members' domestic lives: imbalanced marriages marked by greater material resources for the men and greater domestic responsibilities for the women. Just as in other contexts, the country clubs represent a case where a progressive official organizational message is drowned out by norms that are subject to social structural and cultural pressures. And yet, the official organizational message (e.g. of valuing diversity) is itself a response to contemporary cultural pressures. As we've learned here, such contradictions in the discourse of country clubs reflect tensions between differing strains of the popular cultural discourse.

## WHERE DOES THIS LEAVE US?

I do *not* argue that exclusive country clubs deserve special attention because of some sort of causal primacy in the reproduction of inequalities. The search for "root" or "original" causes for race, class, and gender inequalities is beside the point. For each individual, all of these hierarchies present themselves as already formed; my question is which actions help reproduce or diminish them. And this process of (usually) reproduction is a complex one, which takes places on several analytic levels and at multiple sites simultaneously. By the definition of reproduction, these levels and sites tend to reinforce rather than clash with one another.

Clubs like the ones in this study represent one piece of the puzzle. Their primary importance is at the micro and meso levels: micro in the sense that they influence members' self-concepts, and are accounted for partly in service of members' identities; and meso in their functions as cultural and social capital incubators, where networks develop. But zooming out, these clubs also have an indirect macro effect, as they contribute both to the reproduction of the dominant inequality ideology, and also (through the micro and meso phenomena) to the inequalities themselves.

Panning, I have shown some of the ways in which these clubs link to other sites. They connect with affluent, largely segregated neighborhoods, which are a primary way that new members are drawn in. The clubs connect with workplaces, which are both another source of new members, and also a place where club members reap material rewards for the cultural and social capital they've developed at the club. Clubs also connect with home and family: for one thing, members refer to their parenting to explain their club involvement. Also, the effect of the typical (asymmetrical, procreative, heterosexual) marriage of club members is clear in the male dominance at the club. In these connections, the exclusive clubs are usually in mutually reinforcing relationships with the beliefs and patterned behaviors at other sites.

I have also shown some ways in which patterns seen here echo patterns seen elsewhere in social life. Concerning the clubs themselves, we see a familiar site where class consciousness is developed in a racial and gender specific way. There is also the accumulation of advantage, which has parallels elsewhere. And, the recent changes at the clubs represent a familiar tendency to make reforms without any restructuring.

There are also familiar patterns in the accounts given for club operations. Overall, we see how the dominant culture serves both as a call to account and as a toolkit for shaping effective accounts. At clubs, as in other organizations, the talk represented in interviews and even in official documents does not always match the reality of the action. We see talk of exclusion which echoes the talk of comfort and compatibility in workplaces; the internal exclusion of women differs from the class and race exclusion from membership. There is also, in the accounts, the use and reproduction of a dominant ideology of inequalities, which emphasizes meritocratic individualism. Much of this accounting sounds similar across the three axes, with the embrace of natural differences between men and women making gender somewhat exceptional. And, these accounts are offered more for personal than interpersonal reasons, so participants can come to terms with the morality of their clubs. But the consequences of well accounted for exclusion ramify well above and beyond the individual level.

The camera work of zooming and panning is useful: it can improve scholarship on any subject. Though this study has been mainly "zoomed in" on the things people say about each other, it's important to zoom out. Then we see macrostructure, including the ways that resources are distributed unevenly among groups of people. We must consider both how the up-close action influences the wide-angle action—for example, accounts can influence ideologies and policies—and the reverse: resources and laws help people draw exclusionary social boundaries.

Panning across sites and institutions is helpful too: studying country clubs (or anything!) in isolation wouldn't do much good. But as we see the connections of club membership with exclusive neighborhoods, with marriage, and with other means of intergenerational reproduction, we get a better picture of how people reproduce intersecting inequalities. In addition to surveying across sites, surveying across inequalities is also crucial. This study has shown the interdependence of hierarchies of class, race, gender and sexuality, and the importance of considering the unmarked as well as marked groups.

This research has shown the complexity of the talk surrounding class and cultural exclusion, racial-ethnic boundaries, and gender regimes. Though my interviewees are unusually powerful, they feel mostly constrained by outside forces. These forces, that keep them mostly reproducing the status quo, include the following: the weight of club traditions, the preferences of the "old guard," and peer pressure; the norms of exclusivity and male dominance learned in other contexts; the power of the almighty dollar in dictating the subordinate status of (most) nonwhites and women; and an ideology that hegemonically gives all of the above the stamp of normalcy. Last but not least, for this population to fight the status quo would generally present them with the prospect of diminishing the material and psychological resources they now enjoy. This research has taught us three things: it conveys the voices of country clubs' members in explaining themselves and their clubs; it critiques those accounts as often self-serving and incomplete; and then again, it shows the understandable reasons why even these good people (many of whom embrace the label "liberal") persist in contributing to the reproduction of class, race, and gender inequalities.

## NOTES

1. "Generic Processes in the Reproduction of Inequality" is the title of Schwalbe, Godwin, Holden, Schrock, Thompson, and Wolkomir. "Generic Processes in the Reproduction of Inequality: An Interactionist Analysis." *Social Forces* 79 (2000): 419.

2. Kendall describes this norm, and calls it taken-for-granted (*The Power of Good Deeds: Privileged Women and the Social Reproduction of the Upper Class.* Lanham, MD: Rowman & Littlefield, 2002, page 97).

3. Kendall (2002:75).

4. These reports are in Kendall (2002) and Ostrander (*Women Of The Upper Class.* Philadelphia: Temple University Press, 1984), as well as here.

5. Collins, *Fighting Words: Black Women and the Search for Justice.* Minneapolis: University of Minnesota Press, 1998, page 210.

6. Hochschild, *Facing Up to the American Dream: Race, Class, and the Soul of the Nation.* Princeton: Princeton University Press, 1995; and Smith and Stone, "Rags, Riches, and Bootstraps: Beliefs About the Causes of Wealth and Poverty." *Sociological Quarterly* 30 (1989): 93.

7. Bettie, *Women Without Class: Girls, Race, and Identity.* Berkeley: University of California Press, 2003; Brantlinger, *The Politics of Social Class in Secondary School: Views of Affluent and Impoverished Youth.* New York: Teachers College Press, 1993; Stuber, "Talk of Class: The Discursive Repertoires of White Working- and Upper-Middle-Class College Students." *Journal of Contemporary Ethnography* 35 (2006): 285.

8. Lorber, *Paradoxes of Gender.* New Haven, CT: Yale University Press, 1994; and Risman, *Gender Vertigo: American Families in Transition.* New Haven, CT: Yale University Press, 1998.

9. MacKinnon, *Feminism Unmodified.* Cambridge: Harvard University Press, 1987, page 8.

10. Mills, "Situated Actions and Vocabularies of Motive." *American Sociological Review* 5 (1940): 904; and Scott and Lyman, "Accounts." *American Sociological Review* 33 (1968): 46.

11. "Every account is a manifestation of the underlying negotiation of identities" (Scott and Lyman 1968:59).

12. Ryan, *Blaming the Victim.* New York: Vintage Books, 1976, page 20.

13. Myers, "Ladies First: Race, Class, and the Contradictions of a Powerful Femininity." *Sociological Spectrum* 24 (2004): 11.

14. Hochschild (1995), Hyde (*Holding Disillusionment at Bay: Latino/a Immigrants and Working Class North Carolinians Expose and Reinforce the American Dream's Discrepancies.* Doctoral dissertation, North Carolina State University, 2002), Rubin (*Worlds of Pain: Life in the Working-Class Family.* New York: Basic Books, 1976), Sennett and Cobb (*The Hidden Injuries of Class.* New York: Vintage Books, 1972).

15. The phrases come from Hyde (2002) and Sennett and Cobb (1972), respectively.

16. The fallacy of racial pluralism is noted in Bonilla-Silva (*Racism Without Racists: Color-Blind Racism & Racial Inequality in Contemporary America,* 3rd

ed. Lanham, MD: Rowman & Littlefield, 2010, page 36), and similarly, false parallels in Schwalbe (*The Sociologically Examined Life: Pieces of the Conversation.* 2nd ed. Mountain View, CA: Mayfield, 2001, page 182).

17. Della Fave, "The Meek Shall Not Inherit the Earth: Self-Evaluation and the Legitimacy of Stratification." *American Sociological Review* 45 (1980): 955; Lamont, *Money, Morals, and Manners: The Culture of the French and American Upper-Middle Class.* Chicago: University of Chicago Press, 1992; Rubin (1976); and Sennett and Cobb (1972).

18. Rubin, *Families on the Fault Line.* New York: HarperPerennial, 1994, page 239.

19. Wright, *Class Counts: Comparative Studies in Class Analysis.* New York: Cambridge University Press, 1997.

20. Useem (*The Inner Circle: Large Corporations and the Rise of Business Political Activity in the U.S. and U.K.* New York: Oxford University Press, 1984) pointed out the importance of, and some mechanisms for, building upper-class loyalty beyond family or firm.

21. On schools, see Cookson and Persell (*Preparing For Power: America's Elite Boarding Schools.* New York: Basic Books, 1985); philanthropy, Daniels (*Invisible Careers: Women Civic Leaders From the Volunteer World.* Chicago: University of Chicago Press, 1988) and Kendall (2002); exclusive locations, Domhoff (*The Higher Circles: The Governing Class in America.* New York: Vintage Books, 1971), Higley (*Privilege, Power, and Place: The Geography of the American Upper Class.* Lanham, MD: Rowman & Littlefield, 1995), and Mills (*The Power Elite.* New York: Oxford University Press, 1956).

22. Through neighborhood choice, elite parents "make sure that their children have only limited and highly structured involvement with people of other social classes or racial-ethnic groupings" (Kendall 2002:84).

23. Kohn and Schooler, *Work And Personality: An Inquiry Into the Impact of Social Stratification.* Norwood, NJ: Ablex Publishing, 1983; and Morgan and Schwalbe, "Mind and Self in Society: Linking Social Structure and Social Cognition." *Social Psychology Quarterly* 53 (1990): 158.

24. Cookson and Persell (1985); Ostrander, "Class Consciousness as Conduct and Meaning." *The Insurgent Sociologist* 9 (1980): 38.

25. Granovetter (*Getting A Job.* Chicago: University of Chicago Press, 1995) shows systematically how better social capital yields better jobs.

26. Tilly, *Durable Inequality.* Berkeley: University of California Press, 1998.

27. My discussion of the accumulation of advantage owes a debt to Schwalbe (2001, chapter 11).

28. Bourdieu, "Cultural Reproduction and Social Reproduction." In *Power and Ideology in Education*, edited by Jerome Karabel and A. H. Halsey. New York: Oxford University Press, 1977; and DiMaggio, "Cultural Capital and School Success: The Impact of Status Culture Participation on the Grades of U.S. High School Students." *American Sociological Review* 47 (1982): 189.

29. Risman (1998:36).

30. On hiring decisions, see Browne and Kennelly ("Black Women in the Labor Market: Stereotypes, Employer Perceptions, and Worker Profiles." Paper presented at the 93rd annual meeting of the American Sociological Association, San

Francisco, 1998) and Reskin and Roos (*Job Queues, Gender Queues: Explaining Women's Inroads Into Male Occupations*. Philadelphia: Temple University Press, 1990); on selective sponsorship, Cockburn (*In The Way of Women: Men's Resistance to Sex Equality in Organizations*. Ithaca, NY: ILR Press, 1991) and Jackall (*Moral Mazes: The World of Corporate Managers*. New York: Oxford University Press, 1988).

Occupational segregation is covered in Reskin and Roos (1990) and Tomaskovic-Devey (*Gender and Racial Inequality at Work: The Sources and Consequences of Job Segregation*. Ithaca, NY: ILR Press, 1993); comparable worth discrimination in England (*Comparable Worth: Theories and Evidence*. New York: Aldine de Gruyter, 1992); definitions of firms and workers in Acker ("Hierarchies, Jobs, Bodies: A Theory of Gendered Organizations." *Gender & Society* 4 (1990): 139); and employers' use of gender in Padavic and Reskin (*Women and Men at Work*. Thousand Oaks, CA: Pine Forge Press, 2002).

31. DiPrete and Eirich, "Cumulative Advantage as a Mechanism for Inequality: A Review of Theoretical and Empirical Developments." *Annual Review of Sociology* 32 (2006): 271.

32. Schwalbe et al. (2000:432), drawing on Bourdieu, *Distinction: A Social Critique of the Judgment of Taste*. Cambridge: Harvard University Press, 1984.

33. This analysis corresponds to, and owes a debt to, that of Zweigenhaft and Domhoff (*Diversity in the Power Elite: How It Happened, Why It Matters*. Lanham, MD: Rowman & Littlefield, 2006, chapter 7) on the diversification of the power elite.

34. See Fischer, Hout, Sánchez Jankowski, Lucas, Swidler, and Voss, *Inequality By Design: Cracking the Bell Curve Myth*. Princeton: Princeton University Press, 1996.

35. Cookson and Persell (1985, chapter 9).

36. Wilkins, *Wannabes, Goths, and Christians: The Boundaries of Sex, Style, and Status*. Chicago: University of Chicago Press, 2008, page 257.

37. Cockburn (1991), Padavic and Reskin (2002), Tomaskovic-Devey (1993).

38. Tomaskovic-Devey (1993:157). Cockburn (1991:45) notes that there are both institutional and cultural reasons for the difficulty in implementation.

# Methodological Appendix

As a graduate student, I heard the call to "study up" in stratification systems, and noticed the idea appearing repeatedly. For the scholarship on this subject, please see chapter 1. Here in the Methodological Appendix it's time to get personal: doing research reflexively means acknowledging the influence of one's biography on the research question, analysis, and access to subjects.[1]

(Interestingly, reflexive scholars also recommend problematizing the researcher's authority and working more collaboratively with subjects. This advice doesn't apply to my work, but it reflects the presumption— often accurate—that the researcher has more power than her subjects.)

The call to study superordinates resonated with me, partly because of my own social location. My graduate experience at a large state university was eye-opening in terms of my position on the socioeconomic scale. Coming from an upper-middle-class background, my privileged socioeconomic position had been invisible for me. Now I recognize its significance: first, that as a member of unmarked groups (affluent and white), one of my privileges has been never to think about that group membership; and second, that my life was organized in ways, such as attending an expensive private college, that preserved that obliviousness well into my twenties.[2]

I did not grow up going to country clubs, except a few times as the guest of a friend. I think it would have been financially possible, but didn't appeal to my parents and grandparents culturally. My mother and father both say that they are "not a joiner," and take pride in being nonconformists. Besides, they prioritized their spending elsewhere: I have great childhood memories of all sorts of sports and travel experiences.

Given the way my life was organized, I shared with my interviewees the truncated vision of stratification. When Steve said that Suburban dues were reasonable because they compared to renting a beach house, I actually thought he had a decent point, until I checked in with my dissertation committee.

## ACCESS AND ITS IRONIES

While scholars of inequality recommend studying the unmarked, they acknowledge that it can be more difficult than studying members of subordinated groups. Especially when it comes to class, the privileged are thought of as elusive subjects of study. I thought that my own social location—being white, knowing some people that are rich and/or powerful, and having the cultural capital to interact with them smoothly—might enable me to overcome that elusiveness.

Having targeted people with race, class, and gender privilege, I now needed a context in which to study them. I attended an elite boarding school, and I considered doing research at that school or a similar one. But, I was more interested in the doings of adults than teenagers. I'm familiar with a destination for wealthy vacationers to the northeast, and I considered studying its social life. But, anybody can visit that place, and the wealthy vacationers don't all know each other, so it's not exactly a coherent community. I settled on something that's convenient and concrete: a study of country clubs in one area of the Northeastern United States. These private clubs provide a specific context for the social lives of people who are advantaged rather than disadvantaged.

My initial research design called for an ethnography of one country club: I hoped to do fieldwork there, attend board meetings, and interview members. This plan met with initial resistance from the Oldfamily club (described in chapter 1). I did not pursue it because it was also rejected by my university's Institutional Review Board (IRB), and so the research design changed to an interview-only study.

Did the considerable power of the research population contribute to the IRB's reluctance to approve ethnographic research? I don't know for sure, but I'd speculate that it was a factor. If so, then this hesitance is an example of the obstacles that restrict scholarship on the wealthy. Such research is stunted often because it includes unique risks—real or imagined—for the researcher and her university. These risks—of social sanctions, of lawsuits—are significant even though they are not common.

Noticing which groups do and do not get studied, and why, is one part of understanding how inequalities get reproduced.

I resigned myself to an interview study, but always wished for data on "the action itself," meaning the transactions wherein candidates for club membership are rejected or approved. Future research could investigate this action, although the researcher would first need a better transaction with their IRB than the one I had. "Undercover" work (without prior informed consent of subjects) has ethical dilemmas, but is a possibility given this sort of research.[3]

My initial population of interviewees was people who belong to exclusive clubs whose membership is by selective invitation only. I eventually focused on five country clubs' members or former members (and three club managers). The data collection took place in 2000 and 2001 in the Northeastern United States, primarily in a single urban area.

I had found the initial key informants through personal acquaintances. Then I used snowball sampling, asking club members to identify each other. The snowball sampling method could account for the interviewees' career concentrations in law, finance, insurance, real estate, and institutional administration. As with any nonrandom sample, generalizability is limited. However, I know of no particular sampling bias here that would necessitate a caution that this sample is not representative of the population.

The snowball sampling technique relies on club members' social networks, precisely the same tool used to determine club membership. As such, I consider this sampling design a strength rather than a drawback. I moved well beyond the original key informant network. I had no trouble securing interviews, probably because I always introduced myself using one or more names of previous interviewees.[4] Of fifty-six requests, forty-seven people happily granted interviews. The remaining nine either declined or were so difficult to reach that I took it as an indirect refusal.

So, I use cultural capital and social capital to conduct my research; and then I critique as unjust the ways those tools are used in the country clubs. Am I biting the hand that feeds me? I suppose I am to some extent. But at the risk of seeming defensive, let me make a distinction. As individuals, we can and do disagree with each other's behavior. But we can legitimately object to unfair behavior if it is institutionalized in a formal organization. Imagine a group of friends who are entirely homogeneous, and keep their social circle closed for years. While our opinions of this circle of friends may vary, its social significance is minor. But on the other hand, country clubs are institutions—having amassed considerable bureaucracy, human resources, and other capital—that serve the exclusion of outsiders and the reproduction of privileges. As other researchers have shown, the social significance is now on a level well above our imaginary circle of friends. While individual use of exclusive networks may be disagreeable, institutionalizing nonmeritocratic processes is more significant and thus more deserving of our critical attention.

## ANALYSIS

The interviews, in subjects' homes and offices, usually lasted between sixty and ninety minutes. All interviews were tape-recorded, transcribed, and pseudonymized, with field notes attached. I sent a handwritten thank you note after each interview.

The field notes included, as well as direct observations, my impressions and thoughts on how each interview compared to others. From these seeds grew analytic memos, in which I identified emergent patterns, contradictions in the data, and potential explanations.[5] Focusing on subjects' talk, I came to an emphasis on the accounts they offer in three subjects: accounts for the exclusiveness of their clubs, for the racial-ethnic composition of the membership, and for women's status in their own and other clubs.

I made use of the QSR N5 software for qualitative data analysis. I coded the interviews thematically according to these three subjects and several sub-topics within each. For example, under the heading of "women's status" there is coding for the role of the men in the club, the role of the women in the club, marital power, and so on. These codes emerged and were adjusted in the course of reading and re-reading interview transcripts.

When material under a code seemed promising, and complex, I printed all of its output to review and analyze it further. For instance, it was during this step that I saw within the topic "there is no exclusion" the following specifics: there is no exclusion except affordability; there is no exclusion that I know of once someone has been proposed; and, there is no exclusion as long as you just know some people. In reviewing the output of "no exclusion" (not during the coding process itself), I saw interviewees' blind spots concerning stratification and social capital.

Overall, the analysis done here grows from a reiterative process of studying the results of my coding, plus consulting the relevant literature for comparison, plus corresponding with my dissertation advisory committee.

## STUDYING A LIMITED POPULATION AS A SEMI-INSIDER

As I gathered data, I felt that my social location gave me a good combination of outsider and insider perspectives. As an outsider to country clubs, processes that members had taken for granted for decades were not automatic and invisible to me. (My outsider status also enables the criticism written here, since I have little to lose if club members are antagonized by reading it.) But as a fellow insider to the Yankee upper-middle class, I had smooth interactions and received a warm welcome.

But studying near-peers also has its difficulties. As a relative insider to interviewees' cultural milieu, I sometimes shared their assumptions: for example, I was initially receptive to club members' contentions about how affordable their club fees are. I was unintentionally sharing interviewees' truncated vision of stratification. And although I have no experience as a country club member, my relative-insider status may have limited how aggressive I was in interviews.

I also took care not to antagonize anyone, because I knew I was interviewing in a limited population with dense network ties. In fact, if anything I was more meek in interviews than necessary. I knew that word was spreading about my project, and I feared that a negative reputation would make it almost impossible to secure interviews.

Besides, I found that this population is aware of some negative public opinion about exclusive private clubs. Some even seemed to grant the interview so as to publicize their own side of the story, to counter the criticism that fails to consider the insider perspective. Another reason I was amiable in interviews was to calm their fears that I was doing a damaging exposé.

Reflecting on the completed project, I know that my own social location has been influential in my choice of research topic and pursuit of subjects to interview. In reporting on the research, I have sometimes felt pulled in two directions. On one hand, critical sociologists encourage me to emphasize the harmful consequences of the talk and action of country club members in reproducing inequalities that serve themselves above others. It would be an easy next step to impugning this population as especially scheming and selfish.

But on the other hand, these people are somewhat "close to home" for me. [6] This closeness is literal as well as figurative, as I have at times lived among the population I studied. They seem like decent people; most seem like people I would enjoy spending time with. There are two reasons that I am reluctant to condemn them. The first is that, if they read this, they could be outraged and somehow hurt me. (I'm not sure exactly what could happen, but I could earn a bad reputation in the collective unconscious of the local elite.) But the second reason is more important: I do not believe that the evidence merits their condemnation. Along with other scholars of inequality, I have tried to suggest that people's behavior is overwhelmingly a product of their social location. I believe that good sociology gives the reader a better understanding of the subjects, whoever they are, and maybe even the thought that if the reader were located in the same web of identities, opportunities, and constraints, he or she would behave quite similarly.

And yet, I do not want to portray this population as automatons in machinery beyond their control. Sociologists do well to study not just the constraints upon, but also the agency of their subjects. Agency looms larger among people like these who have disproportionate influence and control of resources. But, the dominant American ideology provides more obfuscation than it does illumination. The people in this study are not critical sociologists and therefore do not see all the ways in which their behaviors serve to reproduce inequalities. I cannot really blame them individually; and yet, I would certainly like to spread the sociological perspective to them and beyond.

Is the behavior of exclusive club members ethical? The question is a difficult one, and a question for all of us with somehow privileged identities. The concept of justice here goes beyond the highly individualistic American concept of justice. As complicated as the reproduction of inequalities is, I have no simple answer for the ethical questions raised here. I simply hope that the insights of this book can be helpful in some small way.

## NOTES

1. Hesse-Biber and Yaiser, "Difference Matters: Studying Across Race, Class, Gender and Sexuality." In *Feminist Perspectives on Social Research*, edited by Hesse-Biber and Yaiser. New York: Oxford University Press, 2004, page 115.

2. See McIntosh ("White Privilege and Male Privilege: A Personal Account of Coming to See Correspondences Through Work in Women's Studies." In *Race, Class and Gender: An Anthology*, edited by Margaret Anderson and Patricia Hill Collins. Belmont, CA: Wadsworth, 1992) for a classic statement on privileges of whiteness, including not having to think about it.

3. For examples of "undercover" research, see Graham (*Member of the Club: Reflections on Life in a Racially Polarized World*. New York: HarperCollins, 1996) and Kendall (*The Power of Good Deeds: Privileged Women and the Social Reproduction of the Upper Class*. Lanham, MD: Rowman & Littlefield, 2002); for a rationale for it, see Myers (*Racetalk: Racism Hiding in Plain Sight*. Lanham, MD: Rowman & Littlefield, 2005, page 31).

4. Ostrander ("'Surely You're Not in This Just to Be Helpful': Access, Rapport, and Interviews in Three Studies of Elites." *Journal of Contemporary Ethnography* 22 (1993): 7) similarly recommends using referrals when interviewing elites.

5. Qualitative analysis techniques drawn from Emerson, Fretz, and Shaw (*Writing Ethnographic Fieldnotes*. Chicago: University of Chicago Press, 1995, chapter 6); and Lofland and Lofland (*Analyzing Social Settings: A Guide to Qualitative Observation and Analysis*, 3rd edition. Belmont, CA: Wadsworth, 1995, chapter 9).

6. The phrase is from Davidman, "Studying Close to Home: The Intersection of Life and Work." *Sociology of Religion* 61 (2000): 425.

# References

Acker, Joan. "Hierarchies, Jobs, Bodies: A Theory of Gendered Organizations." *Gender & Society* 4 (1990): 139.

Aldrich, Nelson W. Jr. *Old Money: The Mythology of America's Upper Class*. New York: A. A. Knopf, 1988.

Andersen, Margaret L. "Thinking About Women: A Quarter Century's View." *Gender & Society* 19 (2005): 437.

Anderson, Dave. "Woods is Not Obliged to Boycott." *New York Times*, 8 December 2002, 8-1.

Anderson, Kristin L. "Gender, Status, and Domestic Violence: An Integration of Feminist and Family Violence Approaches." *Journal of Marriage and the Family* 59 (1997): 655.

Araton, Harvey. "Other Women's Issues Need A Voice." *New York Times*, 8 December 2002, 8-1.

Baca Zinn, Maxine. "Chicano Men and Masculinity." *Journal of Ethnic Studies* 10 (1982): 29.

Baca Zinn, Maxine, and D. Stanley Eitzen. *Diversity in Families*. 5th ed. New York: Longman, 1999.

Baltzell, E. Digby. *The Protestant Establishment: Aristocracy and Caste in America*. Glencoe, IL: Free Press, 1964.

Bettie, Julie. *Women Without Class: Girls, Race, and Identity*. Berkeley: University of California Press, 2003.

Blalock, Hubert M. *Toward A Theory of Minority-Group Relations*. New York: Wiley, 1967.

Blau, Peter M. *Inequality and Heterogeneity: A Primitive Theory of Social Structure*. New York: Free Press, 1977.

Blumer, Herbert. "Race Prejudice as a Sense of Group Position." *Pacific Sociological Review* 1 (1958): 3.

Blumstein, Philip and Pepper Schwartz. *American Couples: Money, Work, Sex.* New York: William Morrow, 1983.

Bonacich, Edna. "A Theory of Ethnic Antagonism: The Split Labor Market." *American Sociological Review* 37 (1972): 547.

Bonilla-Silva, Eduardo. "Rethinking Racism: Toward a Structural Interpretation." *American Sociological Review* 62 (1997): 465.

———. *White Supremacy and Racism in the Post–Civil Rights Era.* Boulder, CO: Rienner, 2001.

———. "'New Racism,' Color-Blind Racism, and the Future of Whiteness in America." In *White Out: The Continuing Significance of Racism,* edited by Ashley W. Doane and Eduardo Bonilla-Silva. New York: Routledge, 2003.

———. *Racism Without Racists: Color-Blind Racism & Racial Inequality in Contemporary America,* 3rd ed. Lanham, MD: Rowman & Littlefield, 2010.

Bonilla-Silva, Eduardo and Tyrone Forman. "'I Am Not a Racist but . . .': Mapping White College Students' Racial Ideology in the USA." *Discourse and Society* 11 (2000): 50.

Bourdieu, Pierre. "Cultural Reproduction and Social Reproduction." In *Power and Ideology in Education,* edited by Jerome Karabel and A. H. Halsey. New York: Oxford University Press, 1977.

———. *Distinction: A Social Critique of the Judgment of Taste.* Cambridge: Harvard University Press, 1984.

Bourgois, Philippe. *In Search of Respect: Selling Crack in El Barrio.* New York: Cambridge University Press, 1996.

Brantlinger, Ellen. *The Politics of Social Class in Secondary School: Views of Affluent and Impoverished Youth.* New York: Teachers College Press, 1993.

Bravin, Jess. "How A Jewish Man Got Into a Ritzy Club in Palm Beach, Fla." *Wall Street Journal,* 28 February 2001, A-1.

Brekhus, Wayne. "A Sociology of the Unmarked: Redirecting Our Focus." *Sociological Theory* 16, no. 1 (1998): 34–51.

Brines, Julie. "Economic Dependency and the Division of Labor." *American Journal of Sociology* 100 (1994): 652.

Brown, Clifton. "Augusta Answers Critics on Policy." *New York Times,* 10 July 2002, D-4.

Browne, Irene and Ivy Kennelly. "Black Women in the Labor Market: Stereotypes, Employer Perceptions, and Worker Profiles." Paper presented at the 93rd annual meeting of the American Sociological Association, San Francisco, 1998.

Business Week. "Rule No.1 at This New Club: No Dames." *Business Week,* 21 January 2002, p. 10.

Carr, Leslie G. *"Color-Blind" Racism.* Thousand Oaks, CA: Sage, 1997.

Choo, Hae Yeon and Myra Marx Ferree. "Practicing Intersectionality in Sociological Research: A Critical Analysis of Inclusions, Interactions and Institutions in the Study of Inequalities." *Social Forces* 28 (2010): 129.

Christopher, Robert C. *Crashing the Gates: The De-WASPing of America's Power Elite.* New York: Simon and Schuster, 1989.

Cockburn, Cynthia. *In The Way of Women: Men's Resistance to Sex Equality in Organizations.* Ithaca, NY: ILR Press, 1991.

Coleman, James S. "Social Capital in the Creation of Human Capital." *American Journal of Sociology* 94 (1988): 95.

Collins, Patricia Hill. *Black Feminist Thought: Knowledge, Consciousness, and the Politics of Empowerment*. New York: Routledge, 1990.

———. *Fighting Words: Black Women and the Search for Justice*. Minneapolis: University of Minnesota Press, 1998.

Connell, R. W. *Gender and Power*. Palo Alto, CA: Stanford University Press, 1987.

———. "Live Fast and Die Young: The Construction of Masculinity Among Young Working-Class Men on the Margin of the Labour Market." *Australian & New Zealand Journal of Sociology* 27 (1991): 141.

Cookson, Peter W., Jr. and Caroline Hodges Persell. *Preparing For Power: America's Elite Boarding Schools*. New York: Basic Books, 1985.

Crenshaw, Kimberle W. "Mapping the Margins: Intersectionality, Identity Politics, and Violence Against Women of Color." *Stanford Law Review* 43 (1991): 1241.

Daniels, Arlene Kaplan. *Invisible Careers: Women Civic Leaders From the Volunteer World*. Chicago: University of Chicago Press, 1988.

Davidman, Lynn. "Studying Close to Home: The Intersection of Life and Work." *Sociology of Religion* 61 (2000): 425.

Davis, Kathy. "Intersectionality as a Buzzword: A Sociology of Science Perspective on What Makes a Feminist Theory Successful." *Feminist Theory* 9 (2008): 67.

Della Cava, Marco R. "Men Tee Up As Critics Tee Off." *USA Today*, 4 October 2002, A-1.

Della Fave, L. Richard. "The Meek Shall Not Inherit the Earth: Self-Evaluation and the Legitimacy of Stratification." *American Sociological Review* 45 (1980): 955.

———. "Toward an Explication of the Legitimation Process." *Social Forces* 65 (1986): 476.

———. "Ritual and the Legitimation of Inequality." *Sociological Perspectives* 34 (1991): 21.

Denis, Ann. "Review Essay: Intersectional Analysis: A Contribution of Feminism to Sociology." *International Sociology* 23 (2008): 677.

Deutsch, Francine M. *Halving It All: How Equally Shared Parenting Works*. Cambridge: Harvard University Press, 1999.

DiMaggio, Paul. "Cultural Capital and School Success: The Impact of Status Culture Participation on the Grades of U.S. High School Students." *American Sociological Review* 47 (1982): 189.

DiPrete, Thomas A. and Gregory M. Eirich. "Cumulative Advantage as a Mechanism for Inequality: A Review of Theoretical and Empirical Developments." *Annual Review of Sociology* 32 (2006): 271.

Disch, Estelle. "General Introduction." In *Reconstructing Gender: A Multicultural Anthology*, 4th ed., edited by Estelle Disch. Boston: McGraw-Hill, 1997.

DiTomaso, Nancy, Rochelle Parks-Yancey, and Corinne Post. "White Views of Civil Rights: Color Blindness and Equal Opportunity." In *White Out: The Continuing Significance of Racism*, edited by Ashley W. Doane and Eduardo Bonilla-Silva. New York: Routledge, 2003.

Doane, Ashley W. (Woody). "What Is Racism? Racial Discourse and Racial Politics." *Critical Sociology* 32 (2006): 255.

Doane, Ashley W. (Woody) and Eduardo Bonilla-Silva, eds. *White Out: The Continuing Significance of Racism*. New York: Routledge, 2003.

Dolgon, Corey. *The End of the Hamptons: Scenes from the Class Struggle in America's Paradise*. New York: NYU Press, 2005.

Domhoff, G. William. *Who Rules America?* Englewood Cliffs, NJ: Prentice-Hall, 1967.

———. *The Higher Circles: The Governing Class in America*. New York: Vintage Books, 1971.

———. *The Powers That Be: Processes of Ruling Class Domination in America*. New York: Random House, 1979.

———. *Who Rules America Now?: A View for the '80s*. New York: Simon & Schuster, 1986.

Dye, Thomas R. *Who's Running America?: Institutional Leadership in the United States*. Englewood Cliffs, NJ: Prentice-Hall, 1976.

Eliasoph, Nina. "'Everyday Racism' in a Culture of Political Avoidance: Civil Society, Speech, and Taboo." *Social Problems* 46 (1999): 479.

Emerson, Robert M., Rachel I. Fretz, and Linda L. Shaw. *Writing Ethnographic Fieldnotes*. Chicago: University of Chicago Press, 1995.

England, Paula. *Comparable Worth: Theories and Evidence*. New York: Aldine de Gruyter, 1992.

Fantasia, Rick. "From Class Consciousness to Culture, Action, and Social Organization." *American Sociological Review* 21 (1995): 269.

Feagin, Joe R. and Eileen O'Brien. *White Men on Race: Power, Privilege, and the Shaping of Cultural Consciousness*. Boston: Beacon Press, 2003.

Feagin, Joe R. and Hernan Vera. *White Racism: The Basics*. New York: Routledge, 1995.

Fine, Michelle. "Working the Hyphens: Reinventing Self and Other in Qualitative Research." In *The Handbook of Qualitative Research*, edited by Norman K. Denzin and Yvonna S. Lincoln. Thousand Oaks, CA: Sage, 1994.

Finkelstein, Joanne. *The Fashioned Self*. Philadelphia: Temple University Press, 1991.

Firey, Walter I. *Land Use in Central Boston*. Cambridge: Harvard University Press, 1947.

Fischer, Claude S., Michael Hout, Martín Sánchez Jankowski, Samuel R. Lucas, Ann Swidler, and Kim Voss. *Inequality By Design: Cracking the Bell Curve Myth*. Princeton: Princeton University Press, 1996.

Frankenberg, Ruth. *White Women, Race Matters: The Social Construction of Whiteness*. Minneapolis: University of Minnesota Press, 1993.

Giddens, Anthony. *The Constitution of Society*. Berkeley: University of California Press, 1984.

Glenn, Evelyn Nakano. "The Social Construction and Institutionalization of Gender and Race: An Integrative Framework." In *Revisioning Gender*, edited by Myra Marx Ferree, Judith Lorber, and Beth B. Hess. Thousand Oaks, CA: Sage, 1999.

Gordon, Avery F. and Christopher Newfield, eds. *Mapping Multiculturalism*. Minneapolis: University of Minnesota Press, 1996.

Gordon, Ted and Wahneema Lubiano. "The Statement of the Black Faculty Caucus." In *Debating P.C.: The Controversy Over Political Correctness on Campuses*, edited by Paul Berman. New York: Dell, 1992.

Gould, Stephen Jay. *The Mismeasure of Man*. New York: W. W. Norton, 1981.

Graham, Lawrence Otis. *Member of the Club: Reflections on Life in a Racially Polarized World*. New York: HarperCollins, 1996.

Granovetter, Mark. *Getting A Job*. Chicago: University of Chicago Press, 1995.

Gubrium, Jaber F. and James A. Holstein. *What Is Family?* Mountain View, CA: Mayfield, 1990.

Harrington, Michael. *The Other America: Poverty in the United States*. 2nd ed. New York: Penguin Books, 1981.

Hays, Sharon. *The Cultural Contradictions of Motherhood*. New Haven, CT: Yale University Press, 1996.

Hertz, Rosanna and Susan M. Reverby. "Gender, Gentility, and Political Protest: The Barbara Bush Controversy at Wellesley College." *Gender & Society* 9 (1995): 594.

Hesse-Biber, Sharlene Nagy and Michelle L. Yaiser. "Difference Matters: Studying Across Race, Class, Gender and Sexuality." In *Feminist Perspectives on Social Research*, edited by Hesse-Biber and Yaiser. New York: Oxford University Press, 2004.

Higley, Stephen Richard. *Privilege, Power, and Place: The Geography of the American Upper Class*. Lanham, MD: Rowman & Littlefield, 1995.

Hochschild, Arlie with Anne Machung. *The Second Shift: Working Parents and the Revolution at Home*. New York: Viking Penguin, 1989.

Hochschild, Jennifer. *Facing Up to the American Dream: Race, Class, and the Soul of the Nation*. Princeton: Princeton University Press, 1995.

Hondagneu-Sotelo, Pierrette and Michael A. Messner. "Gender Displays and Men's Power: The 'New Man' and the Mexican Immigrant Man." In *Theorizing Masculinities*, edited by Harry Brod and Michael Kaufman. Thousand Oaks, CA: Sage, 1994.

hooks, bell. *Feminist Theory: From Margin to Center*. Boston: South End Press, 1984.

Horowitz, Ruth. "Barriers and Bridges to Class Mobility and Formation: Ethnographies of Stratification." *Sociological Methods and Research* 25 (1997): 495.

Howard, Johnette. "Shoal Truth: This Is The Same." *Newsday*, 12 April 2003.

Huber, Joan and William Form. *Income and Ideology: An Analysis of the American Political Formula*. New York: Free Press, 1973.

Hull, Gloria T., Patricia Bell Scott, and Barbara Smith. *But Some of Us Are Brave*. Old Westbury, NY: Feminist Press, 1982.

Hyde, Katherine Ann. *Holding Disillusionment at Bay: Latino/a Immigrants and Working Class North Carolinians Expose and Reinforce the American Dream's Discrepancies*. Doctoral dissertation, North Carolina State University, 2002. Available at www.lib.ncsu.edu/theses/available/etd-11122002-220157/.

Jackall, Robert. *Moral Mazes: The World of Corporate Managers*. New York: Oxford University Press, 1988.

Johnson, Heather Beth. *The American Dream and the Power of Wealth: Choosing Schools and Inheriting Inequality in the Land of Opportunity*. New York: Routledge, 2006.

Kanter, Rosabeth Moss. *Men and Women of the Corporation*. New York: Basic Books, 1977.

Keller, Suzanne. "The American Upper Class Family: Precarious Claims on the Future." *Journal of Comparative Family Studies* 22 (1991): 159.

Kendall, Diana. *The Power of Good Deeds: Privileged Women and the Social Re-production of the Upper Class.* Lanham, MD: Rowman & Littlefield, 2002.

——. *Members Only: Elite Clubs and the Process of Exclusion.* Lanham, MD: Rowman & Littlefield, 2008.

Kerr, Bob. "A Casualty of the Trial Suffers Quietly." *Providence Journal,* 3 May 2002, B-1.

Kessler, S., D. J. Ashenden, R.W. Connell, and G. W. Dowsett. "Gender Relations in Secondary Schooling." *Sociology of Education* 58 (1985): 34.

King, Valarie and Holly E. Heard. "Nonresident Father Visitation, Parental Conflict, and Mother's Satisfaction: What's Best for Child Well-Being?" *Journal of Marriage and the Family* 61 (1999): 385.

Kluegel, James and Eliot Smith. *Beliefs About Inequality: Americans' View of What Is and What Ought to Be.* Hawthorne, NY: Aldine de Gruyter, 1986.

Kohn, Melvin L. and Carmi Schooler. *Work And Personality: An Inquiry Into the Impact of Social Stratification.* Norwood, NJ: Ablex Publishing, 1983.

Kuczynski, Alex. "It's Still A Man's, Man's, Man's World." *New York Times,* 21 July 2002, 9-1.

Labovitz, Priscilla. "Immigration—Just the Facts." *New York Times,* 25 March 1996, A-15.

Lamont, Michèle. *Money, Morals, and Manners: The Culture of the French and American Upper-Middle Class.* Chicago: University of Chicago Press, 1992.

——. "Above 'People Above'? Status and Worth among White and Black Workers." In *The Cultural Territories of Race: Black and White Boundaries,* edited by Michele Lamont. Chicago: University of Chicago Press, 1999.

——. *The Dignity of Working Men: Morality and the Boundaries of Race, Class, and Immigration.* New York: Russell Sage, 2000.

Lamont, Michèle and Marcel Fournier, eds. *Cultivating Differences: Symbolic Boundaries and the Making of Inequality.* Chicago: University of Chicago Press, 1992.

Lareau, Annette and Elliot B. Weininger. "Cultural Capital in Educational Research: A Critical Assessment." *Theory and Society* 32 (2003): 567.

Litsky, Frank. "Women's Group Vows to Pressure Augusta." *New York Times,* 13 July 2002, D-6.

Lofland, John and Lyn H. Lofland. *Analyzing Social Settings: A Guide to Qualitative Observation and Analysis,* 3rd edition. Belmont, CA: Wadsworth, 1995.

Lofland, Lyn H. *The Public Realm: Exploring the City's Quintessential Social Territory.* Hawthorne, NY: Aldine de Gruyter, 1998.

Lorber, Judith. *Paradoxes of Gender.* New Haven, CT: Yale University Press, 1994.

——. *Breaking the Bowls: Degendering and Feminist Change.* New York: W. W. Norton, 2005.

Mac an Ghaill, Mairtin. *The Making of Men: Masculinities, Sexualities, and Schooling.* Philadelphia: Open University Press, 1994.

MacKinnon, Catharine. *Feminism Unmodified.* Cambridge: Harvard University Press, 1987.

Majors, Richard and Janet Mancini Billson. *Cool Pose: The Dilemmas of Black Manhood in America.* New York: Lexington Books, 1992.

Martin, Patricia Y. "Gender as a Social Institution." *Social Forces* 82 (2004): 1249.

Massey, Douglas S. and Nancy A. Denton. *American Apartheid: Segregation and the Making of the Underclass*. Cambridge: Harvard University Press, 1993.

Mayo, James M. *The American Country Club: Its Origins and Development*. New Brunswick, NJ: Rutgers University Press, 1998.

McCall, Leslie. "The Complexity of Intersectionality." *Signs* 30, no. 3 (2005): 1771.

McCloskey, Laura A. "Socioeconomic and Coercive Power Within the Family." *Gender & Society* 10 (1996): 449.

McGrath, Charles. "Why don't men and women play golf together?" *New York Times Magazine*, 29 July 2001, p. 16.

McIntosh, Peggy. "White Privilege and Male Privilege: A Personal Account of Coming to See Correspondences Through Work in Women's Studies." In *Race, Class and Gender: An Anthology*, edited by Margaret Anderson and Patricia Hill Collins. Belmont, CA: Wadsworth, 1992.

McLanahan, Sara. "Family Structure and the Reproduction of Poverty." *American Journal of Sociology* 90 (1985): 873.

McPherson, Miller, Lynn Smith-Lovin, and James M. Cook. "Birds of a Feather: Homophily in Social Networks." *Annual Review of Sociology* 27 (2001): 415.

Messner, Michael A. "Men as Superordinates: Challenges for Gender Scholarship." In *Privilege: A Reader*, edited by Michael S. Kimmel and Abby S. Ferber. Boulder, CO: Westview Press, 2003.

Mies, Maria. *Patriarchy and Accumulation on a World Scale: Women in the International Division of Labour*. London: Zed Books, 1986.

Mills, C. Wright. "Situated Actions and Vocabularies of Motive." *American Sociological Review* 5 (1940): 904.

———. *The Power Elite*. New York: Oxford University Press, 1956.

Morgan, David L. and Michael Schwalbe. "Mind and Self in Society: Linking Social Structure and Social Cognition." *Social Psychology Quarterly* 53 (1990): 158.

Morris, Martina and Bruce Western. "Inequality in Earnings at the Close of the Twentieth Century." *Annual Review of Sociology* 25 (1999): 623.

Morrison, Toni. *Playing in the Dark: Whiteness and the Literary Imagination*. New York: Vintage, 1992.

Moss, Philip and Chris Tilly. "'Soft' Skills and Race: An Investigation of Black Men's Employment Problems." *Work and Occupations* 23 (1996): 252.

Moss, Richard J. *Golf and The American Country Club*. Urbana: University of Illinois Press, 2001.

Myers, Kristen. "Ladies First: Race, Class, and the Contradictions of a Powerful Femininity." *Sociological Spectrum* 24 (2004): 11.

———. *Racetalk: Racism Hiding in Plain Sight*. Lanham, MD: Rowman & Littlefield, 2005.

Nader, Laura. "Up the Anthropologist: Perspectives Gained from Studying Up." In *Reinventing Anthropology*, edited by Dell Hymes. New York: Vintage, 1969.

Nash, Jennifer C. "Re-Thinking Intersectionality." *Feminist Review* 89 (2008): 1.

Neckerman, Kathryn M. and Joleen Kirschenman. "Hiring Strategies, Racial Bias, and Inner-City Workers." *Social Problems* 38 (1991): 433.

Odendahl, Teresa. *Charity Begins at Home: Generosity and Self-Interest Among the Philanthropic Elite*. New York: Basic Books, 1990.

Oliver, Melvin L. and Thomas M. Shapiro. *Black Wealth/White Wealth: A New Perspective on Racial Inequality.* 2nd ed. New York: Routledge, 2006.

Orbuch, Terri L. "People's Accounts Count: The Sociology of Accounts." *Annual Review of Sociology* 23 (1997): 455.

Osmond, Marie Withers and Barrie Thorne. "Feminist Theories: The Social Construction of Gender in Families and Society." In *Sourcebook of Family Theories and Methods,* edited by Pauline Boss et al. New York: Plenum Press, 1993.

Ostrander, Susan A. "Class Consciousness as Conduct and Meaning." *The Insurgent Sociologist* 9 (1980): 38.

———. *Women Of The Upper Class.* Philadelphia: Temple University Press, 1984.

———. "'Surely You're Not in This Just to Be Helpful': Access, Rapport, and Interviews in Three Studies of Elites." *Journal of Contemporary Ethnography* 22 (1993): 7.

Padavic, Irene and Barbara F. Reskin. *Women and Men at Work.* Thousand Oaks, CA: Pine Forge Press, 2002.

Portes, Alejandro. "Social Capital: Its Origins and Applications in Modern Sociology." *Annual Review of Sociology* 24 (1998): 1.

Pyke, Karen D. "Class-Based Masculinities: The Interdependence of Gender, Class, and Interpersonal Power." *Gender & Society* 10 (1996): 527.

Reay, Diane. "Rethinking Social Class: Qualitative Perspectives on Class and Gender." *Sociology* 32 (1998): 259.

Reskin, Barbara F. and Patricia A. Roos. *Job Queues, Gender Queues: Explaining Women's Inroads Into Male Occupations.* Philadelphia: Temple University Press, 1990.

Rich, Adrienne. "Compulsory Heterosexuality and Lesbian Existence." In *Powers of Desire: The Politics of Sexuality,* edited by Ann Snitow, Christine Stansell, and Sharon Thompson. New York: Monthly Review Press, 1983.

Ridgeway, Cecilia. "The Social Construction of Status Value: Gender and Other Nominal Characteristics." *Social Forces* 70 (1991): 367.

Risman, Barbara J. *Gender Vertigo: American Families in Transition.* New Haven, CT: Yale University Press, 1998.

———. "Gender as a Social Structure: Theory Wrestling With Activism." *Gender & Society* 18 (2004): 429.

Rubin, Gayle. "The Traffic in Women: Notes on the 'Political Economy' of Sex." In *Toward an Anthropology of Women,* edited by Reyna Reiter. New York: Monthly Review Press, 1975.

Rubin, Lillian B. *Worlds of Pain: Life in the Working-Class Family.* New York: BasicBooks, 1976.

———. *Families on the Fault Line.* New York: HarperPerennial, 1994.

Ryan, William. *Blaming the Victim.* New York: Vintage Books, 1976.

Sandberg, John F. and Sandra L. Hofferth. "Changes in Children's Time with Parents: United States, 1981–1997." *Demography* 38 (2001): 423.

Satow, Roberta. "New Yorkers in the Countryside: Status Conflict and Social Change." *Journal of Contemporary Ethnography* 22 (1993): 227.

Schuman, Howard, Charlotte Steeh, Lawrence Bobo, and Maria Krysan. *Racial Attitudes in America: Trends and Interpretations.* Cambridge; Harvard University Press, 1997.

Schumer, Fran. "A Peek Inside the Country Club." *New York Times*, 16 March 2003.

Schwalbe, Michael. *The Sociologically Examined Life: Pieces of the Conversation*. 2nd ed. Mountain View, CA: Mayfield, 2001.

Schwalbe, Michael, Sandra Godwin, Daphne Holden, Doug Schrock, Shealy Thompson, and Michele Wolkomir. "Generic Processes in the Reproduction of Inequality: An Interactionist Analysis." *Social Forces* 79 (2000): 419.

Schwalbe, Michael and Michelle Wolkomir. "Interviewing Men." In *Handbook of Interviewing*, edited by Jay Gubrium and James Holstein. Thousand Oaks, CA: Sage, 2001.

Schwartz, Pepper. *Peer Marriage: How Love Between Equals Really Works*. New York: Free Press, 1994.

Scott, Janny. "Debating Which Private Clubs are Acceptable. And Private." *New York Times*, 8 December 2002, W-5.

Scott, Marvin B. and Stanford M. Lyman. "Accounts." *American Sociological Review* 33 (1968): 46.

Sennett, Richard and Jonathan Cobb. *The Hidden Injuries of Class*. New York: Vintage Books, 1972.

Smith, Kevin B. and Lorene H. Stone. "Rags, Riches, and Bootstraps: Beliefs About the Causes of Wealth and Poverty." *Sociological Quarterly* 30 (1989): 93.

Stuber, Jenny M. "Talk of Class: The Discursive Repertoires of White Working- and Upper-Middle-Class College Students." *Journal of Contemporary Ethnography* 35 (2006): 285.

Swidler, Ann. "Culture in Action: Symbols and Strategies." *American Sociological Review* 51 (1986): 273.

Szinovacz, Maximiliane. "Family Power." In *Handbook of Marriage and the Family*, edited by Marvin B. Sussman and Susan K. Steinmetz. New York: Plenum Press, 1987.

Tilly, Charles. *Durable Inequality*. Berkeley: University of California Press, 1998.

Tomaskovic-Devey, Donald. *Gender and Racial Inequality at Work: The Sources and Consequences of Job Segregation*. Ithaca, NY: ILR Press, 1993.

Useem, Michael. *The Inner Circle: Large Corporations and the Rise of Business Political Activity in the U.S. and U.K.* New York: Oxford University Press, 1984.

van Dijk, Teun A. *Elite Discourse and Racism*. Newbury Park, CA: Sage, 1993.

Vanderpool, Tim. "Lawsuits Tee Off Against Male Golf Clubs." *Christian Science Monitor*, 16 October 2001, p. 3.

Warner, W. Lloyd and Paul S. Lunt. *The Social Life of a Modern Community*. New Haven, CT: Yale University Press, 1941.

Weber, Lynn. *Understanding Race, Class, Gender and Sexuality: A Conceptual Framework*, 2d ed. New York: Oxford University Press, 2009.

Wellman, David T. *Portraits of White Racism*, 2nd ed. Cambridge: Cambridge University Press, 1993.

West, Candace and Don Zimmerman. "Doing Gender." *Gender & Society* 1 (1987): 125.

Wilkins, Amy. *Wannabes, Goths, and Christians: The Boundaries of Sex, Style, and Status*. Chicago: University of Chicago Press, 2008.

Wilkinson, Doris. "The Clinical Irrelevance and Scientific Invalidity of the 'Minority' Notion: Deleting It from the Social Science Vocabulary." *Journal of Sociology and Social Welfare* 29 (2002): 21.

Willis, Paul E. *Learning to Labour: How Working Class Kids Get Working Class Jobs*. New York: Columbia University Press, 1977.

Wise, Tim. "Breaking the Cycle of White Dependence: A Call for Majority Self-Sufficiency." *ZNet*, 19 May 2001. www.zmag.org/weluser.htm. Accessed on

———. "Whites Swim in Racial Preference." *Alternet*, 23 February 2003. http://zmag.org/content/showarticle.cfm?SectionID=30&ItemID=3113. Accessed on

Wright, Erik Olin. *Class Counts: Comparative Studies in Class Analysis*. New York: Cambridge University Press, 1997.

Yodanis, Carrie L. "Producing Social Class Representations: Women's Work in a Rural Town." *Gender & Society* 16 (2002): 323.

Zerubavel, Eviatar. *The Fine Line: Making Distinctions in Everyday Life*. New York: Free Press, 1991.

Zweigenhaft, Richard L. and G. William Domhoff. *Diversity in the Power Elite: How It Happened, Why It Matters*. Lanham, MD: Rowman & Littlefield, 2006.

# Index

accounts, xiv, 25–29, 56, 67, 115, 126–30
African American. *See* black
appearance (dress), 1, 10–11, 46–48, 69, 77

black, 4, 70–71, 82
Bonilla-Silva, Eduardo, 64, 70, 76, 80, 81, 84
boundary maintenance. *See* symbolic boundaries
business. *See* career

career, 2, 11–14, 38, 135
Catholic, 7, 21n2, 72
children, 35–40
class: definition of, 17–18; structure, 33, 78, 132, 137; upper, 28, 57, 105, 112, 130, 133–34,
colorblindness: in the clubs, 66, 77, 80, 137; in society broadly, xv, 64–66, 69, 78, 83–85, 90, 128, 133
compulsory heterosexuality, 19–20, 101
cultural capital, 10, 16, 38, 45–46, 57, 71, 79, 134–35, 136

diversity, xiv, 64–66, 79–88, 89, 90, 138

dominant inequality ideology, 128–29, 130, 132–33
dominant stratification ideology, 28, 58, 64, 78, 87
dress. *See* appearance

elites, 7, 15–17, 65, 66, 89

femininity, 105–8. *See also* wives

golf, 12, 26, 34–35, 38

Heights, 2–3
heteronormativity. *See* compulsory heterosexuality
homogeneity: in the clubs, 19, 35, 44, 67, 68–70, 81, 89–90, 127; consequences of, 15–17, 35, 57, 134; in society broadly, 57, 82,
husbands, 19, 99, 103, 112, 119, 131, 135. *See also* masculinity

intersectionality. *See* matrix of privilege
Italian, 3, 69–70, 113–14

Jewish, xiii, 7, 69, 92n13, 70, 87

# About the Author

**Jessica Holden Sherwood** has been observing the upper class ever since she attended Phillips Academy Andover, class of 1989. From there she went to Wesleyan University in Connecticut and on to North Carolina State University for a PhD in sociology. She now works as executive officer of Sociologists for Women in Society (SWS), an international association of feminist sociologists. Jessica lives in New England with her husband, Jesse, and daughters Abigail and Ellie, and enjoys gardening and other outdoor activities.

LaVergne, TN USA
16 September 2010
197309LV00002B/4/P